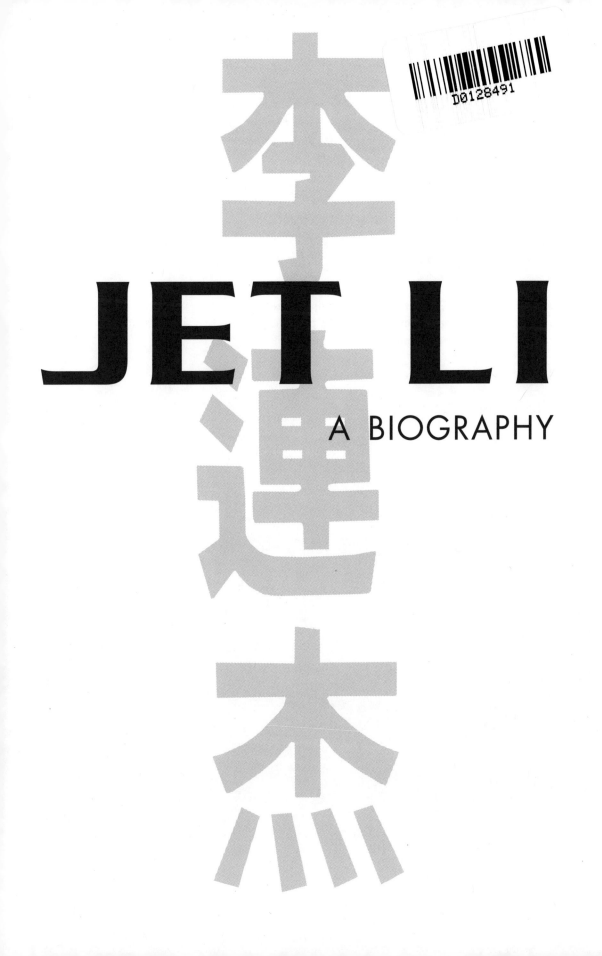

李連杰

JET LI
A BIOGRAPHY

Jet Li

© 2002 by James Robert Parish

Published by
Thunder's Mouth Press
An Imprint of Avalon Publishing Group Incorporated
161 William St., 16th Floor
New York, NY 10038

Library of Congress Control Number: 2002103620

ISBN 1-56025-376-2

9 8 7 6 5 4 3 2

Designed by Paul Paddock

Printed in the United States of America

Distributed by Publishers Group West

JET LI

A BIOGRAPHY

JAMES ROBERT PARISH

THUNDER'S MOUTH PRESS

NEW YORK

李連

CONTENTS

ACKNOWLEDGEMENTS

Academy of Motion Picture Arts & Sciences—Margaret Herrick Library, Sheila Benson, Billy Rose Theater Collection of the New York Public Library at Lincoln Center, Bobo Peng, Chen Wen, John Cocchi, CollectRareStuff.com, Bobby Cramer, Ernest Cunningham, Frank Djeng (Tai Seng Video Marketing), Leo Fang, Colin Geddes, Stephen L. Grossman, Pierre Guinle, Stefan Hammond, Jane Klain, Richard Krevolin, Frederick Levy, Howard Mandelbaum (Photofest), Alvin H. Marill, Jim Meyer, Su Mrozinski, Hubert Niogret, Michele Olivieri, Albert L. Ortega (Albert L. Ortega Photos), Barry Rivadue, Jonathan Rosenthal, Brad Schreiber, Arleen Schwartz, Sam Sherman, Michael Shulman (Getty Images), Walter Smalling, David Stenn, Bob Tamkin, Allan Taylor (editorial consultant/copy editor), Dr. Bryan Taylor, Vincent Terrace, Graham Uden, Norman Wang, Dr. Gerald Weales, Buddy Weiss (Photofest), Steven Whitney, and Valerie Zars (Getty Images).

Special thanks to my agent, Stuart Bernstein, and to my editor, Daniel O'Connor.

For Jet Li
and all those who have been a part of
China's long and honorable history of martial arts

The World of Jet Li

Today Jet Li is an internationally known movie star. A man of considerable prowess in martial arts, he has utilized these skills to become a major screen celebrity around the globe. The path to such acclaim has not been an easy or simple one. The fork in his road to success occurred three decades ago in the mid-1970s when he was a youngster growing up in Beijing, China.

At the time, for many, particularly in Western countries, who did not follow the world of martial arts, the name Li Lian-jie meant little. They did not know that this remarkable youth was already winning top prizes in major martial arts competitions in his homeland. Then, in 1974, the eleven-year-old made a splash in the global media. While on a goodwill tour of the United States with a Beijing martial arts team, he performed his wushu routines and steps on the White House lawn for a prestigious audience. News outlets around the world carried the details when this remarkable adolescent from the Far East rejected impressed President Nixon's suggestion that he someday become the Chief Executive's bodyguard.

Next, in the early 1980s this same young man captured the hearts and imagination of millions of filmgoers in Asia with *The Shaolin Temple*. However, this feature made in mainland China only found distribution in those Western nations with cities that boasted sizeable Chinese populations that supported Chinese-language movie theaters.

Still later, in the early 1990s, this determined twentysomething man (now known professionally as Jet Li) reinvented his movie image by starring in the hugely popular *Once Upon a Time in China*. In this screen saga, he portrayed the legendary nineteenth-century Wong Fei Hung—a Robin Hood–type defender of

Romance enters the picture for Jet Li's vengeance-bound hero in *Shaolin Temple* (1982).

the poor and an arch advocate of removing foreign influences from China. Jet quickly became a film icon in Asia. On the other hand, Li remained a largely unknown quantity to mainstream filmgoers in the West.

Throughout much of the 1990s, Jet continued making martial arts screen entries at Hong Kong film studios. He often reappeared in the rich historical role of the traditionalist Wong Fei Hung, who, in the progression of the *Once Upon a Time in China* series, slowly came to accept western technology and to became more tolerant of foreigners. In other movie showcases, Jet starred in contemporary actioners (1994's *The Bodyguard from Beijing*), adventure yarns (1996's *Dr. Wai in the Scripture With No Words*), or even as a comic-book hero (1996's *Black Mask*).

Outside of Asia, however, most of these popular Hong Kong–made pictures were still being shown only at Chinese-language theaters or at an occasional film festival. At the time, Western audiences in general were stymied by several limiting factors of Hong Kong cinema. These included the lack of Caucasian leading players with which to empathize and the inability of most Western filmgoers to comprehend the Chinese subtitles or the Chinese dialogue track. (The latter created another problem as it was customarily dubbed in after the feature was completed and usually utilized different players to provide the voices.)

Then too, there were such other conventions of Hong Kong cinema which included hastily shooting the picture and then rushing it through post-production. Such economic measures led to a finished product often filled with continuity gaps and abrupt editing. In addition, there were the genre's preference to include overstated villains and often distracting lowbrow comedy interludes. Above all, these releases reflected an Asian sensibility that was too unfamiliar to moviegoers with different cultural backgrounds. (A certain amount of this Western parochialism would diminish in later years as television and the Internet made the world more of a global community. Then, too, as the colorful Hong Kong film product gained in popularity it, in turn, influenced Hollywood-type productions. As such, audi-

The airborne Jet Li in *Kids from Shaolin* (1984).

ences in the West became more comfortable with these foreign movies by the 1990s. Thanks to these changes in attitude, dubbed or English subtitled versions of Asian movies became more available to non-Chinese speaking audiences through theatrical, TV, or home entertainment outlets.)

With such a long history of resistance against Hong Kong cinema in the West, it was not until Jet played the villain in the American-made *Lethal Weapon 4* (1998) that, finally, he became a mainstream global film celebrity. (He was then in his mid-thirties.) Soon Li switched his base of operations from Hong Kong to Hollywood and turned out more movies for the international marketplace. This created a growing interest around the globe in learning more about him. People were intrigued to know what brought a boy born in humble circumstances in Beijing, China, to such exalted international fame. Was he truly the successor to the celebrated Bruce Lee (1940–1973) who had popularized martial arts movie around the world in the 1970s? In addition, how did Jet Li measure up against two other major Asian action stars (Jackie Chan and Chow Yun-fat), who were already receiving international acclaim?

For anyone familiar only with the generally simplified kung fu demonstrated in the movies by Chuck Norris, Steven Seagal, and Michael Dudikoff, or by David Carradine in the TV series *Kung Fu* (1972–75) and *Kung Fu—The Legend Continues* (1993–96), seeing Jet Li in action on screen is a true revelation. It is like watching poetry in motion. Li's martial arts style is more traditional and stylized than that of the mythical Bruce Lee, but it is equally spellbinding. Jet brings his own unique, masterful blend of martial arts to his action pictures. As such he emerges an agile giant on screen—although he stands only five feet, six inches tall.

Over recent years, many impressed film critics have analyzed Jet Li's amazing physical dexterity and strong camera presence. For example, Sean Macaulay of the London *Times* observed, "If Bruce Lee was the Mick Jagger of kung-fu, Jet Li is the Billy Joel of wushu." Macaulay added, "It is only when he moves that it all makes sense. He is a compact powerhouse of chops, jabs, kicks, and spins. He claims that he prefers a slightly slower style than his contemporaries, the better to showcase the 'flavour' of his movies, but to the naked eye, without slow-motion, he is like the cloud of dust that signifies Tom and Jerry [cartoon figures] coming to blows."

An impressed Stephen Hunter (*Washington Post*) said of Jet: "Man, can he do stuff. An extraordinary gymnast, he's weirdly able to change direction in midair, or catch himself between pillars in a leg-spread iron cross, or duck a blade by

Jet Li as the master of martial arts in *Swordsman II* (1992).

leg-spreading on the ground (ouch!) then skip back to his feet. He frequently takes on gangs of 30 or 40, and he's so fast, elegant and coordinated that he makes you believe in the reality of what you're seeing." Meanwhile, Michael Lamb, in New Zealand's *Sunday Star Times* praised the talent for his "precision, pace, and a strange sense of dignity."

Richard Corliss told his *Time Asia* readers, "Li in repose is a cool star; Li in action is a hot one. It is a deep movie pleasure just to watch him scale a flight of stairs . . . by vaulting over a railing, taking a long, lithe step up and then pushing himself over the top rail. His martial poses with their wonderfully expressive names (the Rotation of the Stars, the Essence-Absorbing Stance, the ever-potent Wonder Screw), have classical beauty and power. His spin-kicks flout all laws of physics, if not metaphysics; there's nothing like Jet Li in a foot fight. His slippered feet (in *Once Upon a Time in China 3* [1993]) vs. four baddies with sabers: no contest! Four other miscreants (in *Fong Sai Yuk II* [1993]) rush at Li while he is holding a squirmy princess on a raft; he throws her high in the air, disarms the quartet and catches the girl before she falls. In *The New Legend of Shaolin* (1994) he fights off a dozen attackers with his infant son strapped to his back."

Roger Ebert (*Chicago Sun Times*) rates Jet as "compact, quiet, good-looking, not a show-off; the Alan Ladd of the genre." For Jonathan Ross of London's *Mirror*, "Jet is probably the last of the great martial artists we'll see in the movies. Long gone are the days when an actor actually had to be capable of the remarkable feats that launched the careers of Sammo Hung Kam-bo, Jackie Chan and, of course, Bruce Lee. With computer-generated effects and digital film-making, it's possible to make even a lumpy old plank such as Keanu Reeves look capable of dynamic martial artistry—as seen in *The Matrix* [1999]." This led Ross to alert moviegoers, "So savour the screen performances of Jet while you can."

Marveling at the highly polished gymnastics of Jet Li on screen does not take into account the full dimension of this complex personality who overcame great odds to become a martial arts champion and, later, to emerge as an international movie star. To appreciate his depth, one must take into consideration the tremendous discipline and drive needed for the young Lian-jie to master the martial arts and to excel among champions—some competitors many years his senior.

One of the interesting personality facets of Li is that, while his on-screen alter egos often tackle several opponents simultaneously, in real life Jet is a man of peace. He has said, "I myself have never been in a fight in real life, nor do I wish to be in one. When someone comes up to me, threatens me, wants to challenge me—I do whatever is possible to avoid conflict. Because it is never worth it. I never say to myself I'm the best fighter in the world. In this day and age, martial arts is a sport that is popular in competitions and in moviemaking. And as a form of exercise, as an interest, and as a means of maintaining or improving one's health, the learning of martial arts can be invaluable."

His serene approach to life and people—no matter the circumstance—has become more entrenched in recent years as he renewed his study of Buddhism. This has shaped his present point of view: "As a Buddhist, I believe strongly in the concept of karma. What you do will come back to you eventually, as is the universal balance. You can win today, but tomorrow, your choice to use violence will return to you, perhaps in a form ten times stronger."

While an American star with comparable status to Jet would long ago have been fully interviewed, analyzed, dissected, and served up by the media for public consumption, Jet comes from a traditional Chinese background. Shy and reserved by nature and from his culture, he has not always had an easy time dealing with the press, a fact which has limited what the public at large knows about the off-camera celebrity. In more recent years, when he began to capture the attention of Western audiences, there was the added language difficulty with non-Asian media as Li was not fully articulate in English. It led him to become, generally, reticent in such interviews, wary that he might not communicate his thoughts properly.

In addition, as Li's prominence spread in the 1990s to include Western countries, there was that unstated undertone of racial bias towards this man who spoke English in such an accented manner. In Hollywood, for example, with the exception of such silent cinema talents as Japanese-born Sessue Hayakawa and Chinese-American Anna May Wong (who carried their careers over into talkies), rarely was a personality of Asian heritage been allowed to play major roles in Americans films (or later on TV). For instance, American-born Bruce Lee had to relocate to Hong Kong in the 1970s and make kung fu action movies there before his action fare was deemed acceptable and commercial enough to be distributed in the United States. Even when Hollywood attempted over the decades to make crossover mainstream stars of talents with Asian backgrounds, the efforts generally failed. These included such performers as James Shigeta (1959's *The Crimson Kimona*, 1961's *Bridge to the Sun*), France Nuyen (1958's *South Pacific*, 1962's *Diamond Head*), Russell Wong (1987's *China Girl*, 1995's TV series *Vanishing Son*), and Jason Scott Lee (1993's *Dragon: The Bruce Lee Story*, 1994's *The Jungle Book*). Thus ethnic discrimination—as reflected by Jet's casting as a stock Asian villain in *Lethal Weapon 4*—limited the options for Li's transition to international box-office success. That he has not been outspoken about this situation does not lessen its impact on either his career or the man himself.

Thus it is not a simple matter to understand the still-boyish looking Jet Li of today, a phenomenon who has bridged cultures and moved from the world of martial arts to the movie sound stages. One must consider his modest origins, ethnic roots, and driving need to compensate for the loss of his father at an early age. On top of all this is his strong belief in the honor and pride in following traditional Chinese customs which, in turn, dictates complete respect for the martial arts school and its master. Understanding Jet's deep sense of obligation to family and authority figures gives one more insight into his years of devout dedication to acquiring and always improving his martial arts skills. Appreciating his penchant for promoting his life's interests (e.g., the skills of martial arts, the rich traditions of his Chinese heritage, and the principles of Buddhism), one can more readily

Jet Li in a romantic but pensive moment from *Fong Sai Yuk II* (1993).

comprehend what led Jet to choosing his previous screen roles and what shapes his career choices today.

Tracing Li's past gives a filmgoer an even greater appreciation of Jet's special screen presence. On camera, he typically portrays a man of few words, one who is moral and serious. This posture has allowed him in his best screen roles to project an enigmatic, sexy presence, one that exemplifies conviction, firmness, honesty, and power. Mick LaSalle (*San Francisco Chronicle*) recognized this charisma when he wrote that Jet Li is "a man whose presence—like that of Harrison Ford— radiates integrity. He has a great stillness as an actor, which he breaks only occa- sionally and with great effect. In the course of a film he'll smile perhaps twice, but each time he does, the whole audience warms up and relaxes." In his 2001 *Playboy* interview with Li, Matthew Polly observed that the key to Jet's path to stardom in the crowded (but relatively small) field of martial arts movie stars was that "while

Bruce Lee was ferocious and Jackie Chan funny, Jet Li developed a reputation for being something quite shocking in the kung fu genre: a genuine character actor, Jet consistently subsumed himself into each role rather than bending it to his persona."

These days, Li, a man of practiced modesty, devotes himself regularly to communicating with and understanding his worldwide fan base who visit his Internet website. It has made him increasingly shrewd about his box-office image. Here is a man who has displayed a sizeable range of emotions and warmth in several of his screen roles. (It is a flexibility which movie watchers and critics alike often overlook because of his attention-grabbing displays of martial arts skills.) Yet Jet realizes that he must meet his public's expectations in order to keep their loyalty over the long haul. For him, "The audience is the real boss. People pay $10 to watch your movie. What do they want to get? You need to understand them. They want to see action, they see me. If they want to see comedy they see Jim Carrey. If they want to see drama, they see Tom Hanks. Much better than me. Why go see me do drama?"

These then, are just a few of the multilayered aspects of the continuously intriguing Jet Li.

Humble Beginnings

2

To comprehend Jet Li, one must appreciate his place of birth, the tumultuous economic and social changes, and severe governmental control that was synonymous with China during the twentieth century, especially during the years that Li grew up there.

With its 3.7 million square miles of territory, China is the third largest country in the world, slightly bigger than the United States. However, with its population today of over 1.318 billion people it far outranks the United States in people with the latter's mere 285 million inhabitants.

For many centuries, China was a leading civilization in the world, far ahead of most countries with its arts and sciences. Under its several dynasties of rulers, the country underwent varying degrees of national unity as it stood off a host of invaders. During the Qing Dynasty (1644–1911), the last such in China history, the country's insularity from the world was broken to a degree by the desires of foreign nations (such as England, France, Russia, and the United States) to carry on lucrative trading with this aloof country. This interaction led to a rising nationalistic hatred of outside influences and paved the way in the late 1890s for the Boxer Rebellion, which targeted for extermination those external and internal forces within China (including all foreigners) which were challenging the traditional ways and control of Chinese life. Nevertheless, by 1912 such outside modernizing influences on China led to the formation of the Republic of China with Dr. Sun Yat-sen as its first president.

During the first half of the twentieth century, China suffered large famines, growing civil unrest, several major military defeats, and tyrannical foreign

11

occupation, including that by Japan before and during World War II. Following the global armistice in the mid-1940s, a ravaged China underwent new civil wars, with the Communist faction winning out over the Nationalist party. On October 1, 1949, Mao Zedong's Chinese Communist Party proclaimed the founding of the People's Republic of China (PRC). During Mao's dictatorial leadership, the nation embarked on ambitious economic measures to modernize the country. In the process, the PRC exercised extremely strict controls over its population and was responsible for the deaths of millions of dissidents—real or alleged. Chairman Mao resigned as head of state in 1959, but instigated the Cultural Revolution in 1966. In this cultural upheaval, government power intensified as the regime sought to "reeducate" (or eradicate) adherents of, and destroy symbols to, China's past rich civilization. After Mao's death in 1976, Deng Xiaoping, who had been discredited during the Cultural Revolution, became China's de facto leader. He introduced many economic reforms but he and his supporters maintained a tight political hold over the country, a vast land in which the national welfare was paramount and the individual secondary.

It was into this complex and bewildering period that Li Lian-jie, the future martial arts film star, was born on April 26, 1963, in Beijing, China. He was the fifth child (there were already two boys and two girls) in the household. Two years later, the father, an engineer, died and the mother, age thirty-two, became burdened with further pressures as she struggled to keep her family together and to provide for her five offspring in Beijing.

Beijing is located in northeast China, with Mongolia and Russia to the northwest, the Yellow Sea and Korea to the east, and to the south, the mighty Huang He River and the Chinese port city of Shanghai. Further southeast—beyond China's borders—lie the island nations of Taiwan and the Philippines. (Off the southeast coast of China are the island cities of Hong Kong and Macao which, until the late 1990s, were dependencies of Great Britain and Portugal respectively.)

With its population of just under seven million people, Beijing (formerly known as Peiping and also called Peking) is China's second largest city (Shanghai is the largest). At the start of the Ming Dynasty in 1421, the metropolis was made the country's capital. Over succeeding centuries Beijing became China's cultural and political hub and, by the twentieth century, an industrial hub.

As the center of China's government, the huge and sprawling Beijing—for so long subjected to devastating dust storms from the Gobi Desert—is filled with notable landmarks. These range from the Forbidden City (the elaborate palaces of the Ming and Qing dynasties which took a million laborers to construct), the

Temple of Heaven (built on the site of the "meeting" of Heaven and Earth by Emperor Yongle in the fifteenth century), the Summer Palace (on the lake shores of Yiheyuan), Tiananmen Square (an enormous expanse bordered by many monuments and the site of many momentous political events over the years), and portions of China's Great Wall.

As the youngest child—both small and slight for his age—Lian-jie was constantly supervised by his overprotective mother and by his pampering siblings. When his mother was not working (selling bus tickets) to support her children, she was closely monitoring her last-born's *every* activity. He has recalled, "Because I was the smallest my mother never allowed me to go swimming or ride the bicycle [or go ice skating]. Any risky activity—any kind of physical exercise that was even slightly dangerous—was off-limits. So while kids my age were out playing in the street, this docile little boy stayed inside." Even inside the family's extremely modest living quarters, the youngster endured constant strictures: "Don't touch that!" "Don't eat that!" Rebelling against such (over)care was not only *not* in the tradition of his culture which highly respected family and elders, but Lian-jie was born with an extra sense of duty to oblige commands from those in charge of him. It never occurred to him to do any forbidden activity behind his mother's back. According to the future celebrity: "I was a poster child for obedience. The mischief came later. . . ." (Lian-jie did not learn to ride a bicycle until he was fourteen or fifteen.)

It was not until Li was eight years old—over a year after most other children his age had started their formal education—that Lian-jie began attending the Changqiao Primary School of Beijing. His shielding parent hated letting go of her little boy. In one way, beginning at one of the city's primary schools was not such a major transition for the youngster. He was merely substituting his mother's supervision for that of his teachers. On the other hand he had other situations to which he had to adjust. For example, there was the matter of clothing: "We were poor. In my family, my older sister wears pants. Then when she gets taller, they go to my other sister. Then to my brother. Then to my other brother. Then he gives them to me. So I wear them to school. Eight years old, I wear girls' pants to school. The schoolchildren say, 'Oh, you wear your sister's pants.'" To this day Lian-jie remembers how, as an eight-year-old, he used to walk around school holding his hand over his pants' side zipper (made that way for females), hoping to disguise the gender construction of the trousers.

If the hand-me-down clothing reflected his impoverished family's struggling finances, that was something with which he could deal, as many or most of his classmates in his section of Beijing came from low-income households. But Lian-jie felt very much apart in another way from his classmates, a factor emphasized by his listening to accounts of their home life. Unlike most of them, he had no father. Being so young when he lost his dad, he did not even have any real remembrance of the man, memories that could sustain him through life. (Li reflected in later years: "I don't have a picture in my mind what, who is my father. I always remember my mother in my heart.") It prompted the youngster to overcompensate for his missing parent. He has explained, "I do everything I need to win, to do the best. I want to try to give my father a feeling [of being] proud of me. . . . So that's why I always tried so hard when I was young."

In the classroom, though small for his age, Lian-jie quickly became a favorite among his instructors. They were impressed by his disciplined behavior and understood its origins in his obvious need to please others. The situation soon fed on itself—the more the boy received the teachers' approval (and became the recipient of preferential treatment), the harder he worked to be a model student who "was always honest and did what I was told." Regarding his drive to be at his obedient best at school and to "work harder than everybody," Li has said that not only did it help him make up for not having a dad, but he also accepted the need for his disciplined behavior, "Because I don't want my mom to feel sad."

Having his teachers' approbation, however, did not guarantee that his peers would always treat Li with equality. One week, for example, Lian-jie was chosen to be a teacher's helper. He noticed that one of the boys was being a little tyrant at the Ping-Pong table. Li rushed over to the table and sprung up on it with a single leap and proceeded to give the little bully a well-placed kick. His teary-eyed victim yelled out, "Damn you! It serves you right to have lost your father!" Lian-jie chased after the offender who ran into a nearby teachers' room. These actions led other classmates to be unruly and the young monitor promptly charged into their number to restore calm. Eventually the offenders were urged to apologize to Lian-jie. It was an early example of Li fighting for right, a habit that would occur frequently on screen when he later became a major martial arts star of the Chinese cinema.

It was not long before the dutifully obedient Lian-jie was rewarded by his teachers and made a regular monitor. Some monitors were assigned to record attendance, keep order, etc. at math, reading, or for one of the other daily school activities. Li was picked to be a physical education monitor. In China, at that time, during each school day, after the morning's first two class periods there was a recess and all of the students would file out into the schoolyard. There they performed state-required daily exercises all done in synchronization to recorded music from a radio broadcast played on the school's loudspeakers. As a physical education monitor young and little Lian-jie daily stood on a platform leading his schoolmates in these mandatory national calisthenics.

While the young student was superior in deportment, enthusiasm, and effort, he was not above being the recipient of teachers' favoritism when it came to academics. Looking back, years later, the star remembered, "I might forget to write a dash or a decimal. When I would go up to the teacher's desk to turn it [the test] in, she would ask me, 'Are you sure you want to turn that in? Are you sure you've thought everything through?' Lying directly in front of me was a copy of a perfectly-scored test. 'You sure you're ready to turn in your test? . . . Have you checked everything?'"

Even with such well-intentioned academic coaching, Li still had problems with one class in particular—music. (He claims he had no sense of pitch.) One day a dreaded music test was to be given. The boy was very anxious about the exam. Soon it was his turn to sing in front of the class. The teacher called his name and he stood up. The instructor said, "You have a sore throat today. Isn't that right?" Lian-jie was perplexed. As he explained, "Here was my chance to escape. But my mother had raised me not to lie, so I just stood there with my mouth open in confusion." The teacher repeated the rhetorical question: "You have a sore throat today, isn't that right?" As a result, Lian-jie did not have to perform the much-feared vocal exam.

In 1971 at the end of Lian-jie's first academic year, all the students at his school (which covered grades one through six), along with youngsters from fifteen other similar institutions in his Beijing district were dispatched to mandatory attendance at sports summer school. (The officials reasoned that a month of such activity would help to keep the youths away from the city's streets and out of potential trouble.) The youngsters were assigned arbitrarily to different sports—e.g., some to soccer, others to swimming, basketball, etc.—where about 1,000 students in each activity spent two-and-a-half hours of their daily schedule participating in their prechosen sport.

When he was randomly allocated to wushu, young Lian-jie said, "Oh. What is martial arts? I don't know. Tell me and I'll learn." The boy had no idea that this was an intensely physical sport based on very traditional martial arts forms. In wushu—a Chinese general term for martial arts which derives from "wu" (military) and "shu" (art)—the choreographed routines of kung fu were developed as both a martial art and an energetic, acrobatic type of entertainment. A person adept in wushu will combine deadly kicks and jet-fast hand and head strikes at opponents with the use of martial arts weapons (e.g., swords, staffs, spears, axes). When executed properly the blend of force, agility, and speed—in tandem with stylized head twists and dramatic facial gestures—create a spellbinding spectacle. This mixture of martial arts and theatrics (codified in a stylized performance routine as done by, for example, members of the famed Peking Opera), had developed over time into a high art in China. Although by the twentieth century, modern weapons, especially guns, had turned the practice of wushu into a spectator sport rather than remaining a practical means of self-defense in combat, it still carried with it deeply traditional elements tied to Chinese history, religion, and philosophy.

To Li's (and most everyone else's) surprise, he did quite well with his wushu training which included leg presses, somersaults, and bending. Here his natural agility, sense of discipline, and commitment to meet this latest challenge from authority figures stood him in very good stead. In fact, at the end of the "vacation," he was among the thirty other participants from the group of 1,000 pupils chosen from the ranks to have more such training. For a first grader to be so singled out was considered a great honor. Thereafter, when he returned to his regular school, each day he waited after classes for the older pupils assigned to pick him up and escort him to wushu training. As Lian-jie said later, "The other students looked at me enviously, which I enjoyed."

During the next three months the boy underwent rigorous training after school with the other martial arts students. The instruction was exacting and the trainees were expected to become proficient, disciplined practitioners despite their youth. For example, there was the perfecting of hand slapping the opponent. If it was executed too hard (which caused both the doer and recipient to suffer a strong sting) it caught the attention of the stern instructor, who disciplined his erring disciples severely.

Soon there were more elimination rounds and only four survivors were left from the original thirty. Lian-jie was one of them. They joined other winning students who had begun wushu during the previous year's winter "vacation." Li's growing success in the sport elevated further his status at school where no one now looked down on him as some had just a year ago. The sweet victory among his peers would have been more delicious but for the fact that, each day, Lian-jie was enduring a double session of schooling: the regular school day and then the martial arts training supplement to his education.

When he was nine Lian-jie was preparing to enter his debut martial arts competition. He was to contend in the first national wushu competition held in China since the tide of Chairman Mao Zedong's growing Cultural Revolution had stopped such "inappropriate" events two decades earlier. At the big event, no prizes or official standing was to be offered. Rather it was more an opportunity to demonstrate form in the art in front of a major audience. It was determined that only a single honor was to be given—one based on overall excellence. The much-discussed competition was to be held in Jinan, the capital of Shandong province in east China, some 300 miles to the southeast of his home city. Not only was it the first time that Li had been on a train, but it was also the first time the excited boy had traveled out of Beijing.

In retrospect, even given the boy's natural ability, determination to excel, and his need to make a mark for himself, it was still an amazing accomplishment that young Lian-jie won the award for excellence. Returning to Beijing in triumph, he was instructed by school officials that now he need attend school for only half a day. With more of his daily life devoted to wushu, Li threw himself into the regimen with a fierce pride, bent on not displeasing his superiors or bringing embarrassment to his family. Lian-jie soon learned that there was a special reason for his being excused from so much of the day's classroom lessons. Mainland China had closed its diplomatic doors to outsiders for many years. Now, however, for economic reasons, the need for trade became clear and the country was more receptive to foreign influences. As such the nation had chosen to host the Pan-Asian-African-Latin American Table Tennis championship. For China, which placed great importance to the sport of Ping-Pong, this was a significant event. As such the government invited a small number of contestants from other countries to come to China for the competition.

For the pending occasion it was determined that the opening ceremonies would include a demonstration of various artistic performances, all designed to showcase the best of Chinese culture. This prelude to the main event was to include dance, Peking opera, and, especially, wushu. Lian-jie's group was assigned to perform in five programs, and Li was in three of these offerings. If normal wushu workouts were rigorous and exhausting, the preparation for this event was even more so. Li recalls, "Practice was impossibly tiring; our motherland was expecting us to give a performance that was nothing less than perfect. We rehearsed the forms and routines countless times."

As the crucial festivities showcase ceremony—to be held in Beijing's largest stadium—drew near, the wushu group found itself being constantly inspected during their heavy-duty training by high-ranking government officials. Lian-jie said years later: "This was the first time I felt the pressure of representing many people with my performance. There was no room for mistake." Striving and driven to perfection, the youngsters made a fine showing at the large pre-ping-pong demonstration.

One reward given the well-honed troupe was that, after their appearances, they had the great honor of meeting Zhou En-lai (Chou En-lai), China's prime minister and current highest-ranking official, now that the ailing Mao Zedong was in seclusion. Another result of the youngsters' fine work was that Lian-jie was asked to join the Beijing Sports and Exercise School. It would mean leaving his classroom studies altogether and living at the institution full-time except for weekends.

The offer/command was considered a great tribute, one definitely *not* to be taken lightly. The ever-so-obedient and very ambitious youngster pliantly agreed to the request. Without fully realizing it, he was choosing a path that would inextricably alter his life. At the time, however, he knew only that it would be dishonorable not to comply with this decision from his government. It was, after all, unthinkable for a humble boy from the poor district of Beijing to reject such a golden, if arduous, opportunity.

Wushu As a Way of Life

3

When Li Lian-jie was asked to join the Beijing Sports and Exercise School, his family, like the boy, did not seriously consider they had any option but to accept the state's request for their honored son to participate in the program. Much as Lian-jie's mother hated having her boy away from home six days a week, she knew it was a good opportunity for her son to be well-fed, clothed, and supervised during the work week, and that he would return to her for Sundays.

The regimen for the young pupils at the School was arduous to say the least. Each training day they were awakened at 6:00 A.M. by a loud bell. Within ninety seconds they had to dress and be lined up outside in the field, at full attention. After one hour of practice, they were given the opportunity to wash up and then eat breakfast. Thereafter, from 8:30 A.M. till noontime, they practiced wushu. After lunch, they rested for a set time. However, by now the School had developed into a tourist site for foreigners and the students were required to perform for such unexpected visitors. Often just as the youngsters were taking a postlunch nap, they'd be summoned by a loudspeaker announcement stating "tour group." That was the alert that they must rush outside and perform for the new arrivals. After more training and dinner, there was additional practice—from 7:30 P.M. until usually 10:30 P.M. One benefit of the night instruction was that then the wushu pupils could work in the inside gym out of the often cold weather. (There was only one gym facility at the institution and other sports—such as volleyball, gymnastics, and basketball—took priority for using the inside facility during the days.) Such was a typical training day for the students.

One break in the youths' workweek routine came on Friday nights. At the time, China's power plant facilities had not been able to keep up with the country's fast-growing demands for electricity, so there were scheduled rolling blackouts in the city and the rest of the country. Friday nights was the appointed time for the School to be without electricity. On this evening, with no lights, it meant no training. For Lian-jie, "We loved it. Friday night never came soon enough." After Saturday's training, the pupils were allowed to return to their homes for Sunday. (Always the dedicated student, Lian-jie often spent part of his day off practicing his routines.)

With such an arduous physical program the students were bound to suffer injuries. For example, one evening, the dreaded alarm bell summoned the trainees from their dormitory to the darkened exercise field. In their haste the youngsters had rushed out in their slippers rather than putting on their athletic shoes. As punishment for their lack of foresight, the coach demanded that they run around the darkened track. Using a flashlight to guide the thirteen pupils to their starting positions, the coach ordered them to start running and had them continue at full speed in the dark for quite a while. None of the boys dared to slacken off because they had no way of anticipating when the instructor would suddenly shine the light on one of them to see how he was doing at the moment.

During this rigorous punishment exercise, Lian-jie made a misstep in the blackness and twisted his ankle. Nevertheless, he kept going, limping with each step. The next day he attended regular morning practice outdoors; that afternoon he and the others performed for a tour group—and that evening for yet another batch of gawking visitors. By now the pain in his ankle had worsened. He had not alerted his coach to his injury because typically any such complaint led to a grueling set of exercise, which might be an order to do thousands of stances or kicks. The future film star would say later, "Whatever reason you came up with to shirk training, the coach was ready with ten alternatives to counter you. He didn't care whether the injury was real or faked."

By the time Lian-jie reached home on Sunday after the accident, he could not walk on his badly swollen foot. (As Li described it, it had "swelled up like a loaf of steamed bread.") He somehow managed to limp back to the School on Monday. The unrelenting coach ordered the boy to practice upper body exercises rather than join his peers in the normal activities. It happened that day that another coach was visiting the institution and he inquired why Lian-jie was not training with the other students. Finally, Li's instructor had him taken to the hospital where an X-ray revealed that the boy's bone had cracked right through. The doctors outfitted him with a big plaster cast. For the next weeks, an older classmate carried Lian-jie piggyback to the practice field daily and set him down. There Li would perfect arm movements all day long. After the practice a classmate would carry Lian-jie back to the dormitory.

This was but one example of the strictness and seriousness in which the boys underwent their training. Sometimes the coaches would use corporal punishment on nondiligent pupils. Lian-jie was only infrequently the subject of such treatment. The Jet Li of today explains why that was so: "Because my instructors knew that it wasn't the best way to make me learn. Words alone could shame me into training harder. I had a strong sense of pride. The coach didn't need to hit me; a few sarcastic comments questioning my ability to work hard would get the same results. Other people, though, were different. They needed to be physically reprimanded before they would change their behavior."

Over the years, as Lian-jie began to gain fame as a practitioner of wushu, it became standard practice for the media to refer to him as a child prodigy in the arena of martial arts. The Jet Li of today has said that such labels "annoyed me beyond measure. It was simply not true. Like everyone else, I came across numerous problems in the course of training and many a time I wavered and thought of dropping out."

There were, however, several reasons that Lian-jie stayed the tough course which even he has described as "bitter" and "harsh." For one thing, he regarded the acceptance to the Beijing Sports and Exercise School an obligation to fulfill to the state, to his family, and to himself. He found ways to make the grueling course more appealing. For example, unlike say swimming or basketball, there are a tremendous number of elements to learn in wushu. The future movie star once explained, "You have hundreds of styles: monkey-style, tiger-style, short sword, hard, longer, many kinds. So today you're learning this. Tomorrow you're learning [that]. . . . Very interesting."

The boy also began to perceive the complexities between the internal and external styles of wushu, and how much the right philosophical approach to the art not only made the physical acts more endurable but, also more successful in execution. According to Li, "A few of my classmates trained much harder than I did. If the teacher told them to drink water, they would run off and drink three cups of water! But they never got the point. And they didn't know why they were drinking three times as much. In martial arts, you need to think about what makes a man different from other people. My approach to training is what made me different from my classmates."

Another key factor in Lian-jie's growing success in his training was his coach (i.e., master) Wu Bin who had graduated from the Beijing Sports University Wushu Department in 1963. Their relationship soon became symbiotic with the dedicated and talented young coach taking special interest in his talented pupil, and adolescent Li coming to regard his mentor as a father figure. From his instructor the boy learned the elder's philosophy: "Fists swift as meteors and eyes quick as lighting, back as agile as a snake and feet always in position." Then, too, since Lian-jie had dropped his academic education at such an early age, he found Wu Bin a willing teacher to help him with his Mandarin language conversation, with understanding life better, and with appreciating the golden chance wushu offered to make him a strong man of self-worth. According to Li, it was Wu Bin who "helped me steer clear of all obstacles and encouraged me never to give up. His admonitions and his patience in guiding me along will always remain in my heart of hearts." (The future Jet Li has also noted of his early training: "I learned many kinds of martial arts, picked up many styles of kung-fu—different names but the foundations are the same. Wu Bin helped me establish that foundation.")

On the other hand, Lian-jie did not always appreciate that his coach was far more solicitous to his teammates than to him. For example, "When he saw they were too tired, he advised them to take a break. But he seemed to be quite another person when he talked to me. Often he would snap at me, 'Do you think that's the correct movement?' 'How come the more you practice the worse you become?' . . . To be frank, I didn't quite like the way he treated me. But now I understand he did it all for my good. Whenever he took on a new trainee, the first thing he did was to get to know his character so he could deal with him accordingly. Seeing that I was a bit 'ambitious' and proved a willing trainee, he applied the rigorous method of training toward me. This was described by him as: 'A resounding drum must be struck with a heavy hammer.'"

As the kinship between Lian-jie and Wu Bin grew stronger, the coach devised extra training for his talented, persistent pupil. The additional work helped to refine the youth's abilities in martial arts. One thing soon puzzled the elder. He noticed that the boy lacked the full strength needed for kicking and striking. One day while visiting the boy's family, he discovered that no one in the household ate red meat and that their diet was somewhat lacking in proteins. (It was explained to the coach that this habit was a carryover from an aged grandmother who, when she had been ill, had been advised by a doctor not to eat much pork, mutton, or beef. This habit, so the coach was told, was carried on by the family even after the grandmother recovered. However, the astute instructor perceived quickly that the true reason for this practice was that the family was too poor to include meat in their diet.) Diplomatically the coach began bringing food packages to the struggling Li household and helping out Lian-jie and his family with financial aid, clothing, etc. This kindness would continue for several years.

During three years of training at the Beijing Sports and Exercise School, Lian-jie continued to excel as he grew more sophisticated in wushu skills. While other students dropped out due to the rigors of the course, Li continued his daily practice—kicking, punching, learning agility and flexibility with swords and spears, etc. Under Wu Bin's guidance, Li began the needed combining of kung fu styles. He developed the inner energy of Tai Chi Chuan, the strength and power derived from Dragon Boxing, the briskness of Monkey Boxing, the precision afforded by Crane Boxing, and the benefits of Gun Boxing. Thanks to his capacity for enduring the punishing routines and his need always to learn more, the talented fledgling became very proficient in the varieties of forms, postures, movements, and imitations of animals that combine to make an outstanding exponent of wushu.

It was also during these demanding and exhausting years of wushu instruction that young Lian-jie began to have a better sense of his self and to put his life into a perceptive relationship to those around him in Beijing. Despite his status as a student at the Beijing Sports and Exercise School and the special treatment/ training he received from coach Wu Bin, Li found that he still harbored those early, inner resentments about being different from others because he had no father and because his family had such a financial struggle. Now, he began to understand these angers of his. He perceived, "Others had what I didn't and I felt jealous of them. I felt that society wasn't fair to me—that I had been dealt a bad hand. In comparing my circumstances with others, I brought a lot of unhappiness upon myself which in turn caused many emotional ups and downs." Then, "After several years, I used my philosophy and began to view these same issues in a different light. I believe my key failing was in comparing my perceived difficulties (what I didn't have) with others' perceived abundance (what they had that I did not). By basing my emotional well-being on the perceptions I had about material abundance, I experienced those emotional peaks and valleys—I brought about my own unhappiness."

By 1974 Li Lian-jie had already completed three years of intensive training at the Beijing Sports and Exercise School. By now he had progressed admirably, having learned the integration of the forms of running, springing, and leaping with a sense of beauty, and was accomplished in many of the requisite, intricate movements of martial arts. As such the talented youth was entered by his wushu superiors into the Youth National Athletic Competition being held by the Chinese government for contestants under the age of eighteen. The eleven-year-old took first place in the compulsories, winning the highest marks in Pu swordsplay, spearplay, routine boxing, two-man sparring, etc., to his and everyone's amazement. Later in life, when he had become a staunch Buddhist, Li would attribute his talent and success in martial arts to reincarnation and karma. He reasoned, "I learned wushu before—in my past life. I must have brought something with me to this life. This didn't happened just to me. For instance, Mozart composed music at five years old. Many children can't even read at that age. How could he possess such talent? Maybe his soul was nurtured in music in his past life. I probably have genes that allow me to learn things quickly, especially physical techniques. But I also learn[ed] the inner energy or feelings behind the movements. I think the reason I could win was because people could feel my punch was different from other people's punches—they could see the energy released from inside."

As such a young winner, Lian-jie gained visibility with the media, the public, and, of course, the government. At the time, China was preparing to send a group of its best young wushu students on a goodwill tour of the United States, part of its détente program with that country. Once selected, Li and the thirty other youths selected from throughout China underwent further martial arts training. In addition, the young Chinese were given extensive lessons in Western etiquette so they would not be an embarrassment to their nation in any public social situation. For the unsophisticated Li and most of the others, it meant learning the use of Western eating utensils and which fork, knife, or spoon to utilize with which course in a fancy meal. The training also included learning a few practical words of English, a language with which he and most of his comrades were unfamiliar, since at the time English-language movies or television programming (for those who had sets) were not yet shown in the People's Republic of China.

Once in the United States, the excited group of young Chinese goodwill ambassadors performed their martial arts skills in forums across the United States. Before departing China the youths had been warned by their elders that their activities—even in private—might be monitored by American officials as both nations considered this venture a very high security operation. This fact stuck in Lian-jie's mind. One morning after his arrival in the United States, the youth—who had grown to a degree rambunctious and playful since coming into his own—decided to try an experiment in his hotel room. "I spoke to the flowers in

Chinese. 'I like chocolate ice cream.' I said to the mirror, 'I like banana.' When I [returned] to the hotel [later that day], I opened the door, and everything I'd mentioned was on the table as if I'd ordered it.' 'It's true,' I thought. 'They are listening.'" The youths were given $5 a day as spending allowance by the Chinese government. Lian-jie used this luxury to buy his mother a Swiss watch. (When he later presented it to her, she hugged him and told him he was "a good boy.")

The highlight of this special delegation's American trek (which included New York City and San Francisco) was a command performance in Washington, D.C., for President Richard M. Nixon. Thus one morning, Li and the other young martial artists were driven to the White House where on the stately lawn Nixon, Secretary of State Henry Kissinger, and many others, including reporters and news cameramen, were gathered for the event. After Lian-jie (dressed in a bright red outfit) and another did a two-man exhibition of kung fu (which included brandishing broad swords at lightning speed), an impressed President Nixon approached Li and asked through an interpreter, "How would you like to be my bodyguard when you grow up?" Without much hesitation, Lian-jie blurted out in Chinese (which was duly translated), "Nope. I don't want to protect one person. When I grow up I want to protect billions of Chinese people."

Everyone present was amused by the teenager's response. It led Kissinger to say to Lian-jie, "Little boy, when you grow up, you should become a diplomat instead of a bodyguard." The media on hand duly reported the exchanges of conversation and the cute item made news around the globe. In China, the government was very pleased with Lian-jie's response of putting his country's people first and ahead of a foreign leader. It made Li a celebrity of the moment in his homeland.

The exciting trip for the youths ended in Hong Kong where their American State Department bodyguards (who had been assigned to the exhibition tour) finally had an opportunity to see their charges perform their martial art skills. They were duly impressed by these young Chinese and it led to a teary goodbye when the youths and their protectors said goodbye. (A few years later, President Gerald Ford made a trip to China and Lian-jie—thanks to his international fame due to the Richard M. Nixon exchange back in 1974—was on the list to attend banquets for such important visitors. At the dinner, the young man spotted a few of the bodyguards from his American tour. When he and the government men began whooping it up in an impromptu reunion, it caused momentary consternation when their yells of joys was assumed by others in the room to be yelps of alarm.)

• • •

Growing in stature and fame over the next few years, Lian-jie participated in several martial arts competitions in his homeland. In 1975 China began preparation for staging its Third National Games, a domestic version of the Olympics for all competitive sports and held every four years. (Since the founding of the new China in the late 1940s, however, only twice in the 1950s had the nation held such games; thereafter the Cultural Revolution had put such activities on hold. Thus the upcoming games were very important.)

Because Lian-jie had recently won the Youth National Athletic Championship there was much anticipation and expectations of him for the Third China Competition. Thus, the officials made an exception, allowing the twelve-year-old to jump into the eighteen and over category. As the competition neared and his training accelerated, Li felt the pressure mounting on him. Not only was Wu Bin coaching him, but he had other instructors teaching this prize pupil. One positive result of this intensified training was that it broadened his vision of martial arts as he interacted increasingly with other rising martial arts talents.

In a warm-up to the upcoming big event, Li was entered in an important invitational tournament held in Kumming in Yunnan province in Southwest China. There were participants from eight large cities. In the five events, Lian-jie won first place in each category.

During a qualifying practice session for the national competition, Lian-jie gashed himself in the head but was so focused on his performance that he had no idea of what damage he'd done, even when the audience went "waah" in horror. At the time he thought the substance (i.e., blood) dripping down his head was sweat. As the contender finished his form, he noticed that several of his female teammates were crying. Then he began to realize something was wrong. Trained not to use physical pain as an excuse, he wanted to ignore his condition, but his trainers rushed him to the hospital where his wound was cleaned and stitched. He was then sent to recoup back at the Sports School. Hearing of the accident, Li's elder brother immediately visited his brother's school dormitory. When he saw his bandaged sibling, he immediately ran home to tell their mother. The concerned parent hurried to meet with school officials to discuss her boy's condition. They finally persuaded the mother that Lian-jie was okay and would be fit to compete. As for Li's brother, Lian-jie's martial arts master took him outside and punished him for causing the ensuing scene.

The day of the crucial competition Lian-jie appeared on time. He knew that he had to remove his wound dressing or it would have spoiled his balance in the competition. With this in mind, he put himself into a proper focus for the contest, and when he walked up to the platform to engage his opponent, he ripped off his bandage. A nurse was on hand with disinfectant and a syringe full of antibiotics. She had instructed him, "Immediately after you finish, come over here so I can clean your wound and cover it up again." As she explained, exposure to dirt and sweat could infect the cut which had not yet healed. Obedient as always, after finishing his form, Lian-jie left the platform, ran down to where the nurse waited, pulled down his pants to get an injection, and then had the nurse sponge his head wound and rebandage it.

When the events were finished, Lian-jie was announced as the first-place winner. When the twelve-year-old hastened to the winners' stand to accept his prize, he was shorter than his two other competitors, both in their mid-to-late twenties. As China's national anthem played, Li recalls being overcome with emotion. He had the urge to cry. As his eyes watered up, he thought, "This medal is for you, Mom! You didn't raise me in vain! Without your sacrifices, I couldn't have made it to this point."

4
The Wushu Winner

A s an accomplished wushu champion, Li Lian-jie and several of his peers were sent by the Chinese government on a goodwill tour in 1976, which included stopovers in several cities in Europe, Asia, Africa, and the Middle East. For Li it was an amazing opportunity to explore the world. Being a world traveler allowed him to gain a cosmopolitan attitude that living in Beijing as a poor student attending the public schools could never have afforded.

On this 1976 excursion, the group went to Iraq. It was so enormously hot there that the inventive young Chinese teammates began pouring buckets of cold water on their bedding at nighttime so they could sleep for a while at least during the stifling evenings. On this trip the group also visited the Philippines. There the honored team was received by President Ferdinand Marcos and his wife Imelda. Later the guests were taken on a tour of the capital. While visiting local shops, the owner of one clothing store offered each of the Chinese visitors a free suit. At a local shoe factory, the proprietor volunteered to make a custom-made pair of leather boots for each of the kung fu talents. The young people accepted the hospitality graciously. In their glee they "forgot" about the rule in China that prohibited athletes and performers who represented China abroad from accepting any gifts valued at more than a few dollars. Such extravagant gifts had to be relinquished to the nation. When the travelers returned to China, they were told that had to turn all their gifts over to the state. Dispirited, the team went outside and rolled on the ground. Now they could offer the state their torn and dirty new clothing. Next they went out to a field to play soccer in their leather boots, trying their best to scuff them up. To complete the process, they kicked at walls and ground the boots into the dirt. By day's end they had spitefully destroyed these valuable possessions. The next day, their coach gathered together his crew. He said, "Team, you all worked really hard on this last tour and made a special contribution to the nation. And I know that you were not happy about having to give up the presents you received in the Philippines. So I decided to apply for a special exemption on our behalf. And in light of our excellent performance, I'm happy to report that the authorities have agreed—just this once—that you can keep all your gifts."

In 1977, the increasingly proficient Li Lian-jie won his second Gold Medal at China's National Martial Arts competition. Again, the celebrity, now fourteen, was requested by the government to tour the world. The excursion this time included a visit to Zaire (once called the Democratic Republic of the Congo). As the plane reached its African destination, Lian-jie noticed that the craft was circling over the airport for what seemed to be a long time and that the flight attendants were looking worried. Soon thereafter the captain informed the passengers that the plane's landing gear would not descend. With this dire announcement, the flight attendants distributed stationery so that all aboard could write their wills. Young Li's writing skills were very rudimentary from lack of classroom practice, and he feared he would be unable to fulfill this directive—this assignment—satisfactorily. He has described, "I started to feel extremely anxious—not because I was being told to write my will, but because I was staring at a blank sheet of paper. It was like being given a pop quiz [in school]! I had no idea what to write. I have no clear recollection of how people around me were reacting to the crisis— I just remember panicking: 'I would so much rather be practicing a [martial arts] form or doing drills right now. Anything but writing!' As it turned out the landing gear function[ed] after all."

While in Africa, the Chinese guests had a sharp awakening to their relative values to the locals. On one jaunt between African cities, the choice middle section of the plane was used to ship cattle, while the martial arts team were seated in front of and behind the livestock.

On another exhibition trek, Li and his teammates flew to England to perform. Their accommodating hosts arranged a big banquet in the Chinese visitors' honor after their impressive performance. The British was toasting the team with beers and offered Lian-jie and the others some. Li did not drink liquor and politely refused. The English then suggested, "Alright then, for every bottle of beer that we drink, you'll have to match us with a bottle of cola." During the next two-and-a-half hours, the challengers drank down eight bottles of beers apiece. Therefore Li had to match it with his swigging down Coca-Colas. Later, during the extended car ride back to the hotel, Lian-jie went through an excruciating hell with his gaseous stomach. He took several showers and tried soaking in the tub to curb his discomfort. After an hour or so in the hot water he began to breathe comfortably again. A much relieved teenager swore never to drink that much cola again at one time.

In 1978 Lian-jie again emerged Gold Champion of China's National Martial Arts competition, an achievement he duplicated yet again the next year. Also in 1979 he was the victor in the Fourth China Martial Arts "Olympics." It was an extremely impressive array of victories for the young Chinese man who was now sixteen.

Each year as Li won more honors the media referred to him as the "All-round Wushu Champion of China." This caused Lian-jie to ponder. "I thought I should live up to my title. If I was going to be truly all-capable, I would have to know something. All I had to do was to learn what I didn't already know. As soon as I started learning, though, I realized I didn't know anything. 'So I'm not all-around,' I said to myself. 'I'm not well-rounded enough.' Now I knew there was a lot I was not yet capable of—a lot I hadn't yet mastered."

As he continued to learn more from master Wu about the art and philosophy of wushu, Lian-jie began attending the city's famed Opera to study the actors and dancers as they performed their elaborate, stylized routines. He began talking with the opera performers afterward, gaining insights he could incorporate into his forms. Just as he had done as an eight-year-old schoolboy, he was determined to meet and exceed any expectation made on him. This need made him determined always to improve his skills and never to be satisfied with his current degree of abilities. He was still a man possessed.

As Lian-jie's fame increased so did his career options, ranging far beyond wushu. One area into which he had an entrée was government work. As he explained to *Playboy* magazine's Matthew Polly not long ago, "I have no interest in politics. If I'd had an interest, I could have become a politician when I was young. In China if you are successful professionally, the government likes to train you to become a leader of a department. Instead, I became interested in promoting wushu, and that's what I have been doing." As such he continued his goodwill tours both abroad and home, always eager to gain new converts to the virtues of martial arts.

As the 1970s came to an end, Li Lian-jie observed how the world of wushu competition was subtly changing. Up to that point such contests only occurred in China so the contenders' forms were judged by one set of rules formulated by the Chinese. Li detailed, "Everybody had to compete in broadsword, spear, straight sword, cudgel, and empty-hand form. Why, in our day, we had to learn all of the Eighteen-Arms [i.e., axe, battleaxe, cudgel, fork, halberd, hammer, hook, long-handled spear, mace, meteor hammering, saber, short cudgel, stick, spear, sword, talon, trident, and whip], internal styles, external styles, everything. That was our curriculum. Nowadays, if you want to go to the Olympics, you learn the compulsory forms, and that's it." He explained further, "I believe that deep inside, wushu is much worse than before. I'm talking about the inside knowledge, the part of wushu that does not involve the physical body. Inner cultivation is the most important part, and it's definitely lacking nowadays." As he explained, today participants have "got to take the time to bring their whole energy together with their mind to finish every movement. The speed nowadays is so fast and the jumps are so high and yet, the details in between are not perfected at all."

In 1979 when Lian-jie was sixteen—the age when most teenagers in much of the world are high school students and may be just learning to drive a car—Li Lian-jie was at a professional crossroads. While many of his wushu school teammates would continue in the field—some becoming teachers of martial arts in China or abroad—others gravitated to different career paths. As for the stalwart Wu Bin, he continued coaching at the Beijing Amateur Sports and Exercise School. Each year, until 1985, he entered his Beijing team into China's National competition, winning an impressive ten continuous national championships. That year he retired, but came out of retirement in 1994. (Among the other notables he coached over the years in wushu besides Li were actors Michelle Yeoh and Russell Wong.)

Now in 1979, Lian-jie took on a brand new and exciting career path. He had been given the opportunity to star in a mainland China feature film. It was too tempting an offer to refuse. The goal-oriented young man had decided to become a movie star.

A Bright New Career 5

When Li Lian-jie was born in the spring of 1963 in Beijing, China, across the globe in Seattle, Washington, twenty-three-year-old, San Francisco–born Lee Siu-lung was ending his philosophy studies at the University of Washington. Siu-lung, the son of a veteran of the Cantonese Opera and his Shanghai-born wife, had already appeared in several Hong Kong–made features (e.g., 1953's *The Guiding Light* [Foo Hoi Ming Dang]; 1956's *Too Late for Divorce* [Cho Chi Dong Choh Ngo Lut Ga]. In these entries he typically played a surly teenager or a short-fused, scowling ruffian. Later, while attending Saint Francis Xavier College in Hong Kong, Lee Siu-lung studied martial arts. As a student of the ancient discipline he found a peace of mind which helped to end his years as a troublesome punk.

In 1958 Siu-lung returned to San Francisco and, after matriculating at the Edison Vocational School in Seattle, had gone on to the local university. To support himself, he gave dance and martial arts instruction and soon opened his own martial arts academy. His version of martial arts was an amalgam of assorted forms of kung fu, following his stricture: "Absorb what is useful. Discard what is not. Add what is uniquely your own." In 1964 Lee wed the Caucasian Linda Emery, one of his academy pupils and they had two children (Brandon in 1965, Shannon in 1969).

Despite the strong prejudice that existed against non-Caucasians in the Hollywood film and TV industry, ambitious, confident Siu-lung set his goals on returning to filmmaking—this time in America. Spotted by TV producers while competing at a martial arts tournament in Long Beach, California, he was hired

Jet Li in his debut feature *Shaolin Temple* (1982).

for the 1966 TV series *The Green Hornet*. He played Kato, the faithful manservant of white Britt Reid (Van Williams), a crusading newspaper publisher who fought the criminal element using his secret guise of the Green Hornet. Paid the modest sum of $400 a week, Siu-lung—now known professionally as Bruce Lee— added energy and spice to the weekly proceedings as the faithful manservant who helped his boss subdue villains by using martial arts and Nunchaku (fighting sticks). Nevertheless, the show lasted only one season on air. Subsequently, after struggling to find meaningful work in Hollywood, Lee and his family relocated to Hong Kong in the early 1970s. There he worked for prolific film producer Raymond Chow Man-wai in the low-budget 1971 entry *The Big Boss* [Tong Saan Daai Fong]. The slam-bang adventure was popular in its Asian release and, under the title *Fists of Fury*, did well in U.S. distribution. This led to more action movies including 1972's *Fist of Fury* [Cheng Miu Moon] which was a big hit with moviegoers around the world, including America where it was distributed as *The Chinese Connection*. Now known as "the fastest fists in the East," Bruce was contracted by Warner Bros. Studios in Hollywood to headline the American-produced, Hong Kong–made *Enter the Dragon* [Lung Chang Foo Dau] (1973).

In May 1973, while starring in *Game of Death* [Sei Miu Yau Fai] in Hong Kong, Lee suddenly collapsed on the set. Some weeks later he died under mysterious circumstances while visiting an actress friend featured in his current picture. Rumors spread quickly that the beloved star had been done in by foul play. One theory insisted that he had been poisoned by jealous martial arts lords who were angered that the celebrity had shared too many secrets of the ancient art with Westerners. (The autopsy revealed that he had died of a brain edema caused in part by an allergic reaction to Equagesic, a pain remedy he had been given to relieve a severe headache.) After his regal funeral in Hong Kong on July 25, 1973—where fans mobbed the streets near the funeral parlor—Lee's body was flown to Seattle, Washington, for burial at the Lake View Cemetery.

Both before and after Bruce Lee's tragic demise, there had been a host of imitator actors cashing in on the new martial arts film craze that was sweeping the globe. Even Lee made a "new" such movie when footage from the uncompleted *Game of Death* was incorporated into a revamped plot line and stand-ins were used to add Bruce to a few of the newly filmed sequences. Released in 1978, *Game of Death* helped to perpetuate the myth of the legendary Lee who had become a major icon to fans all over the world.

When *Fist of Fury* played in China in 1972, twelve-year-old Li Lian-jie was among the multitude who saw the film. Li has recalled that this action flick—the first of its genre he had viewed—filled him with great excitement. The enthusiastic youngster, who had already made his mark in the world of martial arts competition, had adolescent ambitions of becoming an action movie star like high-kicking, hand-punching Bruce Lee. These thoughts were strengthened when TV and movie news cameramen photographed him practicing wushu or at home with his family celebrating his mother's birthday with a feast of dumplings and birthday cake. (Later on, when he had become famous in the world of cinema, such footage would be incorporated into a host of movie documentaries, including, in 1988, *Dragons of the Orient* [Dong Fang Ju Long], *Abbot Hai Teng of Shaolin* [Shao Lin Hai Deng Da Shi], *This Is Kung Fu* [Chung Wa Miu Sui], in 1992, *The Lucky Way* [Daai Baat Gwa], in 1994, *Shaolin Kung Fu* [Li Lian Jie's Shaolin Kung Fu], and *Top Fighters*.

As with so many other ardent fans throughout the world, Bruce Lee's unexpected death affected Lian-jie very strongly. Although his screen idol/role model was now gone, Li did not abandon his dreams of becoming a movie notable. He has detailed, "In 1974, I did a kung fu demonstration in Hong Kong. One of the bigger movie managers came up to me and said, 'Hi, you're pretty good. Want to become a movie star?' I was eleven. Every year, I starred in [exhibition performances in] Hong Kong, they'd look at me and say, 'You're still too young. Why don't you grow up fast?' I ate a lot every day, but it could not help me grow up faster. So until I was seventeen, I waited." By then, Lian-jie had reached seemingly his full adult height of five feet, six inches. He was still an inch shorter than the not-so-tall Bruce Lee.

In 1979 China was enduring persistent political and economic turmoil. Its foreign policies included an invasion of northern Vietnam and efforts to find ways to increase trade with outside nations. Meanwhile, the country sought to rebuild national pride among its citizens and to enhance its reputation with the world at large. This paralleled the country's growing efforts to counteract the dictates of the late Chairman Mao Zedong's Cultural Revolution. Now the country's rich cultural past—even if most of it had occurred under the totalitarian and oppressive reigns of royal dynasties—was deemed increasingly acceptable to receive respect from the government and public alike. As such, mainland China chose to film a property which would explore and exploit the dramatic history of the Shaolin Temple. It was there in the east China province of Hunan in the foothills of the Central Mountains—at the southern foot of Song Shan Mountain—that the famed monks at Shaolin Temple (founded A.D. 495) had elevated the art of wushu to a fine craft, one that government now wanted its citizenry to take great pride in this tradition.

Over the many centuries the Shaolin monks had fought such enemies as Japanese pirates and Chinese rebellious factions that opposed their royal and/or feudal benefactors. In 1736, Emperor Yong Zheng, fearing that the mighty martial arts monks might work against him, dispatched a contingent of 3,000 soldiers who murdered these wushu experts and burned the building. Thereafter, more myths were added to the growing lore about the Shaolin Temple, and the site and its skilled monks became even more celebrated. By the twentieth century the once-again rebuilt temple had become a haven for ex-soldiers who were terrorizing the neighboring area. In 1928 a local warlord led a force to rout the monks and troops there, and the Temple was burned yet again.

Shaolin Temple (1982).

Now in 1979, with the encouragement of the Chinese government, producer Fu Chi teamed with director Zhang Xinyan (Cheung Yam-yim), who had been directing features since the early 1960s, to make this project, a coproduction of mainland China and Hong Kong. The filmmakers soon decided that the key roles should be cast with real martial artists rather than just actors. One of their top choices was Li Lian-jie. The latter was more than willing to accept the offer which would showcase his finely tuned martial arts skills. As such, the seventeen-year-old abandoned the world of wushu competitions as well as, for the time being, his avocation as a goodwill ambassador for his country. He focused himself on his new career. Others added to the joint production included Qiang Hu-jiang (playing the hero's nemesis) who had been China's recent national wushu champion, and Ding Laam (as the film's agile and feisty heroine, the shepherd girl), a star of the Opera in Beijing.

When the cast and crew arrived at the Temple, the shrine and surrounding grounds were in near ruins. As Lian-jie remembered, "There was nothing left inside, and the exterior of the buildings hadn't been kept in very good order either. There were only three monks living at the temple. One was the abbot, one the gatekeeper, and the last one was the caretaker/cook. As far as we knew, none of them had any particular martial prowess and nobody in the area practiced wushu."

In the wake of the Cultural Revolution, mainland China was reinventing yet again its film industry and this project was slow in getting organized in front of the cameras—in sharp contrast to the rapid filming and quick distribution procedures of the Hong Kong moviemaking business. To begin with, many of the young people in the cast had never before acted in front of a camera, and it took time to get them to relax enough for the needs of the on-camera story line. Then too, cast members such as Li Lian-jie, who had had condensed formal educations

Shaolin Temple (1982).

and who mostly spoke the Mandarin dialect of Chinese, had problems under-standing Cantonese, the latter most often used in film productions. Although, as in standard China/Hong Kong filming methods, the actors' dialogue would be dubbed in during postproduction (along with Chinese—and sometimes English language subtitles which could be read by any literate Chinese no matter what dialect he or she spoke), it was necessary that Lian-jie converse in Cantonese in front of the camera, if not for his sake, then for that of his coplayers. This helped to make his first acting assignment a chore.

Regarding this language roadblock, the star has explained, "To this day, I still wouldn't say that I'm very comfortable speaking Cantonese. When I was making my first movie, I could understand Cantonese when it was spoken to me, but I never seriously studied it myself. Later, Hong Kong people would sometimes make fun of me for speaking 'Jet Li language.' You know, half-Mandarin, half-Cantonese, mix the two together and hope the people understand. Anyway, people who are familiar with me know what I'm trying to say."

Since *The Shaolin Temple* was a fledgling modern martial arts project for the mainland Chinese government forces, there was little consideration given to hav-ing seasoned action choreographers/directors assigned to the movie as was done, for example, in the Hong Kong filmmaking process. According to the star: "The director told us the basic story, and we took what we had learned in [martial arts] class to design our own fight scenes. We'd show the director what we had come up with, and he'd say, 'Well, in this scene, you have the advantage' or 'your char-acter should be more vulnerable. Make the villain stronger.' And we'd go back and change it. Come back for more feedback. Go back and change it again. Before the movie even began shooting, we'd already choreographed all our fights scenes. . . . We didn't know any better and we had no experience, so we made up most of it ourselves. It was a good learning experience."

While making *The Shaolin Temple*, which took most of 1980 and spilled over into 1981, Li learned just how arduous the moviemaking process could be, espe-cially when novice actors were enacting their self-choreographed wushu forms. He fractured his right leg which slowed down production when the filming reached a point where the moviemakers could no longer work around its star. As one sea-son changed to another, the cast and crew endured the sharp alterations in Chinese climate (which went from extreme cold to hot) without the benefits of modern protective clothing (e.g., thermal underwear, waterproof garments). For Lian-jie who had to shave his head for his role, that was the toughest part of his anatomy to keep warm (or cool). He also had problems with his striking palm which reacted to the intense cold, and he required Chinese medicinal treatment to restore the needed use of his hand. When it came time to shoot the combat scene on the riverside, the intricate action required a week of filming. Every morning dutiful Lian-jie and the others in the sequence, who were supposed to look as if they'd just pulled themselves from the river, had to dose themselves daily with a bucket of water—an act requiring sheer willpower to accomplish in such frigid temperatures.

At one point in production, as the young leading man learned the Shaolin Temple rituals for his character to enact on screen, his temple instructors enthused, "You should become a monk!" However, the concerned movie director broke in hurriedly with, "No, wait! Don't do that. We've got a movie to finish."

This being a state-controlled film project and Lian-jie being a novice movie actor, his salary (or subsidy) for the screen project was less than $750 in total which, when divided by the number of days spent on the movie, left him with a fee of pennies a day. However, it did not dampen the newcomer's spirit. He has acknowledged, "The best part about making that movie was . . . that we didn't have to train anymore! Good-bye to eight hours a day of mandatory drills and practice. Compared to what we'd gone through for the past few years, making a movie was a breeze. Even though we were waking up at five or six to get to the set, and shooting from eight until sunset, this was nothing. This was relaxing. Didn't we have to fight all day? Sure, but this was nowhere near as tiring as wushu class. In fact, after we finished the day's shot, we'd go out again and play soccer or basketball. There must have been about thirty to forty of us young people. It was like we had too much energy."

As to that typical problem of most fledgling actors, Lian-jie did not suffer stage jitters. Because he and many of the other limber, eager martial arts students-turned-actors had been around (news) cameras from early on in life, they were used to working in front of them. Nonetheless, acting was somewhat different and harder than executing wushu forms and had to be practiced and improved upon by the young performer. But in the long run, reasoned Lian-jie, "to be able to take something of your own and put it up there on the big screen—that was a genuine pleasure."

Based on Shaolin Temple folklore, the simplistic plot of *The Shaolin Temple*—which incorporates a brief documentary/travelogue in its opening minutes—focuses on seventh-century China where the people are suffering under a tyrannical ruler. Young Jue Yuan (played by Lian-jie) is severely injured in combat against the sinister Wang and, after witnessing his father's murder, flees the slave labor camp where he had been held prisoner. Taking sanctuary at the Shaolin Temple, he is trained in martial arts by a benevolent monk, Shi Fu. When the latter's daughter, a shepherdess, is captured by Wang, Jue Yuan frees her and then helps a prisoner named Li Shi Min to escape his Sui captors. For their own safety, Shi Fu forces his daughter and Jue Yuan to leave the temple grounds. Thereafter, Wang attacks the Shaolins and Shi Fu dies in the skirmish. Still later, Bai and Jue Yuan return to the Temple where, joined by Li Shi Min and rebel forces, they route their adversaries. Chasing Wang to the river Jue Yuan engages in a fierce battle with him and the cruel despot is killed.

Despite its somewhat basic filmmaking techniques, *The Shaolin Temple*, with its artfully arranged color cinematography of gorgeous terrain, cost several million dollars to complete. It debuted in the winter of 1982 in Hong Kong and mainland China where it proved to be a surprise major hit. *Variety* newspaper reported, "A kung-fu picture is a kung-fu picture, but here's something different. While the Shaolin Temple idea has been done to death in the past [in Hong Kong cinema, not to mention the American TV series *Kung Fu*, 1972–75, starring David Carradine] . . . the plot gives opportunities to show off unique and exotic kung-fu techniques not seen before in the countless cheapies that dominated the local screens. The difference lies in the presentation of the martial arts." As for Lian-jie's screen acting debut, the trade paper enthused, "He has verve, youth, charm, humour and marvelous athletic feats yet is without the cockiness of a Cantonese stunt man turned kung-fu star."

Within its first twenty-seven days of playing just in Hong Kong, over 700,000 filmgoers saw the picture, and the movie, which showcased many different forms of martial arts, went on to be a huge hit. With a take of $16.157 million (in Hong Kong dollars*), it even outgrossed the then-box-office champ—Jackie Chan in *Dragon Lord* [Lung Siu Yau]. Moreover, *The Shaolin Temple* was nominated in the Best Action Choreography category at the Hong Kong Film Awards in 1983.

This was just the beginning of the positive effects from this success. Moviegoers were very much taken by the picture's boyish, charming, and handsome lead actor. With his well-defined physique and his mastery of wushu techniques—especially his prowess with the broadsword, the lance, and three-sectional staff—enthusiastic audiences made Lian-jie a movie star overnight. He was the subject of much media

* The exchange rate on the Hong Kong Dollar to the U.S. dollar has been constant since the 1980s, about 7.8 Hong Kong dollars to the American dollar.

Shaolin Temple (1982).

coverage in generally restrained mainland China and received over 100,000 fan letters (some even reportedly written in blood!). Li would recall, "My house was inundated with sacks of mail and we had no room to move around. I wanted to thank everybody individually, but I soon realized that there was no way to answer every letter. Such an attempt would take up every waking hour and it would be impossible for me to continue making movies."

The film also had a tremendous impact on the Temple shrine itself. The crumbling old monastery quickly became a tourist attraction that drew visitors from all over China, Asia, and the world. So many Chinese youngsters were inspired by the movie to take up wushu training at Shaolin as the screen hero had done, that the government had to issue a strong statement. They requested students to please remain in school and *not* to embark on a pilgrimage to the Temple, dreaming of becoming a disciple there. (Nevertheless, hundreds of young people visited the remains of the shrine, hoping to train in the same manner of Li Lian-jie's celluloid character.) Meanwhile, the Chinese government restored the famed Temple, and with the continuing public curiosity about the site, it became a major tourist attraction. Within months martial arts academies, restaurants, stores, etc., rose up near the Temple and, to this day, for miles around as one approaches the famed landmark, these commercial enterprises crowd the vista.

As the government hoped, *The Shaolin Temple*, mainland China's first modern blockbuster screen hit, had a tremendous impact in refocusing Chinese of all ages on the glories of wushu and renewed pride in this traditional Chinese skill. A by-product of this movie success was that audiences were clamoring for the next Li Lian-jie picture. The nineteen-year-old movie recruit was more than happy to oblige.

6

A New Name

The rather leisurely pace of the making of *The Shaolin Temple*—and particularly during the period Li Lian-jie was recuperating from his leg injury sustained during production—gave the teenager ample opportunity to consider the new path his life was now taking. One key element of his new profession that concerned him, and at times depressed him, was the realization that if he continued making such martial arts pictures, no matter how well-trained he kept himself and no matter how careful he might be, there was a strong likelihood that he would undoubtedly suffer new physical mishaps on the film set. In some weaker moments he considered abandoning his new career. At other times, he thought of demanding that more dangerous martial arts work be given over to stunt people, as he had learned was the way of some of the major Hong Kong action stars.

One day, however, Lian-jie had an epiphany: "I just think about it. 'Oh, oh,' I need to tell myself. If I want to become an action actor I need to prefer to break my legs again and again because just like people they want to join the army, they need to think about, if they join the army, they need to go to war to fight, maybe they die. If you want to become a policeman, you already prefer, maybe one day you're going to die on the street. So, I don't have a chance. I love movies, I love action movies, so even broken ten times, I still do it. And I continue to do it."

Within a few months of the winter 1982 release of *The Shaolin Temple*, the Chung Yuen Film Company (which had placed Li under contract during the

Jet Li, as one of the mischievous brothers in *Kids from Shaolin* (1984).

making of his debut feature), began a fresh movie project with its young star. Wanting to tie into the enormous success of *The Shaolin Temple*, they determined the new entry, 1984's *Kids from Shaolin* [Siu Lam Siu Ji], must be a follow-up in subject matter and theme to the original. (By now several Hong Kong film companies had already ripped off the title/concept of *The Shaolin Temple* and there were a spate of such similarly labeled and/or storied martial arts entries in the marketplace.)

While the Chung Yuen Film Company made no attempt to carry forward the same characters from *The Shaolin Temple*, some of the same cast (besides Lian-jie) and crew including director Zhang Xinyan (Cheung Yam-yim), were assigned to the new project. Thus there was an intangible sense of the fresh production being a sequel even though that was not the actual case. (When it came time to market the follow-up picture some distributors wanted to ensure audience identification with the original hit and labeled the movie *Shaolin Temple: Kids from Shaolin* or *Shaolin Temple 2: Kids from Shaolin*.)

Meanwhile, as production was being set for this mainland China/Hong Kong coproduction to commence in August 1982, Li Lian-jie kept himself fit through rigorous daily martial arts practices, a strenuous, demanding task that he continued religiously for many years to come. As the young star was adjusting to his new fame in a new arena, he found himself being given a new name. As legend has it, when the rights to distribute *The Shaolin Temple* were sold in the Philippines, the distributor decided rather than promote the movie as starring Lian-jie Li (since it was the custom in their land to place the first name first, rather than last as in traditional Chinese format), they would advertise the star as Jie Li, which they felt was both shorter and easier for the public to remember. Somewhere along the line, a creative decision-maker, in describing the agile wushu star, enthused that the young man's career was taking off all over Asia as fast as the actor's martial arts moves themselves and that both elements resembled a jet plane zapping skyward. This suggested changing Lian-jie to "Jet Li" and soon the new moniker was being used on posters to advertise *The Shaolin Temple*. (Another variation of his new screen name was Jet Lee, done to tie the screen newcomer with the venerated box-office hero, Bruce Lee.) Thus, supposedly, was the origin's of the Beijing-born celebrity's new screen name.

For plot ideas for *Kids from Shaolin*, the scriptwriters turned to its relatively young cast. The latter recalled mischievous experiences from their childhoods and told the scripters what it had been like to grow up in a wushu school where martial arts was life's top priority. The screenwriters adapted the young performers' anecdotes about impish behavior, enduring friendships (along with the joking and playfulness that accompanies that kinship) and created a tale set in ancient times (although the theme of jovial comradeship was geared to be timeless and universal).

This time the Chinese government subsidized the venture filmed at Hangzhou,

Kids from Shaolin (1984).

the capital of Zhejiang province in East China (and about 100 miles southwest of Shanghai). The crowded city was situated on Hangzhou Bay, an inlet of the Yellow Sea, and the area provided contrasting landscape to allow the story to unfold amidst colorful backgrounds. Once again, the filmmaking process was extremely leisurely and required about ten months to complete. This time around, the cast and crew again experienced all seasonal changes while making the picture. None of them would ever forget the heat of the summer where the temperature averaged well over 104 degrees. (In China, there was a guideline that when the heat reached over 100 degrees, businesses and school would shut down for the day—not true with the shooting of *Kids from Shaolin*.) Sometimes it was so hot that the young performers would crack an egg onto the ground and watch it cook. On the other hand, it was not so amusing when, during shooting, a cast member had to brace his hand against the hot ground to cushion a fall. The earth was so hot that it could easily take off a layer of skin. To remedy the situation, the crew watered the ground continuously. Jet remembered, "During fight scenes, it was not uncommon for one of us to go into shock from heat. . . . You'd be fighting, and suddenly somebody would topple over. Somebody would revive us and then we'd have to shoot the scene again."

Unlike typical action filmmaking today where the editing provides a new camera angle every few seconds to keep audience interest, in *Kids from Shaolin*, the director deliberately filmed relatively long stretches of martial arts interaction from single camera angles so that there would be no doubt in the minds of audiences that the performers were not exhibiting the skills for which they had trained so hard for so many years. This time during the somewhat hazardous stunt work, Jet badly sprained his neck.

As with *The Shaolin Temple* the pay scale for much of the cast was parsimonious at best. Again Jet Li received no more than $750 for the entire project. Also just as before, the perks on location were few indeed. Often the group would camp at a locale where there was no running water and each night each cast and crew member would ladle out his or her apportioned share of hot water which accounted for their bath water for that day. "We lived like the poorest peasants," said Li. "I think actors today might have a hard time imagining the conditions we worked under."

Kids from Shaolin opens with cartoon representations of the characters with an engaging theme song playing as the opening credit roll. It sets the tone for this idyllic fairytale in which San Lung (played by Jet Li) is the eldest of several brothers in a dragon family, descendants of the Shaolins. Their sifu (or teacher) is the man who rescued them years ago from marauders. On the other side of the wide river lives the Phoenix family—in which there are eight girls—and they are descendants of the Wu Tang clan. Much like the American musical *Seven Brides for Seven Brothers* (1954) it is a case of two warring clans who come together as young and older members of each faction pair off, sharing romance together and also their own household's distinctive and highly traditional style of martial arts. Their melding is solidified by a common enemy (a vicious warlord) who is rampaging the countryside and who receives his comeuppance at the film's end.

Within this bucolic action comedy, the still boyish Jet Li not only displays his agility in wushu against male and female opponents, but he further solidifies his image as the earnest, proud, and charismatic country lad who still has much to learn about life—especially about the opposite sex. As would become his cinema trademark in the years ahead, Li's screen alter ego shies away from overt romantic entanglements with his lady love. He remains the good-natured virgin who—at the present time—has more important missions in life than to give into sexual passion. Customary to such Chinese martial arts films, this emerging man has no confusion in treating women warriors as equals (or even superiors) on the battlefield, but regards them as secondary to men off the battlefield.

Kids from Shaolin, with its slowly paced pastoral sequences (including much frolicking in the local river) and its scenes of sibling love, rivalry, and mutual help of one another for the good of the family, was popular with less demanding filmgoers. It did not have, however, the same impact of *The Shaolin Temple*.

Following *Kids from Shaolin*, Jet Li, although still a relative newcomer to making movies, felt the basic formula from *The Shaolin Temple* had run dry. However, by contract he was committed to a third film for the production company. Thus came about 1986's *Martial Arts of Shaolin* [Naam Bak Siu Lam], which some crafty distributors released as *Shaolin Temple 3: Martial Arts of Shaolin*. This time a well-known Hong Kong director, Liu Chia-liang (Lau Kar-liang), a veteran of many Shaw Brothers kung fu epics and, thus, well-versed in the cinema genre, was hired to helm the production. Then too, a lot more Hong Kong talent was used on *Martial Arts of Shaolin* rather than the previous full complement of mainland China cast and crew.

Now in his early twenties, Jet Li had become far more astute about life in general and the business of filmmaking in particular. Although his meager salary of approximately $750 had been nearly doubled for this production, it was still a pittance considering the long period devoted to making the movie. While making *Martial Arts of Shaolin* (which was shot in mainland China and included filming on portions of the Great Wall) the huge discrepancy between his salary as the picture's lead performer and the vastly larger sum doled out, for example, to Hong Kong stunt players who might only be working in the background of scenes which featured him, became clearer. This situation was emphasized when it came time for food breaks on the set. While the mainland Chinese members of the contingent ate their simple fare, the Hong Kong group had far fancier food to consume—edibles provided by a caterer.

The unfairness of such disparate treatment on the project ate away at Li during production. He has recalled, "I began wondering if I wanted to stay in this line of work. . . . Just because I'm a mainlander, I'm supposed to expect this kind of treatment?" As he reasoned, "The studio was depending on me to sell their movie, but

Kids from Shaolin (1984).

they weren't treating me with the most basic level of respect." Jet concluded, "In a capitalist society, this would be unacceptable. In a socialist society, it was intolerable."

Accentuating Li's unhappiness on *Martial Arts of Shaolin* was that, unlike his prior two filmmaking experiences, this time the filmmakers did not allow the cast—some of whom were carried over from the first two pictures—to provide

51

The dexterous Jet Li demonstrates his prowess in *Martial Arts of Shaolin* (1986).

any real input to the story line. For Jet, the final straw came one day when the director scheduled a sequence to be shot at sunrise. This required the actors to arise by 2 A.M. in order to reach the location on time and be in place once the equipment was in position. Daybreak came . . . and went. Still the director did not appear. Finally he arrived around 10 A.M. Then, looking over the locale he said casually, "Oh, the lighting is all wrong now. Let's call it a day." By now the increasingly discontented Li had had enough. He stormed over to the producers and explained what had gone on before. In due course, the director apologized to cast and crew. However, said Li years later, "It was certainly the most tension-filled film I've ever worked on." This time during the production, Jet suffered a badly sprained back.

Despite its production problems, *Martial Arts of Shaolin* benefited from the director's hefty experience with this type of martial arts story. Liu Chia-liang skillfully combined the beauty of the mainland China landscape with the energetic cast's adeptness at action work, and managed to interweave into the proceedings a staple of Hong Kong–made products—slapstick comedy. Under the director's guidance, fluid, fast-paced action, cast/warriors wearing colorful costumes, lots of extras on hand for combat scenes, and quirky but intriguing soundtrack music was the order of the day.

Set in the 1600s during the reign of an infamous dynasty, Jet stars as Zhi Ming, a Northern Shaolin monk with a boyish demeanor and a gift for violent kung fu. Despite having committed himself to the monastic way of life, Zhi seeks to avenge his parents' death by plotting the end of their murderer, a corrupt lord named He Suo. When Suo throws a lavish party in the Forbidden City, Zhi poses as a party performer (undertaking an intricate ceremonial lion dance). However, just when he is about to accomplish his deed of vengeance, two Southern Shaolins accidentally spoil Zhi's undertaking. This duo, a young man and woman, had also made plans to kill Lord Suo. The trio join together and flee the court. Later, the threesome, overcoming the contrasting customs and styles between northern and southern Shaolin temples, repeatedly battle Suo's forces. As the story concludes (upon an elaborate two-tiered royal barge), the evil warlord loses his head in combat with the determined heroine.

Again Jet's screen image is that of a young man full of boyishness (as when he interrupts his intense martial arts training to rescue a little bird that has fallen from a tree). Certain of his abilities as a warrior, Li's character is, however, once again timorous in romance, awkward and adolescent, unsure of how to court persuasively his aggressive young woman friend. This time he has a young rival for his lady's attention, and in the ambiguous finale it appears that his competitor is the one who has won her heart.

Interestingly, in this most agile of the *Shaolin Temple* trilogy, the film seems intent on showcasing Li as celluloid beefcake as he is bare-chested in several

Martial Arts of Shaolin (1986).

scenes. In contrast—and this is the Hong Kong lowbrow comedy influence—there is an extended sequence where, in order to elude the sinister Lord's troops, Jet's Zhi dons the disguise of a peasant girl. While his transformation may be more amusing than convincing for film viewers, the sex-crazed on-camera enemy soldiers are apparently less discerning people. In one scene, the (un)voluptuous farm "girl" who has been leading a flock of sheep (in the midst of which are hidden Zhi's two pals) is almost raped by the troopers until the hero extricates himself from the troublesome situation.

Martial Arts of Shaolin emphasized the different fighting styles of northern and southern China warriors and the cast gave a good account of itself in the fight scenes. This helped to ensure that this picture would be better received than the star's prior entry. Its success promulgated Jet Li's reputation as a young stalwart of the Chinese cinema. By now Li's movies, besides being showcased throughout Asia, were also being exhibited, for example, in the Chinatown theaters of larger United States cities. Mick LaSalle (*San Francisco Chronicle*) in reviewing the picture disparaged the plot, but noted that Li's "technical mastery is astonishing."

Jet's disillusionment with making *Martial Arts of Shaolin* caused the twenty-two-year-old to become quite cynical about his newly launched profession. Again he considered quitting the business. When word of this circulated in the movie industry he received some persuasive offers. One that intrigued him was from his past producer Fu Chi who offered him near carte blanche on a new screen project. Not only could Jet suggest its story line, but the star was granted the opportunity to direct the venture. That, in addition to a salary raise, was too tempting an offer for Li to veto.

Jet saw his new project as a great chance to articulate his growing acrimony with the tremendous contrast between the haves and the have-nots; the Hong Kongers versus China mainlanders. While he intended to emphasize the unfairness of social inequalities he had experienced in moviemaking to date, he (and his advisers) were well aware that if they presented this potentially contentious theme in a contemporary story line, it would meet with severe censorship (or even a shutdown of the picture) from government authorities. Thus, Jet distanced the story back several decades.

As filming got underway on *Born to Defence* [Chung Wa Ying Hung], production was a bit chaotic as novice director Jet sought to guide this ambitious post-World War II tale of American-occupied China. Chui Siu-ming, who had directed such previous early 1980s films as *Gang Master* [Chan Kwai] and *The Fung Shui Master* [Fung Sang Shui Hei] had been brought aboard as action choreographer/director. During one of the several slam-bang kickboxing sequences, Jet Li broke his nose. Besides leaving a slight scar, it put him out of commission for a time. When he returned to the set it was agreed that Chui Siu-ming should take over more responsibilities for directing the picture. As Li would describe the situation: "The producers hired somebody to choreograph our fight scenes, so I started to take a much smaller role in this aspect of filmmaking. Whatever sequences the action directors designed, I learned and performed."

Set in the port city of Qingdao in the Shandong province in East China, the time is the end of World War II as victorious Chinese soldiers return home from the battlefields. They are shocked to find that the Chinese nationalist government seems only to care about pleasing its American allies whose naval forces still dominate the city. As the Chinese veterans enter town they discover quickly that they are second-class citizens compared to the demanding, rapacious American GIs who heap atrocities upon their former Allies. The inequities and indignities continue apace. Meanwhile, Jet Li's on-screen alter ego becomes involved with the prostitute daughter of his army comrade. The latter is disgraced by his offspring's profession and refuses for a long time to accept that she was left with little choice for survival during the war.

Before long, Li's outspoken, prideful Chinese military hero has sparked the enmity of his American compatriots in a local bar. Whenever they encounter the local boy these bullying foreigners seize every opportunity to force him to admit that his U.S. counterparts are much superior to him. As the persecution continues the enraged young man is drawn into (kick)boxing matches with his American "enemies." Taking fierce beatings in the boxing ring from his taller and more robust foes, the brutal fighting continues in other encounters. It ends in an old warehouse (a favorite for such celluloid encounters) where the furious hero battles

Martial Arts of Shaolin (1986).

against a much larger American opponent. As the emotionally and physically exhausted Chinese ex-soldier leaves the scene of mayhem—with his brutish American opponent just barely alive—a freeze frame abruptly ends the narrative.

Before *Born to Defence* was released in 1986, there was some question as to who would receive directing credit for the movie project. However, Chui Sing-ming told Li: "You've started it, so you must be seen to finish it. I'm just helping you out." Thus Jet is listed as director and star of this production, with Chui credited for action choreography/direction.

Born to Defence borrowed in spirit, if not plot, from Jackie Chan's 1980 American-made *The Big Brawl* [Saai Sau Hiu; aka *Battle Creek Brawl*] which in turn would inspire Jean-Claude Van Damme's *Kickboxer* (1989). *Born to Defence* was too downbeat and bitter (and too reflective of past and present conditions in China) to gain much currency with filmgoers of the day. Previously, audiences had thrilled to Li's screen personae in historical epics, where his righteous character emerged victorious from several rounds of stunning traditional combat. In contrast, here his downtrodden hero (who in one screen moment cries) is too depressing for viewers to empathize sufficiently with him. One cannot imagine many young Asian moviegoers relating to this pugnacious soul who, despite his American-style boxing skills and audacity, takes pounding after pounding (and humiliation after humiliation) from the boorish Americans. Not even having the usually fully clad, compact star be shirtless in several scenes did much to help the box office take on this release which opened in Hong Kong in mid February 1988 (where it grossed $11.457 million in Hong Kong dollars, down several million dollars in gross from his first feature, *The Shaolin Temple*).

Years later Jet explained of this venture: "I don't think that I was a very successful director, because I did not achieve my purpose, namely, to get a lot of people to recognize my ideas or understand my point of view. Nor did I attract a lot of attention for trying to tell this story. No, I don't think of myself as a good director. I made the decision not to direct any more movies. Instead I decided to direct my energies back into acting." Summing up the unsatisfying *Born to Defence* experience from the perspective of the year 2000, Jet Li said, "I don't feel this intensely about these issues anymore, but at the time, I was quite young and quite angry. . . . I felt so strongly the need to express my sentiments about social conditions—about how outrageous it was that favoritism for foreigners still existed even after so many years."

The unpleasant and/or chaotic experiences of Li's last films—let alone his declining box-office standing—left Jet very restless. He began to debate mentally the same things that several other Asian movie personalities before him had done: Would he fare better, reach a larger audience, and receive more remuneration if he shifted his focus away from the constraint of mainland China cinema and relocated to Hollywood? If he were going to take such a big chance, now, in his mid-twenties, was an ideal time to do so. Weighing the options, which included an important new woman in his life, Li opted for trying his luck in California.

7

California Dreaming

Having succeeded so spectacularly as a wushu champion at an early age—for which he received tremendous adulation, respect, and worldwide notice—Jet Li was extremely perplexed by his currently fluctuating screen career. After the comparative disappointment of *Born to Defence*, he was finally ready to put into action an idea that had been brewing in his mind since he was eleven and had first come to America. Then, not only did he have a memorable interchange with President Richard M. Nixon on the White House lawn, but the youth briefly sampled the relatively affluent lifestyle that even everyday Americans considered to be a normal way of life.

Also, Jet had heard about the huge salary (in comparison to what Li was being paid per film in China) of $1 million that Hong Kong superstar Jackie Chan was reputed to have received for making his first American-produced feature, *The Big Brawl*. Notwithstanding that that movie, shot in San Antonio, Texas, had not been a huge hit with Americans and Chan had mostly returned to making Hong Kong comedy-action entries. Li, nonetheless, thought his chances might be better in the United States since he was younger (by nine years) than Jackie. Besides, he was constantly being told that, because his martial arts style was purer and more invigorating than what Chan had to offer his filmgoing public, he would be more impressive to American moviegoers.

Another reason for making a fresh start abroad was Jet's personal situation. Despite his early fame, he had been a late bloomer when it came to romance. As a very traditional Chinese man when it came to dating, he would tell *People* magazine in 1998 about the time, years before, when he spent several hours waiting outside a

Jet Li defending the honor of his martial arts sifu in *The Master* (1989; released in 1992).

young woman's house with flowers—hoping to catch a glimpse of her. "Finally," detailed Jet, "her mother came out, took the flowers and went back inside." (This was a rare occasion for the always shy and reticent Li to discuss his personal romantic life with the media.) Now things had changed. By 1987 he was wed to fledgling actress Huang Quiyan (who had been in 1984's *Kids from Shaolin* and 1986's *Martial Arts of Shaolin* with him) and he had responsibilities to be a good provider. (In the next few years Jet and his equally young wife would have two daughters.)

The twenty-four-year-old Li obtained a two-year exit visa from China and came to the United States with his spouse. Before long, the still-naïve Jet discovered that it was not so easy to breach the walls of Hollywood, where the white majority still had a strong bias against casting Asian (Americans) in lead roles in mainstream productions. A rare exception of that time was U.S.-born Russell Wong, a handsome Asian American who alternated his film projects between mainstream ventures such as the American-produced *Tai-Pan* (1986) and *China Girl* (1987) with Chinese-language pictures such as 1986's *Gwai Ma Haau Yuen*. Wong, whose brother Michael had become a Hong Kong movie performer, had lived for a time in that city. During his stay in the Far East, Russell had studied martial arts under Wu Bin, the same master who once instructed Jet Li.

Of course it did not help matters in Tinseltown that unlike American Wong (who spoke fluent English) or Hong Kong's Jackie Chan (whose English was constantly improving), Jet Li had only a sparse command of English vocabulary. In addition, what words he did speak in that language were heavily accented. While waiting for Hollywood to show any interest in him, Li accepted a lead role in a Hong Kong–produced feature. It was to be shot in the United States, although it was to be a Chinese-language project. (In typical Hong Kong fashion the voices would be dubbed in post production with the Asian characters talking Chinese and the Americans in English, and subtitles to help viewers comprehend the story line.) The picture was geared for Asian audiences with the American terrain providing an exotic backdrop.

Dragon Fight [Lung Joi Tin Aai] was made in late 1988/early 1989 in San Francisco with fledgling director Billy Tang Hin-sing in charge of what proved to be a makeshift production. Others in the cast were two performers from Shanghai. One was Stephen Chow Sing-chi, a prolific performer long before he gained his strong following in films. He was to play a comedic type in the proceedings—as the hero's new-found friend, one whose character is soon killed off. The other was attractive Nina Li Chi (as the picture's heroine), who had studied for a time in the Unied States, but had returned to Hong Kong in 1986 where she entered and won the Miss Asia contest. Her early films included 1986's *The Seventh Curse* [Yuen Jan Hap Yue Wai Shut Lee] and 1987's *Seven Years Itch* [Chat Nin Ji Yeung]. The action director was Dick Wei whose early acting credits interestingly included 1977's *The Chinatown Kid* [Tong Yan Gaai Siu Ji]. In this film his kung fu student character is corrupted by the San Francisco scene, similar to the plot elements which found their way into this new Jet Li project.

Made under the working title of *The Defector*, the simplistic tale utilized several biographical elements from Jet's life. He starred as Ah Lap, a wushu performer on tour in the Golden Gate city with his martial arts team from China. One of his group (played by C. L. Tu) defects and, in so doing, accidentally kills a police officer. When Ah Lap is wrongly accused of the crime, he must locate his pal to clear his name. The latter, meanwhile, is rising through the ranks of a local underworld gang which specializes in drug deals.

Outdoor scenes were filmed on the streets of San Francisco and incorporated several landmarks into the backgrounds. Unfortunately, the unsophisticated picture was a hackneyed story with the worst acting being provided by the Caucasian members of the cast. Whether showing careening car chases up and down the city's hilly streets—shades of Steve McQueen's *Bullitt* (1968)—or individuals slugging it out in local (Chinatown) haunts, the uninspired picture lacked pacing or interesting characterizations. Li looks comfortable on camera in the opening scenes which show him and his teammates performing their wushu art in a San Francisco auditorium, but thereafter, like his character, he seems to be a fish out of water. Confused by the bustling American city and daunted by his efforts to clear his name (so he can regain a passport and return to China), he muddles his way through dialogue interchanges. Thankfully, Li comes to life in his climactic confrontation scene with his former wushu pal and underworld thugs in a farmyard barn. At that point, Li's Ah Lap uses every weapon at hand (poles, sticks, a sword hanging on the wall, etc.) to combat the gun-carrying villains. His on-screen fighting includes a variety of styles including dragon and open-handed kickboxing.

As a botched blend of Hong Kong filmmaking and American quickie moviemaking, *Dragon Fight* did not do much to enhance Jet Li's stalled acting career. In the United States it was relegated to Chinese-language movie theaters and, back in Asia, it was just another unremarkable new entry from the one-time star of *The Shaolin Temple*, bolstered strictly by the novelty of the San Francisco on-location shooting. (In its Hong Kong run, it grossed $6.815 million in Hong Kong dollars.)

While this marginal release did little for Li's professional status, on the set the married actor developed a new romance—with his beautiful co-star, Nina Li Chi, who was one-and-a-half years older than Jet. As he described later, "We fell in love right away. Our feelings for each other were very strong. People wondered how long it would last." Still wed at the time, Jet told her, "Let's not rush into anything. What I mean is, if we still feel this way about each other ten years from now, I think we should get married then." Her reply was: "Alright. If you ask me then, I promise that the answer will be yes."

During his stay in the United States when no moviemaking was happening for him, Li and his wife reportedly taught martial arts classes and he worked at turning around his sagging screen career. He also earnestly promoted the wushu competition that was to be part of the Asian Sports convention to be held in Beijing

A romantic interlude within *The Master* (1989; released in 1992) between co-leads Jet Li and Crystal Kwok Gam-yan.

in 1990. By now his marriage was floundering badly as he was pining for Nina Li Chi, who was back in Hong Kong making movies; her career was on a fast rise. Eventually, Jet had a new picture offer, this time from Hong Kong. It was to star in a movie *Ji Lang Hang Tin Gwong*, which would be known to later English-language audiences as *The Master*. It was to be directed by Tsui Hark, the Canton-born filmmaker.

Tsui was raised in Saigon and made his first (home) movie at age ten. After completing his secondary education in Hong Kong, he came to America to be a film major in college. He studied at colleges in Texas for three years, later moved to New York and, by 1976, was back in Hong Kong. He made his feature film directing debut with 1979's *The Butterfly Murders* [Dip Bin] and had a box-office hit with 1981's *All the Wrong Clues* [Gwai Ma Chi Doh Sing], a spy spoof. In the mid 1980s he formed his own highly successful production company (Film

Workshop) with his producer wife (Nansun Shi). In 1986, he created Cinefex Workshop, a high-tech special effects firm. The next year he enjoyed international success by producing/directing *Peking Opera Blues* [Diy Ma Daan], followed by producing 1987's *A Chinese Ghost Story* [Sin Nui Yau Wan]. He also acted in movies, notably in 1987's *Final Victory* [Chui Hau Sing Lei].

According to Lisa Morton in *The Cinema of Tsui Hark* (2001), the director told her that Hong Kong's Golden Harvest film company approached him about the idea of doing a picture with Jet. According to Hark, "I said, 'Jet Li is being wasted. We should . . . do all sorts of things with him [to] restart the action kung fu film again after Jackie Chan.' " So Tsui, well-acquainted with the United States, returned to America to make *The Master*. The film was geared for the Asian market where Jet Li's name meant something, and would likely get distribution in the Chinese movie theater circuit in America. As such the postproduction dubbing would have Asian actors speaking Chinese and the American performers talking

Jet Li doing battle with co-player Jerry Trimble in the American-shot *The Master* (1989; released in 1992).

in English, with subtitles to be utilized. This project was to be filmed in Los Angeles and, if it turned out as hoped, it might get mainstream distribution in the action movie marketplace, following in the path of Jackie Chan's American production *The Protectors* (1985), which, as it turned out, proved not to be a box-office success.

The uncomplicated plot of *The Master* finds old Uncle Tak (played by Yuen Wah) operating a combination kung fu school/herbal store (Po Chi Lam) in Los Angeles. Tak is severely thrashed by arrogant kung fu expert Johnny (played by Jerry Trimble) who runs the all-American School of Martial Arts. Badly in need of assistance, Tak summons Chuck (played by Jet)—his very best student—to fly from Hong Kong to L.A. No sooner does the dutiful young visitor reach his destination then he is robbed by a Hispanic gang, outmaneuvered by a crafty taxi driver, and hounded by a female cop. Most of all he is harassed by the vicious Johnny and his punks who are determined to eliminate (in any way necessary) all rival martial arts school within their turf. Eventually, Chuck's Latino assailants—now his friends and pupils—join with their new mentor and Tak to combat the sinister Johnny in a climactic showdown. Along the way Chuck meets May (played by Crystal Kwok Gam-yan) with whom he forms a growing friendship.

Unfortunately, little went right during the making of *The Master*. For one thing, there was on-set friction between Jet and coplayer Jerry Trimble which failed to translate into an edgy combativeness on camera. For another matter, during production Li broke his right wrist. Thus he could not use that arm for his martial arts routines in this picture as he clashes with Johnny and his thugs. It took a lot of creativity to find ways for the hero to fight his adversaries one-handed, often with the injured limb positioned behind his back or leaning on some prop. (At one time the camera focused on Jet's leg work and stayed away from showing his immobile arm.) In some scenes shot after his injury, Li wore a zipper jacket whose right sleeve was pulled way down over his hand to hide his cast. (It gave the star a very lopsided look in these sequences.) Li has described, with tremendous understatement, the effect of his mishap on this production which displayed few interesting stunt interludes: "It was a terrible inconvenience caused by a not so simple injury."

During his three months in the United States to make *The Master*, Tsui Hark was not only disappointed by the production crew assembled for the project, but he made several discoveries about his new leading man. "I found out there's a lot of things he doesn't do, doesn't like to do, [or] he likes to do." As the director summed up the situation: "I was thinking about something and it didn't work out—the casting, the story, everything. . . . I thought it was supposed to be a comedy, but . . . Jet doesn't act in the way that I expect him to act. And that's something that I realized in the middle of production. I found that it didn't work."

The completed version of *The Master* was so lackluster and full of continuity flaws that the Hong Kong production executives shelved the movie for the time being both at home and abroad. Only after Jet Li reestablished himself at the Hong Kong box office in 1992 was it issued. Then, because of the renewed fame of the star and his work in tandem with the well-known Tsui Hark, was the picture unleashed. It earned a respectable $8.096 million (in Hong Kong dollars) in its Hong Kong exhibition, thanks to the new crest of popularity on which Jet was then riding.

Meanwhile, as Li's exit visa ended and Hollywood had not found a place for him in their production lineup, Jet returned to his homeland. If his marriage to Huang Qiuyan, the mother of his two little girls, was over, there was his growing relationship with Nina Li Chi. She was busily, and successfully, making feature films back in Hong Kong. Moreover, despite the misadventure in his collaboration with Tsui Hark on *The Master*, the prolific filmmaker still believed that Jet had a real future in film—if the right vehicle could be found. It so happened Tsui had one in mind. It was called *Once Upon a Time in China* [Wong Fei Hung].

8
A New Beginning

As the 1990s began, Jet Li's entire life underwent changes. For one thing he had ended his extended stay in the United States and returned to China. It was a land then filled with turmoil. In 1989 his homeland had undergone such key events as the tragic slaying of many hundreds of students and city residents during the student protest demonstration in Beijing's Tiananmen Square. There was also the resignation of Deng Xiaoping as chairman of the Chinese Communist Party. In early 1990 the Chinese government announced a two-year economic austerity program. Later in the year the Eighth Five-Year Plan for China was outlined, a blueprint to make the country more stable and self-reliant.

During all this disorder in mainland China, Jet negotiated permission to relocate to Hong Kong where he had pending film plans. For another thing, Li's marriage to his first wife, Huang Quiyan, was now over and he was soon to be divorced quietly without the media making much note of the situation. (Jet's two daughters would eventually become part of his mother's household.) These days, Li's constant companion was still actress Nina Li Chi, his *Dragon Fight* (1989) co-star. She was now actively pursuing her movie career. For example, among her five 1990 feature films were *The Spooky Family* [Chuk Gwai Gap Ga Foon] and *The Dragon from Russia* [Hung Cheung Fei Lung]. As for Jet, professionally he was winding down his activities on behalf of promoting the Chinese art/sport of wushu and was preparing to start filmmaker Tsui Hark's *Once Upon a Time in China* [Wong Fei Hung] (1991). At the time, no one—including Jet Li—could have anticipated that playing the lead role of Wong Fei

Hung on camera would launch him so quickly into the ranks of Hong Kong movie superstars.

The character of Wong Fei Hung was based on a real-life figure who was born in the Chinese province of Canton in 1847. It is known that Fei Hung's father, Wong Kay-ying, was a well-regarded martial arts master, one of the famous Canton warriors known as the Ten Tigers of Canton. He was also highly regarded for his use of the Hung Kuen (i.e., Hung's Fist) style of martial arts. Because—for motives not recorded in history—he did not deem to instruct his son in the martial arts, the offspring trained under the father's master (Luk Ah-choy). As an adult, Wong Fei Hung gained a strong reputation for his abilities in using Hung Kuen, for his agility of Lion Dancing (a traditional ritual favored in southern China), and for his knowledge and practice of Chinese (herbal) medicine and the healing art of acupuncture. Over the years his fame as a righteous man who, like Robin Hood, championed the poor against the injustices of the rich, made him a legendary figure. Not many other details of his actual life are known beyond the fact that he trained many disciples—whose teaching of Hung Kuen have carried on to the present time—and that his righteous and noble deeds over the decades ensured his immortality to the Chinese. At age seventy-seven, Wong Fei Hung died in 1924.

Both before and after his death, the amazing Wong Fei Hung inspired much folklore which wove fact and fiction about the exploits of this famed figure. He was also the subject of many popular novels by Zhu Yuzhai which extolled the munificent activities of this historical character. In 1949 filmmaker Wu Pang starred Kwan Tak-hing in a movie called *The Story of Wong Fei Hung* [Wong Fei Hung Chuen]. It was so incredibly popular that, in the next twenty-one years, the Yong Yao Film Company made ninety-eight other entries in the film series. A few years later, Kwan Tak-hing made additional Wong Fei Hung entries for Golden Harvest, such as 1974's *The Skyhawk* [Wong Fei Hung Siu Lam Kuen]. Thereafter, the screen property—which had reached over into other media—did not die. Other actors took on the challenging movie role of Wong Fei Hung. Among many, these included Liu Chia-Liang (Lau Kar-liang) in 1976's *Challenge of the Masters* [Luk A Choi Yue Wong Fei Hung] and 1981's *Martial Club* [Miu Goon] and Jackie Chan in 1978's *Drunken Master* [Chui Kuen].

In 1990, film producer/director Tsui Hark was at a peak of activity and success with his Hong Kong–based Film Workshop. Thus, there was great expectation when he announced that he was to revive the Wong Fei Hung legend on film and that Jet Li would star in the coveted title role, playing a man who epitomized the traditional Confucian virtues (such as Charitable Love, Peace, Propriety, and

Righteousness). Li was intrigued with the challenge of tackling the athletic role of Wong Fei Hung not only because it would allow him ample opportunity to display his martial arts skills but also for another key reason. As he explained once: "When I was young, China was very, very poor. Chinese society was completely closed off and we saw nothing of the outside, but now that the country has opened up suddenly the youth are embracing everything that is Western, with the attitude that nothing in the West is bad and all things Chinese are worthless. It's changing now, but that was definitely the attitude when I first started making movies, and so I wanted to let them know that there was value in old characters like [Wong Fei Hung] . . . " In addition, he was naturally eager to get his stalled movie career back on track. Except for several late 1980s martial arts documentaries that incorporated footage of Jet Li performing as a young man, moviegoers had not seen him in a new production since the lackluster *Dragon Fight* of 1989. Meanwhile, such stars as Jackie Chan and Chow Yun-fat reigned as the kings of Hong Kong/China cinema.

Over the years, Hong Kong film production companies could not afford the same large budgets that Hollywood filmmakers enjoyed, and thus they had learned to be inventive in creating viable substitutes for such items as costly computer-generated special effects. By the 1980s it had become an established convention of Hong Kong cinema that, in costumed action entries, to give the on-screen pageantry more fantasy illusion, they would rely on the process of wire work. (In this technique, the actor is attached to heavy wire cables which run through pulleys attached to a huge crane which, in turn, is operated by several technicians. This allows the actor to "fly" through the air—soaring, tumbling, and swooping as he or she combats opponents also harnessed by such wire cables. Through camera angles and lighting, the wire would be generally invisible in the finished filmed scene.) It was a technique that would gain currency later in the West thanks to such international box-office hits as *The Matrix* (1999) and *Crouching Tiger, Hidden Dragon* [Ngo Foo Chong Lung] (2000). One of the big practitioners of this wire-work art in Hong Kong cinema was actor/action director Yuen Cheung-yan. He had been orchestrating such effects on screen from the 1980s onward and had worked with moviemaker Tsui Hark on such pictures as 1987's *A Chinese Ghost Story. Once Upon a Time in China* would give Jet Li his first real experience in wire work, which was such an essential ingredient in creating the magic of the movie.

On the other hand, the Hong Kong filmmakers could afford to use another type of special effect—that of slowing down the speed of the camera from its usual twenty-four frames per second. This was done because action stars, such as Jet Li, were literally so fast in their martial arts moves that the average filmgoer would miss many of the details of their on-camera action work. This, in turn, led the film director to having the cinematographer speed up the frames per seconds when lensing other performers in the scene so that the pacing between characters would appear consistent to viewers.

As Tsui and his screenwriting team prepared the story line for *Once Upon a Time in China*, they, like so many others in the Hong Kong entertainment industry, were ever mindful that, in July 1997, the hundred-year reign of the British over this crown colony would end. Thereafter, Hong Kong would be melded back into the control of mainland Communist China. The upcoming event led many Hong Kong filmmakers to worry about what the transition would mean to their movie industry. In turn, it caused them to reflect on China's history and the repercussions over the centuries of foreign influences and foreign control of the country. (This paralleled life in present-day China, which was undergoing many changes as the current government dealt with the nation's need to interact with foreign countries in order to help modern China cope economically and politically.) Thus Hark set *Once Upon a Time in China* in the late 1870s, a frenzied period in China's history as the Qing dynasty found itself under assault from greedy foreign powers. The moviemaker positioned the picture's hero, Wong Fei Hung, to be the film's commentator and to provide its point of view. Thus Fei Hung, the man of intellect, medical skills, and high martial arts talents, is the key figure who examines what colonialism has done to China. He is the one coping on screen with such weighty issues as the pros and cons of Western values (and technology) which were increasingly impinging on his homeland.

Weeks before *Once Upon a Time in China* started production, Tsui Hark invited Jet Li to his home so they could discuss the epic's action sequences. Once there, his host turned on his VCR and showed the actor a wildlife documentary. It was one in which a lion was stalking its potential next meal in an elaborate ritual of observation, action, and reaction. While Li was interested in the footage, he was not overwhelmed by the subject matter. The action star wondered what this screening had to do with his upcoming movie.

Tsui: Okay? How about it?

Li: How about what?

Tsui: The action scenes that we just went over.

Li: What are you talking about? We never even started discussing the action scenes.

Tsui: You know, the action in a martial arts movie is a display of physical skill. But capturing the disturbing tension of the moment just before a battle—that's pretty important, too.

Suddenly, the real purpose of the screening exercise began to dawn on Jet and he asked to see the documentary again. This time he carefully observed as the lion passed through a stage of growing hunger to one of hunting its next target (an antelope). The wildlife footage now gave Li insight into his screen character as to the tension that should be conveyed *before* the actual on-screen fight with his enemy began. This education would prove very useful to Jet during the filming of combat sequences in the picture. As Tsui had hoped, the tape viewing had been a revelation for Li. Now the actor could say, "Look at the two main characters right before they begin fighting. Circling each other. The wind, the fire, the expressions in their eyes. You know that a fierce battle is already underway. And the inspiration for that scene came from the nature documentary! That's how I learned to view fight scenes from a different perspective. No longer were they just a series of physical movements. . . . You had to take a step back and see the emotions."

As the shooting of *Once Upon a Time in China* began, there were times when Jet questioned the director's approach to a particular piece of action. For example, he observed, "Occasionally, the script demanded that our characters perform bizarre and improbable feats. Case in point: Wong Fei Hung's 'No Shadow Kick.' A few of us [cast members] protested, feeling that the audience would find it impossible to believe that a person could land seven kicks in midair. But Tsui Hark insisted on it. So we all had a lively argument about this issue. Of course, the director's vision always wins out, so we agreed to respect his decision. But I remember asking him, 'Don't you think that this kick is a little too exaggerated?'"

The moviemaker responded to Jet with, "You've forgotten one thing. Once the audience begins to sympathize with the character, he can't do anything wrong. Even if he does something slightly superhuman, they're willing to suspend their disbelief. The audience is already wrapped up in the character and his story; it's not like they're watching the No Shadow Kick out of context. So when I plot out each move, I often ask myself: 'If I were watching this as a member of the audience, would I be able to keep up with the idea that is being conveyed in that instant?' They might miss it altogether. Remember, a fight scene may take one to two months to choreograph and film, but the audience experiences it in a few seconds. It's never just a matter of the physical movements."

For Jet, "These ideas had a huge impact on the way I approached the movies I would make—and the action sequences that I helped create—in the 1990s. I had the chance to put these methods into practice in each movie, and each time, I learned a little more. Even now, while blocking out a fight, I still make a point of pulling back a little and think: If I were watching this for the first time, would I understand what this fight scene is really about?"

One of the opening scenes of *Once Upon a Time in China* required Jet's Wong Fei Hung to balance on ropes (strung taut between poles) as he performed the time-honored Lion Dance. As Li described later, "Lion dancing is based on southern Chinese martial arts and it's used for celebrations and festive days. Because the character of Wong Fei Hung is a southerner, we had to learn it especially for the movie." The star added, "I worked very closely with Yuen Woo-ping, the action director of *Once Upon a Time in China*. We choreographed the movements

Jet Li as the righteous Wong Fei Hung in *Once Upon a Time in China* (1991).

together. Of course, we used a lot of different camera angles to make certain scenes possible. You could search all over the world and you'd never find a teacher who would be able to tell you how to do the lion dance moves that we did in those films! For example, running up the walls and playing on the ceiling—clearly, this is impossible in real life! In the movies, you could do whatever you want. . . . So actually, I didn't put an extensive amount of time and effort into learning lion dancing for the movie. Naturally we still needed to learn a few new movements and techniques: how to fight in the Southern Chinese style, how to use the gongma [a weapon], which is different, etc. These were new skills. But if you've been trained in martial arts, you have the foundation, and that helps you learn very quickly."

During the making of *Once Upon a Time in China*—accomplished relatively quickly as was the style of Hong Kong filmmakers and especially of Tsui Hark, who ambitiously edited the film as he supervised the daily shooting—Li suffered another on-set injury. This time the actor broke his left leg and ankle while undertaking a stunt routine. Because of his limb being out of commission, subsequent sequences had to be rechoreographed (at times using stunt people). Sometimes an ingenious gambit allowed the injured Li to seemingly perform a tough action interlude. For example, "In one fighting scene, I actually sat on a dolly wheeled forward by several assistants. All I did, in that scene, was move my arms around while my legs, contrary to the impression created by the finished product, remained still. I was essentially lying back on a makeshift wheelchair while pretending to be the invincible hero. That scene, not surprisingly, was a difficult one for me." (This moviemaking injury was the last major one to date to befall Li while making his action entries. However, because of his old injuries and his body no longer compensating for his ailments in quite the same manner as when he was a teenager, he began to rely, from time-to-time, on stunt people to help out with aspects of some of his complicated action routines.)

Despite the potential danger of using several different cameramen (with their own styles) to gain the overall vision he demanded, Tsui Hark managed to keep the movie production unified in look and spirit as he quickly assembled the footage into a final cut.

Within *Once Upon a Time in China*, the time is the 1870s in China, where Wong Fei Hung is asked by a local official to form a guard unit to watch over the Chinese in Canton against (invading) foreigners who are corrupting the government and exploiting the people. In his task of righting the political and cultural balance that has been upset, the virtuous and conservative Wong Fei Hung is assisted by self-sufficient Aunt Yee. (She is actually a dear friend, *not* a close relative, who adores the doctor/martial artist.) Yee has just returned from abroad. She sports proper Victorian attire and boasts a new-fangled camera which she uses to photography everything in sight. Others aiding the hero are "Buck Teeth" Sol, who has been educated in Western ways, and the pugnacious "Porky" Lang. (Both of them are comic figures utilized to provide the expected lowbrow comedy, so much a tradition in Hong Kong cinema.)

As events compound and intertwine, Wong must deal with a vicious rival martial arts master ("Iron Robe" Yim). He must also combat local thugs who are extorting profits from the townsfolk, and cope with conniving American slave traders who seek to sell Chinese women into prostitution. In the process Fei Hung is set up by his foes to take the blame for a disturbance. As such, he is placed under house arrest, but later maneuvers out of his detainment. By story's end, Wong has agreed to wear a Western suit that Aunt Yee has arranged to be made, has come to terms with the realization that martial arts cannot compete against firearms, and begun to appreciate Yee's enthusiastic forecast that "China will change with the world."

In the course of the 134-minute saga, Li's stoic, handsome Wong Fei Hung—with his half-shaved head, his ponytail, his bushy eyebrows, and his traditional white street robe—masterfully handles a wide variety of disastrous encounters with enemies, ranging from a restaurant free-for-all, to an ambush at the Opera, and, finally, the rescue of Aunt Yee—who is amazingly trouble-prone—which leads to a showdown with "Iron Robe" Yim and the sinister American, Jackson.

In his moments of combat, Wong Fei Hung, the contemplative folk hero, proves to be a man of practicality whenever he springs into action. If he doesn't have a martial arts weapon at hand, he grabs his umbrella to use as a good substitute. Should his scoundrelly opponent be firing a gun in his direction, the Chinese healer nimbly reflects the oncoming pellet and flicks it back at his enemy with deadly results. Fei Hung's final encounter with "Iron Robe" takes place in a dank warehouse by the docks. Their crucial contest of skills occurs as they fight on ladders in which the benign pieces of equipment become animated weapons of war, with the two opponents flipping, spinning, and whacking away at one another as the ladders see-saw, splinter into pieces, etc. On its own, this is an astonishing sequence, showcasing Jet Li's martial arts skills to a tremendous advantage. (Within this film's heavy-duty action sequences, some of the picture's fight choreographers/directors appear on camera performing very graceful kung fu moves.)

Adding dimension to Li's role as a physician/martial arts master is the responsible young man's hesitant relationship with the very progressive and very lovestruck Aunt Yee. With Rosamund Kwan Che-lam beautifully handling this crucial assignment, she and Wong Fei Hung engage in their tentative (on his part) courtship. The height of their budding romance—slowed down considerably by the hero's traditional propriety and his inexperience in matters of love—occurs when Yee is measuring her beloved for a suit and uses her hand to throw shadows on the wall which suggests she is caressing the object of her affection. (This virginal aspect of Jet's unworldly screen alter ego would be carried forward both in his further playing of the Wong Fei Hung character and in many of his other cinema roles of the 1990s. It became one of his enduring movie trademarks, a trait which has exasperated some reviewers and filmgoers, while endearing him to others.)

Midst the stunning costumes and impressive landscapes of this leisurely paced action adventure, one scene particularly stands out as synonymous with this picture (and the new series)—that of a mass of Wong Fei Hung's followers agilely training on the beach. Beautifully choreographed and lensed, it effectively displays the men's physical prowess. (This impressive sequence with its pulsating theme music would crop up again in later movie entries of *Once Upon a Time in China*.)

With its themes of cultural identity and technological invasion, *Once Upon a Time in China* opened on August 15, 1991, in Hong Kong where the historical epic was an immediate hit with audiences. It ranked #8 for the year on the list of major box-office successes there, grossing $29.672 million (in Hong Kong dollars). The picture garnered several prizes in addition to many other nominations at the 1992 Hong Kong Film Awards.

By 1991, more Western screening venues—not just Chinese film houses in England, the United States, and elsewhere—were showing Hong Kong feature films. Epics such as this began to show up in genre movie festivals in America and abroad. *Weekly Variety*'s Derek Elley, who viewed the picture at the London Film Festival, labeled *Once Upon a Time in China* a "chopsocky epic with a modern message." Granting that the production was overlong, Elley, nevertheless, judged it a "dazzling slice of escapism that could find a limited Western audience with judicious trimming." The critic rated Li as "solid."

When *Once Upon a Time in China* played in New York City in 1992, it was offered in an abbreviated 112 minute-version, chopping twenty minutes off the running time of this intricately plotted spectacle. Stephen Holden (*New York Times*) enthused, "The kung fu fighting sequences . . . are more than just balletic displays of martial-arts prowess. They are extended acrobatic fantasies in which

Wong Fei Hung (Jet Li) an invincible figure from modern Chinese folklore, executes whoshing Superman leaps and in one scene turns an umbrella into a miraculous combination of sword, shield, parachute and human-meat hook." He pointed out, "As in other films of the kung fu genre, the haphazard synchronization of sped-up blows, which often seem to avoid landing on flesh, with the soundtrack's thuds and slaps creates an eerie sense of discontinuity." Thus, for him, "Despite the frantic activity, the combat is strangely nonviolent." Holden concluded, "With its pageantry and battle scenes and its Hong Kong–style version of spaghetti-western music *Once Upon a Time in China* is an unabashedly gaudy film." For J. Hoberman (*Village Voice*): "The action montage is super and Jet Li is impressively acrobatic . . . "

Even after experiencing the truncated version (which confuses the complex plotline) of *Once Upon a Time in China,* a positive Jami Bernard (*New York Post*) had words of advice for American moviemakers: "Hey, Hollywood! Why don't you snap up these filmmakers to give some juice to those boring car-chase movies? If it weren't for our national aversion to reading subtitles, these Hong Kong movies would wipe the American ones off the map."

New York magazine's David Denby found the condensed edition of the picture damaging to the film's continuity. However, "amid the confusion, the great kung-fu star Jet Li, playing the anti-western leader, can be seen doing his [Fred] Astaire-like moves—the fights are what the movie is really about. *Once Upon a Time in China* is a manic mix of melodrama, action, and farce, all of it pitched at a speed that seems to make a mockery of the very notion of coherent narrative. Jokes and 'political' ideas whiz by as fast as the flying feet."

(Several years later in 2001, by which time movie watchers in the West were more accustomed to watching foreign-language films, a restored print of *Once Upon a Time in China* would be issued in DVD and VHS format and new dubbing/subtitling provided so the expanding marketplace for the work of Jet Li and Tsui Hark could enjoy this long-heralded feature.)

Meanwhile, as *Once Upon a Time in China* was being distributed throughout Asia, Jet Li experienced a surge in his box-office popularity. His fans were responding with the same high enthusiasm that had surrounded his screen debut in *The Shaolin Temple* back in 1982. Older and wiser now, the twentysomething Li was better equipped to deal with the frenzy of his public, including the women who wrote him fan letters in blood. Recalling one of his promotional tours for this release, Li described: "It was just crazy. In South Korea I had eight bodyguards, plus 700 policemen. Still the people broke my car."

Such crowd hysteria surrounding Jet's public appearances in Asia substantiated that Li was a key reason for the impressive box-office take on *Once Upon a Time in China*. It clearly demonstrated that Jet was now a martial arts superstar in the Asian marketplace. The result was a huge outcry from the public for more such movies starring Jet Li. The actor was more than willing to oblige his fans.

The Emerging Superstar

9

T he tremendous popularity of *Once Upon a Time in China* made Jet Li a major celebrity in Hong Kong films where Jackie Chan, Chow Yun-fat, and Sammo Hung Kam-bo were among the top echelon at the box office. The hit movie also reestablished the costumed martial arts epic as a viable genre in the current Asian marketplace. Everyone was rushing to jump on this "new" trend, imitating and expanding upon Tsui Hark's original, including the use of wire work (which some termed wire fu) to enhance the entertainment values of their projects' combat sequences. As for Tsui Hark and Jet Li, when *Once Upon a Time in China* burst so successfully onto the cinema scene, they immediately made a sequel to their box-office bonanza. It was entitled *Once Upon a Time in China II* [Wong Fei Hung Ji Yee: Laam Ngai Dong Chi Keung] (1992).

Li, who appreciated and was enjoying his reclaimed fame (despite all its pressures and adjustments), was excited by the thought of playing Wong Fei Hung in a follow-up movie. He explained, "The main character wasn't the typical martial arts protagonist. He was a healer. He doesn't want to kill his enemies; he wants to turn the bad guys into good guys. This film stands out for me because the main character's goal is not to defeat his opponents physically, but rather to influence, in a positive way, their mental and spiritual development."

By now, Jet and filmmaker Tsui Hark had developed a shorthand for working together on the sound stage. Therefore, Hark had no need to reshow his star the wildlife documentary to help the martial arts actor with his character's motivation as, within the plot line, he prepares to engage his enemies in battle. Li had absorbed a great deal during the making of the initial *Once Upon a Time in China*.

Jet Li as the righteous Wong Fei Hung in *Once Upon a Time in China* (1991).

In the new vehicle, Rosamund Kwan Chi-lam returned as the engaging Aunt Yee. This time, however, Max Mok Siu-chung was cast as Leung Foon, the trouble-prone young assistant to the much-respected herbalist/martial arts master, Wong Fei Hung. (Gone for the time being from this big-screen continuation of the Wong Fei Hung saga are two of the hero's past followers, "Buck Teeth" Sol and

"Porky" Lang.) While the first installment of *Once Upon a Time in China* took place in the 1870s, the new edition is set in 1895 China. (Despite the passing of decades, Wong Fei Hung and Aunt Yee's character have not aged a bit.) The new installment occurs in the tumultuous period when the Boxer Rebellion is truly getting underway.

The sequel opens as the White Lotus cult, a murderous group dedicated to removing all things foreign from China, are gathered in a large meeting chamber. They are led by an extreme zealot, the priest Kung. During a rite to stir up further the fervent followers, Kung calls upon the gods as he thunders through a ritual demonstrating dramatically that he is impervious to fire, blades, and even to the foreigners' bullets. Meanwhile, Wong Fei Hung, Aunt Yee, and his helper Foon are traveling by train to Canton for a medical convention. Arriving in the big city, they discover everything in chaos, a state of frenzy sparked by Taiwan being taken by Japan. When Aunt Yee, garbed in Western-cut clothing (which immediately makes her anathema to the White Lotus) attempts to photograph one of the group's rituals, the angered crowd attempts to do away with her and Foon. Wong Fei Hung comes to a timely rescue.

The following day, Wong offers a demonstration of acupuncture to a group of Western doctors. Because he cannot speak English to the attendees, he relies on Dr. Sun Yat-sen (a real-life historical figure who, in 1911, spearheaded the overthrow of the Qing Dynasty and helped to found China's Provisional Republican government). Sun Yat-sen translates Fei Hung's words to the gathering. While Wong's presentation is warmly received, the discussion is interrupted by a raid by the White Lotus group. Wong, Aunt Yee, and Foon narrowly escape being killed as the civil unrest in Canton accelerates.

Lan, chief of Canton's police force, appeals to the local governor for reinforcements, but the executive is focused on capturing the "rebel" Sun Yat-sen and his aide Luke. The next day Wong and his group attempt to leave Canton, but they are sidetracked when they encounter a group of youngsters whose school has been demolished by the White Lotus. When Lan insists to a beseeching Wong Fei Hung that constabulary's priorities do not include helping out the children, Fei Hung has Yee and Foon take the young ones to sanctuary at the British Consulate. When the White Lotus attack the Consulate, Lan is on hand to help their cause. In the process, Lan murders the British Consul, a deed witnessed by Wong.

Pushed to action, the usually restrained Wong, accompanied by Luke, heads to the White Lotus temple. There a now angered Fei Hung does battle with the vicious head priest and Wong emerges victorious. In trying to escape from Canton with a book of vital names that needs to reach Sun Yat-sen, Luke is killed by Lan and his thugs. This leads to a showdown between Wong and Lan, with the latter finally being eliminated by Wong. As Fei Hung reaches the dock, the vessel carrying Aunt Yee and Sun Yat-sen pushes off on its voyage. Wong tosses a folded cloth (which Luke had given him) to Yee. When she unfurls it, it turns out to be a patriotic flag. Yelling from the dock, Wong and Foon announce to Yee that they will meet her at journey's end.

For many viewers, the less complexly plotted *Once Upon a Time in China II*, is a more satisfying screen piece than its predecessor. According to writer Lisa Morton (*The Cinema of Tsui Hark*, 2001), this entry is "that rarest of creatures, a sequel that neither recreates the first film nor expands on the wrong qualities. It manages the nearly impossible feat of continuing the first film's themes and historical setting within the context of a completely new story. . . . It almost completely reverses its hero's moral stance from the first film."

China II certainly expands upon Tsui Hark's recurring theme of old China versus the new, as well as the need to balance the virtues of traditional ways with modern one. Again it is Li's Wong Fei Hung who is the lynchpin upon which this expansive film revolves. (It is a task which the star, increasingly proficient in his acting, is well-equipped to handle.) In this new entry, his Wong has grown far more liberal toward the foreigners' ways (e.g., Fei Hung's willingness to sample Western food on the train trip to Canton). In contrast to his persona in *China I*, here the hero displays a new flexibility of thought. Within the plot, circumstances lead him into joining the foreigners in their struggle against the fanatical White Lotus group, a situation the usually conservative Wong Fei Hung could not have imagined previously. However, having seen how these rebels turned so mercilessly against Aunt Yee (because of her Victorian-style garb), the shocked Wong now (re)examines the actions of his one-time opponents (the British and other foreigners). He soon concludes that they had tried to deal diplomatically with the Chinese but have been met with loathing. With the world topsy-turvy (paralleling the real-life paranoia in 1990s Hong Kong as its return to mainland China in 1997 neared), Fei Hung perceives that it is each side's unyielding principles and ideologies that are at the heart of the chaos, not the Chinese population being subjugated by outsiders.

Within the film's 106 minutes, Jet Li has ample opportunity to display his remarkable martial arts skills. He and his antagonists use a mixture of traditional Chinese weapons, a reliance on any useful object in sight, and, of course, their deadly hands, feet, and heads for body punches. As choreographed by action director Yuen Woo-ping, within this film Jet's protagonist must best two agile and tough adversaries. One is the obsessed White Lotus priest, played by Xiong Xin-xin (Hung Yan-yan), the talent who was often employed as Li's stunt double (and who would later turn up on screen as "Club Foot" in future installments of *Once Upon a Time in China*). In Wong's battle with the arrogant priest the two men fight with balletic precision (using wire work a great deal to give the exciting sequence its fantastic look and feel). Their confrontation ends with the White Lotus leader ironically impaled on an upturned finger of the cult's idol and Fei Hung discovering what is behind the magic that had stopped bullets from penetrating the fanatic's body. (The cult leader had been wearing a metal vest.) Equally engaging are Fei Hung's energetic encounters with the police official, Lan.

As performed by Donnie Yen Ji-dan (born in Boston, Massachusetts), the corrupt policeman Lan, torn between his job and his beliefs, makes a worthy opponent for Wong Fei Hung in *Once Upon a Time in China II*. Lan is the one who battles with Wong at the police station in a supposed exercise match which turns deadly. Near the film's climax—in the grain warehouse—Wong and Lan fight it out to the finish amidst bamboo scaffolds and ladders. In this latter sequence Jet's character attacks his adversary using whatever is handy (a bamboo lance) to fence, to pole vault, and to fight the determined police chief as they attack one another among destroyed shelves and tumbling flows of stored grain.

As impressive as the martial arts displays are in *Once Upon a Time in China II*, the picture focuses a good deal on the characterizations. For example, Aunt Yee, in a smaller role than in the first movie, shines again as the self-willed Chinese woman who is willing to study Western ways and who intends to further her romance with the romantically naïve Wong. The actress demonstrates her acting abilities in the sequence in which Fei Hung calls her by her first name for the first time and she understands that her hoped-for relationship will go beyond the platonic in the future. Yee also demonstrates one of director Tsui Hark's favorite themes (strong-willed, warrior women) when, having been taught the Grappling Hand kung fu move by Fei Hung, she, at the film's finale, uses the move to eliminate a soldier intent on arresting Dr. Sun Yat-sen. There is also comic relief present in the film, provided by Max Mok Siu-chung's Foon, Wong's sometimes addled helper, who has unrequited romantic feelings for Aunt Yee.

In this sequel, Jet's Wong Fei Hung takes on greater dimension. Not only is the character more flexible about topics concerning China versus foreigners, the old against the new, etc., but he also displays strong emotion here. An illustration of that is the sequence where he, opposing the ferocious White Lotus priest, becomes hugely sardonic and pokes fun at his adversary's obeisance to idols. In the process, Fei Hung reveals the zealous side of his nature which previously had been camouflaged beneath pensive calmness, boyish outbursts, and a stance of great responsibility to his fellow beings and to China. As Wong moves from calm to agitation and then on to fierce anger in this film, the viewer witnesses the growing acting acumen of the charismatic Jet Li.

Once Upon a Time in China II proved a strong contender at the Hong Kong box office when it opened there in mid April 1992 (just as Jet Li was reaching his twenty-ninth birthday). It grossed $30.399 million (in Hong Kong dollars). At the city's annual Film Awards it received prizes for Best Action Choreography and nine other nominations. When the movie played in the West (at film festivals, art cinemas, and, of course, at Chinese-language theaters) it received its proper due. Stephen Holden (*New York Times*) rated the picture "a splendid if frankly fake-looking spectacle," while J. Hoberman (*Village Voice*) described it as "one long martial arts fight, kicks, sticks, fists, lance duels interspersed with riffs on English-speaking foreigners."

Already planned before *Once Upon a Time in China II* went into production, 1992's *Swordsman II* [Siu Ngo Kong Woo II: Dung Fong Bat Baai] was a follow-up to the Tsui Hark–produced success, *Swordsman* [Siu Ngo Kong Woo], a 1990 movie based on Louis Cha's epic novel, *The Wandering Swordsman*. The first *Swordsman* picture had been directed by King Hu and several others after the veteran filmmaker abruptly left the project. That costumed adventure was set during the Ming dynasty, and the action revolved around a stolen scroll that was extremely valuable in that anyone who possesses it gains supernatural kung fu powers. Sam Hui Goon-git (a popular singer) had played Ling Woo Chung, the expert swordsman who travels from Wah Mountain with his subordinate Kiddo, and they find themselves involved with a dastardly governor, a power-crazy eunuch, the Sun Moon sect, etc. Filmgoers' positive response to the picture prompted a sequel which Tsui Hark (who chose not to direct this new venture) decided should star Jet Li as Ling Woo Chung. Although several other characters were brought forward from the first to the second *Swordsman* entry, only actress Fennie Yuen Kit-ying as Blue Phoenix, the assistant to the highlander princess (Ying Ying) performed her role in both pictures. Jet Li's co-stars in the new production included Brigitte Li Ching-hsia (as Asia the Invincible), the veteran superstar born in Taiwan. *Swordsman II* also saw the rematching of Jet with Rosamund Kwan Chi-lam in a similar capacity as before—the hero's love interest. (However, this time, as the aggressive Ying Ying, she is only one among several who tempt the handsome, but, at times, reckless warrior.) Yan Yee-kwan, who had appeared as the governor in *Once Upon a Time in China II*, was present now as Master Wu, a capricious and ambitious man.

Production of *Swordsman II* overlapped the wrap-up of *Once Upon a Time in China II*. While Jet Li had grown confident of his portrayal of Wong Fei Hung in the *Once Upon a Time* movie series, he did not feel sufficiently prepared to tackle this new project in which he was thrust so quickly. As he has recalled of the new venture: "I had not read the book that it was based on [*The Proud and Laughing Warrior*, by Louis Cha] and so I didn't have a good sense of the protagonist's inner motivations. And there was no luxury of doing the research on the character or even thinking it through. Going straight from one film set to the other, there was no time to think." It also did not help matters that his very extroverted, swaggering, heavy-drinking character had so many love relationships intricately interwoven into the narrative.

As filming got underway, scenes were shot out of continuity to expedite the hectic production process. According to Li: "I would play a love scene in the morning with one female character; in the afternoon, my character was scheduled to flirt with another. This was nothing like my real life experience! I was not used to this type of behavior. Now, Wong Fei Hong's chaste romance with [the Aunt Yee character in the *Once Upon a Time in China* series] signified a steadfast commitment that I felt was very similar to my own attitude toward women and love. But Ling was mystifying to me. I constantly asked the director [Ching Siu-tung], 'Tell me again why I like this one girl, but start chasing another one as soon as I turn my head?'" Tsui Hark sought to reassure his star with amplifications of the screen hero's dynamics. But parts of the role went against Li's moral grain: "How am I supposed to have so little respect for love? Flirt with one girl, then cozy up with another one behind her back, and as soon as the second one leaves, flirt with the first one again. . . . " While he sought to comply with his director's wishes and tried his best to inhabit this alien alter ego, Jet never felt at one with his character during the intensive making of the costume fantasy adventure.

Also set during the Ming Dynasty, *Swordsman II* tells of Ling Woo Chung who, along with his clansmen and his young woman friend Kiddo, are returning home from their many adventures (in *Swordsman*). It is Ling and his group's plan to retreat into seclusion where they can live in peace and spend their time drinking and contemplating. En route Ling visits with his adored Ying Ying and finds that her clan (the Sun Moon sect) has split into opposing groups who are battling each other. He learns that Ying's father, Master Wu, has been imprisoned by the mighty Asia the Invincible (a renowned male fighter who gained power by castrating himself and who plans to complete the transformation into a woman). Ling is drawn into freeing Wu from Asia's clutches, but, in the process, falls under that female fighter's magical spell. Still later, he finds himself torn between this beguiling "woman" and Ying. However, in a mighty confrontation between Ling and his forces and Asia and her Japanese allies, the conflicted hero must pick between protecting Ying Ying (and Kiddo) or siding with the dastardly but beguiling Asia.

Much as the classic *The Thief of Bagdad* (1940), starring Sabu, had artfully blended exotic settings, colorful costumes, sinister villains with magical powers, along with righteous if flawed heroes and lovely heroines, so *Swordsman II* combines all these elements in its historical Chinese trappings. The film emerges as a swirl of wild, fantastic adventures populated by untypical types. Ling is a hard-drinking soul with no remorse for his wastrel ways. He can be noble (rising to the task of freeing Ying Ying's imprisoned father), but he is an unrepentant womanizer driven by his attractions to several women and his love of wine. The grasping Asia has her masculine side (rapacious, greedy, power-hungry) but this he/she also has her romantic feminine facets. Drawn to the good-looking Ling, she becomes frantic when he wishes to consummate their romance and is forced to send her female underling to substitute for her in the bedroom with an unaware, besotted hero. Meanwhile, there is Master Wu, a veteran fighter and leader who, when once freed from Asia's control, reveals that he is really demented (from torture and confinement?) and wildly crazed for power. In addition, the flavorful cast of characters includes the tomboy Kiddo who is not sure—nor are those around her—what sex she is manifesting.

If *Swordsman II* is filled with ambiguous and ambivalent characters, the overloaded plot is one of crisscrossing (mis)adventures which includes such bizarre occurrences as the decapitation of a eunuch leader and the splitting of a horse down the middle, not to mention the heady display of thunderous combat often accomplished with wire work. (Then too, there are the characters' use of the Essence Absorbing Stance, a move which quickly sucks the life out of the victims.) With such entertaining distractions, it is to Jet Li's credit that, because of his robust performance, he does not sink into the movie's sidelines. This could have easily happened because this fantasy adventure yarn is so dominated by Brigitte Lin Ching-hsia's captivating performance as the beguiling Asia the Invincible. (In the plot, her gender transformation has not yet included the changeover of her masculine voice. As such, Asia remains coyly silent when with Ling. This forces

Jet Li in the fantasy adventure *Swordsman II* (1992).

the actress to rely on intense visual pantomime to convey successfully her character's motivations and reactions.)

By 1992 when *Swordsman* was released, audiences were well accustomed to the fantastic lack of gravity displayed in Hong Kong–made wire fu movies where the martial arts performers never stayed riveted to the ground. However, director Ching Siu-tung shone out here with his mastery of presenting high-flying figures (or sometimes people just skimming above the ground, as when two characters race across the countryside). Li's Ling Woo Chung swoops and darts, sometimes literally jumping into the air with glee over a jug of tasty new wine, when poised for battle, or when he is beside himself as Asia plunges down a cliffside to her apparent death.

Released in Hong Kong in June 1992—nine weeks after the debut of *Once Upon a Time in China II*—*Swordsman II* grossed a whopping $34.462 million (in Hong Kong dollars). At the Hong Kong Film Awards, the movie won two prizes (costumes and makeup design) and was nominated in six other categories (which did not include Jet Li's performance).

Despite the many virtues of this spectacular screen presentation, the trade paper *Daily Variety* had reservations about the entry: Dennis Harvey reported, "A dizzying pileup of hyper-adrenalized action, *Swordsman II* will please ethnic aud[ience]s and fans of the burgeoning Hong Kong cinema's unique brand of spectacle, but narrative incoherency and a rather bleak undertow to all the surface frenzy make this period fantasy an unlikely candidate to break the genre to a crossover Western audience." Harvey further explained: "There's no denying the energy and panache with which all this action is executed. But the script lacks the redeeming narrow focus . . . and its convolutions rob the film of badly needed narrative build." On the other hand, J. Hoberman (*Village Voice*) perceived the picture's many virtues. He labeled it "a funny, fast-moving, slapstick farce," approved of its "relentlessly go-go" pace, and admired the project for being so "splendidly perverse."

The next year Tsui Hark's Film Workshop would make *The East Is Red* [Dung Fong Bat Baai: Fung Wan Joi Hei], which was a further installment in the *Swordsman* series. It again starred Brigitte Lin Ching-hsia as Asia the Invincible, but the new installment—set four months after Asia's supposed demise—would have a totally new plot line and a new (anti) hero in the character of naval officer Koo (played by Yu Rong-guang).

Before Jet Li had been thrust into the making of *Swordsman II*, there was talk of his co-starring with Malaysian-born Michelle Khan (Michelle Yeoh) in *New Dragon Inn* [San Lung Moon Haak Chan] for Tsui Hark's Film Workshop. However, when this remake of *King Hu's Dragon Gate Inn* [Lung Moon Haak Chan] (1967) was released in 1992, the production instead featured Maggie

Cheung Man-yuk, Donnie Yen Ji-dan, Brigitte Lin Ching-hsia, and Tony Leung Ka-fai. It was one of the signs of the growing separation between Jet Li and his mentor Tsui Hark, an escalating difference of opinion about forthcoming screen projects (and some said precipitated because of Li's escalating salary demands and other perks that the film studio Golden Harvest, and in turn, Hark, were not providing him).

Jet's unhappiness over the somewhat negative personality traits of his *Swordsman II* part and the fact that he felt he never really understood the character's motivations, taught him a lesson. He learned that "the actor cannot completely separate himself from the role that he plays." It prompted him to establish his own production firm so he could be more in charge of his professional future. (Ironically, in the period following *Swordsman II*, Li experienced career situations that showed him "that modern day people could still be motivated by power and fame to do some really terrible things." After facing such actions first hand and up close, he suddenly realized more about what his *Swordsman II* hero had been about and why the "warrior laughs and sings. . . . When faced with so much betrayal, how can you not learn to laugh off the vagaries of fate?")

These life revelations were part of many tough situations and adjustments with which Jet Li would have to cope and overcome in late 1992 and 1993.

10
Reaching in New
Directions

I n 1992 Jet Li, now nearing age thirty, ambitiously established his own production company. Called Eastern Production Ltd., it was located at No. 180
Hennessy Road in Hong Kong. (It would later be renamed Eastern Film
Production Ltd., and be relocated to 15 Austin Avenue in that city.) Now that he
was more directly in control of his own artistic fate, some observers said that fame
and the pressure of being an actor/producer were causing the once well-mannered
personality to become more self-involved, more short-tempered with the media,
and more intent on maintaining privacy in his off-camera life. (In 1992, Li's companion, Nina Li Chi, age thirty, retired from moviemaking and turned to the
investment business, focusing on enterprises in mainland China.)

Meanwhile, of pressing concern to Jet was the influence that the criminal triad
gangs were having on the Hong Kong film industry. When the movie business in
this British dependency blossomed once again in the early 1990s (thanks to such
Jet Li pictures as *Once Upon a Time in China I* and *II*, and *Swordsman II*), the
local underworld concluded that moviemaking was a lucrative enterprise in which
they should be involved. As such they muscled their way into the industry using
intimidation and worse to gain a foothold. Becoming de facto movie producers,
they proceeded to enhance the normal industry profit ratio by "suggesting" to big-
name screen talents that they take far less than their usual salaries, with the excess
going into the hoodlums' coffers. It was during this gangster-infiltration period—
in 1992—that Jet Li's business manager was murdered, causing much speculation
that the killing had to do with the mob's stranglehold on the Hong Kong movie
business. (Jet would tell Richard Corliss for *Time Asia* magazine in October 1998,

"When these bad guys would take a gun to rob a bank and fight with policemen, maybe they'd get money or lose their life. But if they put a gun to an actor's head and told them to make a movie for half their regular salary, it was very easy to make money. Easy for them. Difficult for us." Later, on his official Internet website, the actor detailed the departure of underworld elements from the Hong Kong movie business: "Pretty soon [i.e., the mid-1990s] the market got saturated [with too many hastily churned-out features]. When there were no more profits to be made, organized crime left. Only the ones who really loved movies stayed."

Before Jet Li could really branch out on his own in the filmmaking world, he owed one more picture to Tsui Hark. This was 1993's *Once Upon a Time in China III* [Wong Fei Hung Ji Saam: Shut Wong Chang Ba]. In this new installment, set in the late 1890s, Wong Fei Hung, along with his trusty sidekick Leung Foon and the ever-present Aunt Yee, arrive in Peking just as the Dowager Empress announces a Lion Dance contest to choose a new king of the exhibition. The event is designed to show the power-grabbing foreigners just how mighty the Chinese actually are. Meanwhile, Wong is dismayed to learn that he faces a potential romantic rival in a Russian diplomat, Tomanovsky, a former classmate of Yee when she had traveled abroad for studies. As for the Westernized Yee, besides being focused on winning Fei Hung's lasting love, she is delighted to have the use of a new-fangled motion picture camera. Entranced with the new gadget, she busily photographs various staged and candid interludes.

In the interim, a local hoodlum, Chiu Tin Bai, threatens Fei Hung's father, Wong Kay Ying, if the elder dares to enter the Lion Dance competition with his followers. Tin Bai later has his powerful henchman, Club Foot, wreck havoc at Kay Ying's factory where, among other things, the herbalist makes lion heads utilized in martial arts ceremonies. In the devastation, the elder Wong is badly injured. Now aroused by his father's mistreatment and seeing the growing unrest among rival members of the Cantonese Association of merchants (to which his father belongs), Fei Hung makes an appeal to China's President Li for assistance, but is ignored. Thereafter, the younger Wong forges ahead on his own to squelch the vicious Tin Bai. In the process Aunt Yee warns Fei Hung that the Russians—including her duplicitous friend Tomanovsky—plan to use the upcoming pageant as a cover to assassinate President Li. At the crucial moment, the President is saved from the culprits, while Wong and his new ally, Club Foot, defeat Tin Bai and his men and win the coveted contest. When officials present Fei Hung with a coveted medal of honor, the proud Fei Hung refuses it.

He is angered with the royal administration because it does not pay sufficient attention to the people's needs.

As the gun had been the sign of new technology in prior chapters of the *Once Upon a Time in China* movie series, here the novel motion picture camera represents the (intrusive) new way of life being introduced into China. If the thriller plot of the high official being saved from assassination at a public event reminds one of Alfred Hitchcock's two screen versions (1934 and 1956) of *The Man Who Knew Too Much*, so be it. On the other hand there are fresh plot twists to this *China* entry. While Yee is once again pursuing her dear one, this time Fei Hung surprises everyone—including himself—when the usually conservative Wong boldly proposes they marry. One of the entry's romantic highlights occurs as she gazes at her intended in a shadowy room as she hand operates the motion picture projector with the flickering shadows playing on the two lovers' faces. Equally new

Wong Fei Hung and his beloved "Aunt" Yee (Rosamund Kwan Chi-lam) in *Once Upon a Time in China III* (1993).

for the previously reticent Fei Hung is the sequence in which he not only embraces Yee, but does so in public, leaving his father and Foon in total amazement at the young man's daring action.

For many viewers, the picture's dramatic highlight is when Club Foot, badly injured and rejected by his cruel master, Chiu Tin Bai, is tended to by physician/ martial arts master Wong Fei Hung. Later the revived Club Foot crawls out into the rain, too proud to accept further help from his savior. Yee and Fei Hung follow him and, with great compassion, Wong convinces the cripple to let him heal him. The most exciting action set piece in this offering occurs midway through the plot as Wong vanquishes a contingent of cleat-wearing ruffians as he copes (and turns to his advantage) having to conduct his battle on an oil-slick floor. In the humor department there is Aunt Yee's language lesson with Fei Hung as she attempts to teach him to say "I love you" in English. (He pronounces it "I love food," a phrase then repeated by others and causing comical moments.)

When *Once Upon a Time in China III* opened in Hong Kong on February 11, 1993, some critics and viewers complained that there was an overabundance of wire work in the film's martial arts sequences. Moreover, they were disappointed that Wong Fei Hung, who shows himself to be an expert at the martial art of Lion Dancing in this production, had become more a fantasy hero than a beloved man of the common people. Others missed the presence of much social commentary, an ingredient that had appealed to the patriotic nature of many moviegoers. Nevertheless, the slam-bang epic—which does not match the first two parts in structure, excitement, and execution—went on to gross $27.461 million (in Hong Kong dollars). It received a Best Film Editing nomination at the Hong Kong Film Awards.

By late 1992, Jet Li and Tsui Hark had gone their own ways, and Tsui would use Vincent Zhao Wen-zhuo (Chiu Man-cheuk) to take over the key role of Wong Fei Hung in 1993's *Once Upon a Time in China IV* [Wong Fei Hung Ji Sei: Wong Che Ji Fung] and 1994's *Once Upon a Time in China V* [Wong Fei Hung Ji Ng Lung Shing Chim Ba]. As for Li, he now had the artistic freedom to go in any direction he chose. There was a temptation to try a contemporary story, which would have been less expensive to produce for the screen and would have taken him in new creative directions. However, Jet reasoned, "It is easier for me to show my strengths in traditional movies, like the ability to use traditional martial arts weapons. Also, not many people know how to fight with bagua, tai chi, xing yi, or other traditional wushu styles. In modern movies, there are fighting scenes that

Jet Li's hero confronts the enemy in *Fong Sai Yuk* (1993).

a talented actor without a martial arts background can learn to do in three months. But in traditional movies, the audience can tell the difference."

Having resolved to star in another historical actioner, Jet gave some thought to creating a new adventure for his celluloid alter ego, Wong Fei Hung, of the *Once Upon a Time in China* series. Instead, whether out of honor, legality, practicality, or all of these reasons, Jet chose to tackle the playing of another Chinese folk hero: the feisty Fong Sai Yuk, a champion living during the Ching dynasty period. Like Fei Hung, Sai Yuk was also a Robin Hood type (stealing from the rich to help the poor). While Fong was far more of a mischievous, fun-loving soul than Wong, both characters/legends had a healthy respect for the oppressed and took action to help them. Of key importance, Fong Sai Yuk was a martial arts marvel in his own right.

To direct *Fong Sai Yuk* (1993), which was to be produced by Jet's Eastern Production Ltd. company and released by Golden Harvest, Li chose versatile filmmaking veteran Corey (sometimes spelled Cory in on-screen credits) Yuen (Yuen Kwai). Yuen, who had been trained at the Chinese Opera Academy, had risen through the film industry ranks in the middle 1970s, moving from assistant stunt coordinator (1976's *The Secret Rivals* [Naam Kuen Bak Tui]) to actor (1977's *The Invincible Armour* [Ying Chau Tit Biu Saam]) to director (1982's *Ninja in the Dragon's Den* [Lung Ji Yan Che]). Along the way, Corey had been slightly involved with Jet's 1989's *The Master*, that disappointing entry which finally saw release in 1992 as Li's screen fame was growing. Selecting the talented Yuen for his new project was a smart decision on Li's part, and was the start of a prolific working relationship together.

The jubilant *Fong Sai Yuk* presents filmgoers with the playful young hero (with nearly thirty-year-old Jet Li looking the part of a rambunctious youth), a martial arts champion of Canton. He meets an enticing stranger, Ting Ting, and falls

As the title figure riding to the rescue in *Fong Sai Yuk* (1993).

instantly in love with her, but does not even know her name. As it happens, her father, a prominent but crude merchant named Tiger Lu, wants a strong husband for his daughter. To find such a suitor, Lu, who hopes to win the approval of the locals, announces that his beautiful wife, a skilled practitioner of martial arts, will fight any man (from any strata of society) who challenges her. The winner will receive Ting Ting's hand in marriage. Sai Yuk, playing hooky from his studies, enters the competition at the local festival. However, because he mistakes an unattractive young woman as the prize, he deliberately loses the contest. Upset by this loss of face, Fong's mother—disguised as Sai Yuk's brother—enters the competition. While she wins the match against her female opponent, Ting Ting's mother is not upset because she has fallen in love with her agile foe (not knowing that the opponent is actually a woman).

With the martial arts competition now in the past, carefree Sai Yuk boldly announces his love for the willful Ting Ting. Thereafter, complications escalate: Tiger Lu, a supporter of the imperial court, discovers that his future kin, Sai Yuk's father, is a member of the Red Flower Society (a group devoted to overthrowing the Manchu emperor and restoring the throne to the Chinese). In the very nick of time Sai Yuk's dad is rescued from the guillotine. Thereafter, Sai Yuk and his beloved Ting Ting ride off into the sunset looking for new adventures.

With the cast playing their assignments in this extravaganza with relish, the pacing of *Fong Sai Yuk* rarely lags. In turning away from the emotionally controlled, morally proper characterization of the *China* series, Jet Li is here refreshingly buoyant and exuberant. However, it is actress Josephine Siao Fong-fong who steals the show in this saga as the champion's feisty mother. She is the tart-mouthed proprietress of a fabric shop, who is as agile with facial gestures and sharp side remarks as she is in demonstrating her martial arts prowess. While a very liberated, flamboyant woman, she is touchingly devoted to her priggish husband and is especially aroused by his poetic writings. Within this film she is a whirlwind of activity: parent, compatriot, and defender of her energetic, well-meaning, but impulsive son. Also on hand is Vincent Zhao Wen-zhuo (Chiu Man-cheuk) playing the visiting governor, a dastardly Manchu killer. He makes a worthy on-camera opponent for the athletic and skilled Sai Yuk. (It was Man-cheuk who would take over Jet Li's role of Wong Fei Hung in *Once Upon a Time in China IV* and *V* in 1993 and 1994 respectively.)

As the bigger-than-life Fong Sai Yuk, Jet Li discards all his previous seriousness of mind, sense of responsibility, and pensive demeanor in order to play this chipper protagonist—a mama's boy who can be callow one second and goofy the next. In his prankishness, he is not above dressing in a girl's garment and wig to carry out his latest scheme. While he is deeply attached to his mother, this mama's boy treats his parent as his equal on the battlefield or on the home front (where they take turns protecting each other from the rage of exasperated Father Fong).

The two major set pieces of the rollicking *Fong Sai Yuk* are the staggering battle of supremacy between Ting Ting's mother and Sai Yuk's mama. Their encounter occurs on a playing field with a crowd of onlookers. The two women compete against one another on a perilous wooden tower where one misstep could be fatal. Thereafter, the duo continue their nonstop match while positioned on the heads and shoulders of their supporters. It is indeed a masterfully choreographed sequence. The other rousing set piece occurs at the adventure film's finale. Here Sai Yuk and Mother Fong stage a dramatic last-minute rescue of Father Fong who is about to have his head lopped of by the Manchu minions. As the battle rages to free Father Fong, nimble Sai Yuk grabs hold of the guillotine rope which prevents the deadly blade from falling on its victim. As the athletic young man strives to vanquish the enemy, he continually loses and then regains control of the life-or-death blade rope. While a deliberate cinematic teaser, the device nevertheless adds tremendous excitement and suspense to this battle to the finish.

When *Fong Sai Yuk* debuted in Hong Kong on March 4, 1993, it met with a rousing reception from the public who were not disappointed by this costumed adventure, so similar in many ways to Li's earlier Wong Fei Hung series. Li Lin (*Hong Kong Economic Journal*) enthused that "the film maintains a balance between visual delights and the narrative, and simultaneously evokes self-mocking jokes and the story proper. The film creates so much tension that it is a rare case even by Hong Kong cinema standards." As to the superior cast, the critic judged, "Li is simply exuberant."

Fong Sai Yuk grossed $30.667 million (in Hong Kong dollars) in its initial Hong Kong engagements. At the 1994 Hong Kong Film Awards the hit picture won a prize in the Best Action Choreography category and was nominated for Best Actress (Josephine Siao Fong-fong) and Best Editor.

By now, the growing prominence of Hong Kong cinema allowed for this latest product to reach beyond Asia and the Chinese-language theaters in the United States, England, etc., to movie festivals and art houses where it was often titled *The Legend of Fong Sai Yuk*. David Stratton (*Weekly Variety*) rated Jet's new offering as "a breathtakingly energetic mixture of martial arts and comedy." Stratton observed that the picture's "real accomplishment . . . is in its moving effortlessly from knockabout slapstick as broad as an Abbott and Costello comedy, to pathos." (Noted in particular by critics and viewers alike as a dramatic highlight of the picture is the sequence in which a heart-broken Fong Sai Yuk buries his murdered buddy and utters a prayer wishing his comrade's spirit a good journey into the next world and the wish that they will meet there one day. This touching moment disproved the criticism of those who insisted that, when not martial arts chopping, Jet Li was an emotionless performer.)

In rapid succession, producer/leading man Jet Li's next movie, *Last Hero in China* [Wong Fei Hung Ji Tit Gai Dau Ng Gung], opened on April 1, 1993, in Hong Kong. This time he opted to return to his star-making movie role of Wong Fei Hung, with Wong Jing directing the costume action venture. While Dickey Cheung Wai-kin reemerged as the hero's buffoonish helper, "Buck Teeth" Sol, there was no Aunt Yee present in this variation on the formula of the *Once Upon a Time in China* series.

The fanciful plot finds the Canton-based Wong Fei Hung forced to relocate his martial arts teaching school/medical practice shop (a Po Chi Lam). Unknowingly, the proud, moral young man has accepted an offer to rent a location which is adjacent to a brothel. Upon setting up shop, he is frustrated and embarrassed to find his students being distracted frequently by the enticing prostitutes. Meanwhile, Wong is drawn into a violent confrontation with nefarious members of the Boxer Society who have been kidnapping young women to sell into prostitution in south Asia. In this turn-of-the-century China tale, Fei Hung emerges as a one-man war against the ruthless and corrupt Boxer Society criminals. His chief opponent is a corrupt local official, the sadistic and ever-laughing Lui Yat Siu (one of the most memorable villains in the canon of Jet Li pictures). Before Fei Hung's final victory, he has consumed poisoned medicine which causes him to go deaf, until a wiser herbalist/physician than he puts the injured hero through a successful series of curative treatments.

Just as Chinese ceremonial martial arts dances formed such an integral part of earlier Jet Li costumed entries, so it did in *Last Hero in China*. This time around, however, the climactic dance—and the source of a deadly competition between good and evil figures—occurs between characters dressed as a rooster and centipede. The seeds of victory are planted when Wong Fei Hung observes a real-life rooster attacking such a creature and learns from Mother Nature how best to handle the upcoming contest successfully.

Grossing a healthy, if not spectacular, $18.178 million (in Hong Kong dollars) at the box office, it was action directors Yuen Woo-ping and Yuen Cheung-yan (brother of Corey Yuen [Yuen Kwai]) who did a great deal to give *Last Hero in China* its zest, as did Alan Chui Chung-san as the mocking, ever-amused bad guy. When screened later in southern California, Kevin Thomas (*Los Angeles Times*) noted that the new Jet Li entry was "not as complex or as substantial as *Once Upon a Time in China* but it's just as much fun." Thomas pointed out that the film "moves like lightning yet its burlesque humor deftly gives way to moments of unexpected poignancy." *Weekly Variety*'s Derek Elley approved of this picture which "keeps the pratfalls and goofy stuff on a tight rein" and that "the fight scenes are lively and full of character, expressing plot tensions as well as sheer technique." The reviewer also noted, "Chopsocky action star Jet Li looks a whole lot more relaxed in *Last Hero in China*, a semi-comic, well-mounted gloss on his Wong Fei Hung. . . . "

In this highly prolific filmmaking period for Jet Li, his fourth of six (!) 1993 releases was the follow-up to his earlier-in-the-year *Fong Sai Yuk*. In *Fong Sai Yuk II* [Fong Sai Yuk Chuk Chap], the setting is again the eighteenth century when China was ruled by the Manchu Ching dynasty. Candid but naïve Fong Sai Yuk joins the anti-Manchu Red Flower Society, an organization led by his esteemed and famous godfather Chan Ka Lok. After failing at an assignment to take possession of a secret document (which will confirm that Chan Ka Lok is the rightful heir to the Chinese emperorship), Sai Yuk is given a second chance to retrieve the papers. To do so, he must court the governor's daughter, Man Yin, who knows the whereabouts of the valued documentation. Pursuing the love of Man Yin presents problems, since Fong recently had wed his treasured Ting Ting and she is furious at his seeming act of unfaithfulness with Man Yin. In the midst of Sai Yuk's delicate quest, his mother arrives on the scene. She makes it her mission to smooth out the domestic dilemma once her son has fallen in love with the regal and seductive Man Yin. Mother Fong also helps her offspring stay alive as he is pursued by and, in turn, pursues his enemy. In a climactic showdown, Sai Yuk must not only fight the villain(s) to the finish, but at the same time he must prevent his mother—about to be hanged—from choking to death on the scaffolding (perched perilously on a platform which keeps being knocked about as the acrobatic Sai Yuk clashes with his adversaries).

In *Fong Sai Yuk II*, director Corey Yuen (Yuen Kwai) carries forth the same lighthearted tone that he employed so successfully in its predecessor. He gives full reign to Jet's characterization of the boisterous, eager, and often rash (but well-meaning) hero who must deal with two lady loves (quite a feat for the naïve young man who is such a child when it comes to romance). Playing the rival for Fong's heart is Amy Kwok Oi-ming, then a recent Miss Hong Kong beauty pageant winner. Josephine Siao Fong-fong successfully reprised her winning role as Sai Yuk's outspoken and lusty mother who—when not utilizing her martial arts skills to help her boy win the day—finds and loses a new love.

Opening in Hong Kong in July 1993, *Fong Sai Yuk II* grossed $23.013 million (in Hong Kong dollars), a noticeable drop in the take from the first series entry. For *Weekly Variety*'s Derek Elley, however, this second series entry was not to be quickly dismissed. Rightly, he praised, "Action set pieces, including a riverside encounter with some Japanese samurai and a tour de force finale played out on a pyramid of stools, are fully the equal of the first pic's." As to the star, he conceded: "Li makes the most of his limited talents in the acting department, playing Fong as a sexual innocent dominated by his martial-artist mom." When the feature played at the second annual Festival Hong Kong in Santa Monica, California, in December 1993, Kevin Thomas (*Los Angeles Times*) ranked the production "a lively, successful sequel that again demonstrates the zaniness of the uninhibited imagination of director Corey Yuen and his writers." As for Li's appearance, the journalist approved that he played the hero "so winningly." When F. X. Feeney (*Los Angeles Weekly*) caught up with the feature in September 1994 he applauded *Fong Sai Yuk II* for being "so funny and over the-top" and decided that "unlike many other II's and III's, it made me want to see the first film."

Despite the relative success of *Fong Sai Yuk II*, there were clear signs that the sheer weight and number of copycat costumed action films filled with wire fu and lowbrow comedy being churned out by Hong Kong moviemakers was starting to wear out its welcome at the cinema box office. For other stars who alternated between historical action fare, comedies, and (gangland) dramas, it was just a matter of switching their emphasis to genre entries then more in vogue. In contrast, for Jet Li who was so associated now by filmgoers with his performances as heroic Wong Fei Hung and Fong Sai Yuk, this genre oversaturation presented a major career problem. Meanwhile, he was already completing and/or committed to two other martial arts entries for release in late 1993. At least one of the duo was an artistic gem, *The Tai-Chi Master* [Taai Gik Cheung Saam Fung].

A Return to Basics

11

Capitalizing on his immense box-office popularity in Hong Kong and throughout Asia, Jet Li starred in six 1993 releases, the final two appearing that December. The first of these, *The Tai-Chi Master* brought the star back to basics, this time in a tale which imagined the history that developed the tai chi martial arts, both its philosophy and its proper execution. It reflected producer/star Li's desire to make his movies not only exciting but also instructional, and to provide Chinese filmgoers with a sense of pride in their rich culture heritage which included the unique tai chi form of the martial arts.

In contrast to his recent batch of costume action pictures, *The Tai-Chi Master* was shot on mainland China to capture its stunning landscape and give the historical tale a greater ring of verisimilitude. It was directed by Yuen Woo-ping who had been action director on several of Li's earlier productions and who had helmed 1993's *Iron Monkey* [Siu Nin Wong Fei Hung Ji Tit Ma Lau] with Donnie Yen Ji-dan starring as the legendary Wong Fei Hung. In addition, Yuen and his brother (Cheung-yan) served as the picture's martial arts choreographers/directors. Michelle Yeoh (Michelle Khan), a former Miss Malaysia, had returned fairly recently to filmmaking and this well-liked, martial arts-savvy talent was cast as the woman who must choose romantically and ideologically between former friends: Li's Zhang Junbao and Chin Siu-ho's Chin Bo. (Siu-ho's film acting career went back to the late 1970s.)

During production of this dimensional and serious project, the set was alive—ironically—with laughter. According to Li: "The younger brother of Yuen Woo-ping, . . . Michelle Yeoh, and I would banter and joke around the set. And I remember that Michelle always had some hilarious (though dirty) jokes to tell. We laughed so hard. It was not the ordinary laughter that normally accompanies your typical good joke. The humor of it was incredible. Just by looking at one another, we would lapse into spasmodic fits of laughter. It was difficult to get serious on the set, and I remember how badly my belly hurt afterwards from laughing so hard."

Within *The Tai-Chi Master*, Li's Junbao and Chin Bo are youngsters who meet at the Shaolin Temple where they are apprentices. Opposites in many ways, they remain friends into adulthood where they have joined the ranks of devoted students practicing martial arts at the shrine school. Because of Chin Bo's rebelliousness and the enmity of a jealous peer, the two are expelled from the monastery. Tossed into the real world, they are forced to adapt quickly to the practicalities of life, one in which they must earn a living and survive deadly encounters with government troops as well as rebels. It is a task which befuddles the even-tempered and somewhat slow Junbao. In contrast, the more ambitious and cunning Chin Bo acclimates himself far better to their new existence. Before long, the duo come upon an attractive martial arts whiz named Siu Lin who is part of a rebel contingent based at a local eating establishment.

Chin Bo soon joins the corrupt and ruthless military, succumbing to the potential of riches and power. In contrast, the devout Junbao teams with Siu Lin and the partisans as they battle the Royal Eunuch's oppressive government forces. Later, Chin Bo, rising fast in the military ranks, betrays Junbao and his friends to the army which leads to the deaths of many of the rebels. Junbao is so astounded by his ex-friend's treachery that temporarily he falls into a numbing shocked status. As he slowly recovers, he studies the words of wisdom provided in a scroll given to him by a Shaolin monk when Junbao was ejected from the temple. Regaining his reason, Junbao has fresh insights into life which he adapts into the tai chi form of martial arts (in which flowing, circular defensive movements play an important role). Eventually, the occasion arises for Junbao to deal with the traitorous Chin Bo. In their furious battle to the finish, Chin Bo dies. Thus was born the practice of tai chi martial arts, a form taught to new generations over the centuries.

When released in Hong Kong on December 2, 1993, *The Tai-Chi Master* grossed only $12.564 million (in Hong Kong dollars). The relatively mild box-office take was more a product of the glut of costume/action genre pictures in the marketplace than a reflection of the quality of the new film itself. *Weekly Variety*'s Derek Elley pointed out that this mainland China-made picture's lack of Hong Kong moviemaking slickness was compensated for with "old-style, no-nonsense direction . . . and fine action sequences. . . . " As to the cast, "Yeoh is overshadowed by the plot's male rivalry but holds her own in several sequences. Li shows glimmers of personality in the recuperative section played for laughs. Chin makes a fine villain."

By late summer *The Tai-Chi Master* was playing in Los Angeles where Andy Klein (*LA Reader*), a great enthusiast of Hong Kong pictures, rated this a "dazzling period film" and praised the movie's "series of inventive fight sequences." Wade Major (*Entertainment Today*) championed that this Shaolin Temple fable was "one of the best Hong Kong films of the past ten years" and that it was "far and away Li's most impressive film to date—ranking solidly aside *Once Upon a Time in China* and *The Legend of Fong Sai Yuk*." Major reasoned that this offering got Jet away from playing "stone-faced stoics or dopey, wide-eyed youths" and that here the star has a "long-overdue chance to showcase his range as a performer. Junbao's complex spiritual, emotional and physiological journey taps into all of Li's dramatic and comedic strengths. . . . " In conclusion, the reviewer detailed, "At the center of *The Tai-Chi Master* is a voyage of spiritual redemption and enlightenment, growth and discovery that is so uniquely Asian, one would be hard-pressed to find its equivalent in the body of Western film. That *The Tai-Chi Master* manages to make this story work within the constraints of the Kung Fu film genre is yet another testament to the versatility, courage and strength of the world's most exciting film industry."

One of the many pluses of *The Tai-Chi Master* is its demonstration of contrasting styles of martial arts combat, especially in the elaborately staged (with a crowd of hundreds of extras) finale in which the hero utilizes his newly formulated tai chi method against the more traditional Iron Palm (Fist) technique of the chief villain.

Jet Li concluded 1993 with the *The Kung Fu Cult Master* [Kei Tin Tiu Lung Gei Ji Moh Gaau Gaau Chu]. Directed by the prolific Wong Jing (called the Roger Corman of Hong Kong cinema), it was based on a martial arts novel by the director and would additionally be adapted for several other films as well as TV series. As if trying to compensate for the plethora of genre entries swamping the Hong Kong cinema, this feature offered an overabundance of wire work martial arts scenes staged by the renowned Sammo Hung Kam-bo (a director, actor, screenwriter, and producer), who also acted in this project. With all the picture's high-flying activity, Jet Li's hero had too little opportunity to display his tremendous natural abilities in the combative arts.

Set during the Yuan dynasty of the thirteenth/fourteenth century A.D. where there was an enormous rivalry between the Wu Tang and Shaolin clans to gain supremacy, *The Kung Fu Cult Master*—with its circuitous story line—traces the adventures of these opposing martial arts groups, each of whom is tussling to gain possession of prized golden swords (which contain the secret means of dominating the world of martial arts). Caught up in the tumultuous conflict is Chang Mo Kei whose parents are forced by circumstances to commit suicide during the ongoing struggle for power among the warring factions. The boy vows revenge, but unfortunately he has been cursed (by the Jinx's Palm) which gives him chills from a lack of inner strength and prevents him from practicing kung fu. Once grown to adulthood, Mo Kei is cured of his affliction by a voracious Shaolin kung fu master/ monster (embedded in a great rolling boulder) who teaches him the tremendous power of the Great Solar Stance. As the revived Mo Kei prepares to tackle the evil ones he falls in love with Siu Chiu (played on screen by the comely Chingmy Yau Suk-ching). Mo Kei becomes further embroiled in the great war between the traditional martial arts schools. Only later does he discover that the engineered dissension was a government conspiracy to destroy the schools' influence over the splintered clans.

Opening in Hong Kong in mid December 1993, *The Kung Fu Cult Master* grossed only $10.437 million (in Hong Kong dollars). It was rumored that enough additional footage was shot during production to make a follow-up. (This movie does end abruptly with a situation setup that definitely suggests a sequel was contemplated by the filmmakers.) However, when the picture, with its overly convoluted story line, failed to please sufficient filmgoers, any plans for Jet Li to make a continuation of its bizarre narrative and fantastic characters were put to rest. Later, largely because of its kinky plot threads and its frequently horrific ambiance, this picture gained something of a cult film reputation with filmgoers and some critics.

Both director (and scripter) Wong Jing and Chingmy Yau Suk-ching reteamed with Jet Li for 1994's *The New Legend of Shaolin* [Hung Hei Goon], a coproduction between Hong Kong and mainland China. It was yet another revisit to the more traditional story lines of Li's early 1980s movies. (Certainly it did not hurt the box-office take on this project to remind filmgoers of the star's popular "trilogy" of early 1980s Shaolin Temple features, with which Jet had begun his movie career.) In that vein, actor Gai Chun-wa, who had appeared in Li's trio of Shaolin Temple entries, was cast in the role of the poison juice monster in the new big-screen entry.

The premise of *The New Legend of Shaolin* tells of famed Shaolin fighter Hung Hei Goon (played by Jet) who returns home to his village to find it destroyed and his wife murdered. An embittered Hei Goon, a fugitive member of the Red Lotus Society, takes his baby son with him as he wanders about China getting in and out of difficulties. (Sometimes, when he is ambushed, he must fight his attackers with his infant boy still strapped to his back.) Meanwhile, the oppressive imperial forces cracks down on the Shaolin Temple because it fears its members are growing too powerful. Five young monks who have pieces of a map to a buried treasure tattooed on their backs escape the royal forces. Before long, Hung and his boy (now around ten years old) encounter the Shaolin youths as well as a boisterous mother-daughter team of thieves and an old rich buffoon (played in low comedy style by actor Chan Chun-yung). The diverse contingent merge their efforts as they help the quintet of young refugees reach the Niu village where the monks are to reveal the location of the sacred treasure. By the finale the hero and his boy (a miniature carbon copy of his martial arts expert father) conquer the villain. The latter, a longtime foe of Hung, is a character who has turned into a preying monster thanks to the use of magical poison juice.

With its (over)abundance of fast-paced fight scenes (provided by Corey Yuen [Yuen Kwai]) as Li's high-energy movie alter ego clashes with enemies—human and otherwise—the picture had built-in general audience appeal. It also played off the popular early 1970s Japanese movie series about Baby Cart (Lone Wolf and Cubs) by having *The New Legend of Shaolin* tell of a single father-young son team (plus the presence of the preteen monks) successfully battling the odds (which range from dastardly government forces to the hideous ogre).

Following another tried-and-true movie formula, the climax occurs as the hero and fiend battle it out in a dangerous locale. (Here, as they fight to the finish, each adversary repeatedly comes precariously close to tumbling into a vat of bubbling acid—and one of them does just that at the climax.) For balance, this picture offers two offbeat female characters—Red Bean and her conniving mother. They are wily crooks grasping to survive in a difficult world and willing to do whatever it takes to get by. Released in Hong Kong in early March 1994, *The New Legend of Shaolin*, grossed a respectable $19.388 million (in Hong Kong dollars). The picture received a nomination for Best Action Choreography at the Hong Kong Film Awards, and made the rounds of global film festivals including those at Rotterdam and Berlin.

Weekly Variety's David Rooney applauded this "nonstop crowd pleaser" as "a high-kicking historical revenge spectacular with enough accelerated rotary action and slice-and-dice wizardry to put the most high-tech kitchen appliance to shame." Rooney saluted Jet Li for making "a commanding central figure." Mick LaSalle (*San Francisco Chronicle*) was impressed by the picture's action: "Set in ancient times, the film provides a series of lightning-fast, fantastic martial arts encounters, with Hung and his adversaries flying through the air and shooting darts with their fingers and catching them with their teeth." As to its leading man: "One of the biggest stars in Asia, Li is a handsome, compelling screen presence." LaSalle did have a reservation about this entry: "The spectacle comes in endless waves, and although it is well-executed, it gets monotonous."

Walter D. Addiego (*San Francisco Examiner*) noted, "The grim and melodramatic opening is only a setup for director Wong Jing's real interests, which are to stage dazzling and gravity-defying fight sequences and to make us laugh, often at the same time. The humor is broad, to say the least and sometimes crude, but the film is always redeemed by the can-you-top-this martial arts sequences." Regarding the picture's leading man, Addiego reported, "Martial arts idol Jet Li . . . is a pillar of upright fury as a foe of the oppressive Ching Dynasty. . . . " Many critics and viewers alike commented favorably on an early scene in the feature in which the distraught hero must decide if his infant boy will accompany him on his perilous revenge trek. Hung Hei Goon places a rocking horse and a sword nearby. If his child goes to the toy he will die, if he gravitates to the weapon— which he does—he will live and be taught martial arts skills by his parent. (As for the remarkably talented young Tze Miu [Xie Miao], who made such a hit in this production, he would soon be reteamed with Jet Li for a new picture.)

Since Jet Li had returned to his homeland in 1990, he had made ten costumed action pictures (besides newsreel footage of the martial arts star appearing in assorted feature-length documentaries). Li had stuck to a historical period format because it allowed him to promulgate the virtues of traditional martial arts and to play up his talents in that incredibly demanding art form in which he was such an expert. But now times were changing fast and Li noted how the likes of Jackie Chan and other Hong Kong major screen personalities were attracting a more universal audience with their contemporary-set comedies, dramas, and action pictures. As such, Li finally gave in to the trend. With his ambitions geared to the worldwide box office, he now allowed, "It's very difficult to tell older Chinese stories to a foreign audience. They don't know Chinese history, who is the bad guy. In a modern movie, it's very easy to get the meaning. You know, good guy, bad guy. That's why everybody changed."

For his 1994 debut into the new screen mode he chose to make *The Bodyguard from Beijing* [Chung Naam Hoi Biu Biu] with Corey Yuen (Yuen Kwai) at the helm. The entry was an entertaining riff on the Kevin Costner–Whitney Houston Hollywood-made feature, *The Bodyguard* (1992), which had accumulated $410.9 million in worldwide distribution. Actually, the Hong Kong rendition was in many ways an improvement over the overblown, American-produced earlier narrative. The new big-screen rendition cast Li as John Chang, a member of mainland China's high security force. When a businessman is murdered, Chang is dispatched from Beijing to Hong Kong to protect the only surviving witness to the crime—pretty, young Michelle Yeung (played by attractive Christy Chung Lai-tai) whose protector/boyfriend is a wealthy entrepreneur with close ties to the government.

Stern, methodical, and highly practical, Chang is a marked contrast to the two Hong Kong police officers currently assigned to the protective custody detail. (One is fat, jovial, and preoccupied with financing his son's medical school education in America by gambling; the other is younger, slim, but less experienced and too focused on his growing romantic attachment to Michelle.) Before long, it becomes a cat-and-mouse game between Chang and the hired assassin, Wong, a former member of the Red Chinese Army's elite killer squad. Wong has been paid to eliminate the young woman before she can testify in court. The showdown occurs in the confines of Michelle's fancy Hong Kong abode where she, her young school-age brother, the two police, and the ever-vigilant bodyguard are entrenched.

With his brush haircut, form-fitting, sharp business suits, and ever-present sunshades, Li's John Chang makes an extremely cool contemporary hero. Devoted to duty, he breathes his job twenty-four hours a day. He is suspicious of everyone and is ready at a moment's notice to spring into deadly action like a watchful panther. One thing he hasn't counted on is the growing chemistry between he and his beautiful charge, nor that he would develop a friendship with the well-meaning, if sometimes careless, hefty senior member of the Hong Kong police on the joint stakeout. Then too, Chang must deal with the heroine's prankish, ever-curious young sibling as well as the hangdog rich businessman/lover of Michelle. (The latter soon realizes that his beloved is more attracted to handsome, lethal John than to his boring, wealthy self.)

In adapting to a modern plot line, *The Bodyguard from Beijing* scenario cagily finds "plausible" reasons for Li's high-powered protector to turn away from firearms to martial arts to carry out his life-or-death bodyguard duties. Sometimes, for example, his gun jams, other times it runs out of bullets. But whether using firearms or any handy object, Jet's resourceful John Chang proves more than adept for the task at hand. He rolls in and out of the line of fire like a precision robot, agilely moving for cover or to position himself better to go on the offensive. These combat scenes switch from the heroine's home to the Hong Kong streets and, most spectacularly, to a confrontation with murderous thugs at a shopping mall which ends with Chang (and Michelle positioned safely under him) gliding on a skateboard out of harm's way. Frequently the camera pans in on Li's face and in particular his laser-beam eyes as they explore a new situation for any potential danger. Whenever his cold, calculating orbs freeze or do a sudden stealthy side glance, the viewer knows the next moments will bring exciting screen action.

In the final showdown with the highly efficient killer, Wong, and his thugs, Jet's Chang reduces their number one by one. The two Hong Kong cops are both downed (one fatally) by the murderous assailants. As the intruders are felled, Chang and his chief opponent engage in a one-on-one battle, each having to keep his face covered as protection from suffocating gas fumes. Later, the government bodyguard is stabbed in the left shoulder by the killer's knife. Not bothering to remove the blade, the indefatigable protector continues his somersaults, rolls, and dodging the killer's every move. But in a reversal of power, the opponent gains the upper hand by training his gun on a suddenly cornered Michelle. Twice the killer fires at her and twice John jumps in the path of the high-velocity projectile giving new meaning to the expression "faster than a speeding bullet." In a climactic moment, the macho Beijing warrior yanks the knife from his shoulder and with remarkable dexterity, throws it at the killer, thus eliminating his opponent.

Putting aside the low comedy moments of the hefty cop and the overly annoying young brother, what gives *The Bodyguard from Beijing* its grist is the novelty of seeing Jet Li function like a slick human dynamo in a modern setting. In addition, there is the chemistry between him and the heroine. As with most of his costumed action fare, this Li movie entry presents the star (reputedly very embarrassed at doing any type of love scenes on camera) in a growing romance with the spoiled young heroine. Notwithstanding his real-life reluctance (not to mention the Hong Kong cinema custom which did not favor bedroom romps), Li and his leading lady display a credible sparking on camera in their essentially chaste rapport. His sexual urges remain under control because of his character's no-nonsense approach to life and his refusal/inability to put personal satisfaction above his job or his obligation to his wealthy employer who loves his mistress. Despite all this, the nuances of the meaningful looks exchanged between hero and heroine as they each warm to the other provides an intriguing edge to the proceedings. (As in all Jet Li films, the leading lady takes the aggressive romantic posture.) Their relationship is "resolved" in the finale where, his mission accomplished, John Chang returns to Red China. He leaves a gift of money (to his Hong Kong cop pal) and returns the fancy watch that Michelle had given him. In a final shot, repressed John Chang is shown in close-up against the backdrop of an unfurling flag of the People's Republic of China. Evidently, the picture's contrived concluding message is that country comes before individual satisfaction.

Released in Hong Kong on July 28, 1994, *The Bodyguard from Beijing* grossed $11.193 million (in Hong Kong dollars), no longer considered such a modest take as the depression of the Hong Kong economy adversely affected every industry there. For the 1995 Hong Kong Film Awards, this film received a Best Action Choreography nomination for the action direction of Corey Yuen and Yuen Tak. As would become increasingly customary with Jet Li releases—especially those with modern settings—they would be dubbed into English for the TV market in the West and released there in VHS and DVD formats for home viewing. In its English-language dubbed edition, this entry was retitled *The Defender.* Despite its many flaws, *The Bodyguard from Beijing*, in either presentation, is definitely worth careful viewing.

12
Staying the Course

Since childhood days, Jet Li had been inspired by the life, achievements, and screen works of Hong Kong movie star Bruce Lee. Seeing Lee's action movie *Fist of Fury* [Cheng Miu Moon; in the United States: *The Chinese Connection*] when it was released in 1972 had made a tremendous impression on the nine-year-old Jet who was then just beginning a career path in wushu. The impact of the dynamic Bruce on the youngster was intensified when the legendary Lee died unexpectedly in 1973. Later, once Jet himself entered the movie film industry, an idea began to formulate in his mind: One day he would make a feature film that was a direct tribute to his great screen predecessor. Now, as the guiding force of the Hong Kong-based Eastern Production Ltd., Jet was certainly in a position to do so.

As his celluloid accolade to Bruce Lee, Jet Li chose to use the late star's pivotal *Fist of Fury* as his point of departure for his 1994 *Fist of Legend* [Cheng Miu Ying Hung]. What especially appealed to Jet was the 1972 picture's message—"that we Chinese often thought that all Chinese were on our side, and everyone else was the enemy, but that's wrong." Careful reviewings of this cherished Bruce Lee feature, however, led Jet to a fresh discovery: "I found that the topic was too narrow, that it focused on only one point of view. The Japanese were all evil and were portrayed as unsympathetic villains. This, obviously was not the case in real life. In *Fist of Legend*, I . . . hoped for a broader view of the characters. At the time of Japan's invasion of China, not all of the Japanese people wanted to have war. I'm sure there were many who quite opposed the invasion, the expansionist politics and atrocities of their brotherhood armies. . . . "

Jet Li's dashing Chen Zhen and his leading lady (Ada Choi Siu-fan) stare down the opposition in *Fist of Legend* (1994).

Regarding the earlier movie's lead figure, Li explained, "The character of Chen Zhen was interesting in that, though he was highly trained in martial arts, he chose to go to Japan to study engineering. This is a choice that I can relate [to], for I always believe strongly in having a balanced lifestyle. One cannot expect to learn everything just through learning martial arts alone. There are other ways to acquire knowledge, other untapped areas of human resource. . . . "

Another factor entered into the equation that shaped the upcoming *Fist of Legend*. Li detailed, "After the success of *Swordsman II* [1992], the market was flooded with a hundred imitations. Suddenly, everybody could fly: Brigitte Lin, Maggie Cheung, you name it. Without any foundation in martial arts, you could star in an action movie. When I saw what was happening, I wanted to give my fans a more realistic film. Real combat, no flying. That was *Fist of Legend* I poured my energy into. Not only did I produce it, but I was also very involved in the script, the story, the fight scenes, the philosophy. I had high hopes for the movie. I really pushed myself creatively." Of great concern to Jet was his wish that audiences would *not* think that by creating this quasi-remake he was trying to usurp Bruce Lee's lofty place in martial history. Rather, Jet reasoned, it was "to show my respect for his memory."

Gordon Chan Ka-seung, who had written the screenplay for Jet's *The Bodyguard from Beijing* (1994), scripted and directed the new vehicle. Chin Siu-ho, who had made such an impression as the friend/adversary in Li's *The Tai-Chi Master* (1993), was made part of the *Fist of Legend* cast. Ada Choi Siu-fan was hired to play the hero's Japanese lady love. Yuen Woo-ping was again on hand to provide the action choreography/direction. Because of the then shaky Hong Kong financial world and because this was not geared as one of Jet's heavy-duty costume action offerings, the budget for this feature was relatively modest.

Fist of Legend is set in the pre–World War II era. It finds renowned patriot Chen Zhen (played by Jet Li) abandoning his studies in Kyoto, Japan. He feels honor-bound to return home to China because he has learned that his martial arts master died under mysterious circumstances and that his famed training school is in danger of extinction. Determined upon revenge, Chen Zhen begins uncovering the facts in his master's murder, and he discovers a plot to keep China under the iron clutches of expansion-hungry Japan. This forces the hero to battle those enemy Japanese who threaten him, the school, and his homeland. Complicating matters, Chen Zhen's Japanese love has followed him to China, and this interracial romance earns him the enmity of his friends and martial arts school followers. It also leads to a deadly face-off between Chen Zhen and the vicious Japanese officer Fugita (played by Billy Chow Bei-lei). Thereafter, local Japanese authorities insist that the "guilty" must be punished for the general's death and the Chinese officials agree in order to prevent further hostilities between the two countries. As such, the honorable Chen Zhen surrenders himself to the foreigners. Although sentenced to death, the final scene shows him being hurried out of the city, forced to begin life anew elsewhere.

Generally avoiding the use of wire wu, *Fist of Legend* provides a sterling showcase for Jet's superior martial arts skills (including kickboxing) as he battles several Japanese. There are outstanding duels of power between Li and such other cast members as Billy Chow Bei-lei, Yasuaki Kurata, and Jackson Lau Hok-yin.

Debuting in Hong Kong on December 22, 1994, *Fist of Legend* took in $14.785 million (in Hong Kong dollars). For the 1995 Hong Kong Film Awards, the movie was nominated for a prize in the Best Action Choreography/Direction category. Months later, when the picture reached the United States, Mick LaSalle (*San Francisco Chronicle*) wrote, "Li is one of the bright lights of Hong Kong cinema, a man whose presence—like that of Harrison Ford—radiates integrity. He has a great stillness as an actor, which he breaks only occasionally and with great effect. In the course of a film he'll smile perhaps twice, but each time he does, the whole audience warms up and relaxes." LaSalle elaborated, "The seriousness of Li's demeanor keeps the movie from seeming like just an excuse for a lot of fights. Similarly, his good looks and gentle touch serve him well in the romantic scenes, . . . "

For Chris Baker (*Austin Chronicle*), "It took guts to remake a martial arts classic like Bruce Lee's *Chinese Connection*, but *Fist of Legend* is a more than worthy effort. Like Jackie Chan's *Drunken Master II* [1994], it brings modern pacing and stunts to the classic formulas of Seventies kung fu flicks. . . . Actor Jet Li is very

Even blindfolded, Jet Li has the upper hand in *Fist of Legend* (1994).

A proud father (Jet Li) and his son (Tze Miu) in the actioner, *My Father Is a Hero* (1995).

likeable in the lead, and he brings an interesting elusiveness to the fights—he never outright copies Bruce Lee, but an occasional technique or catchphrase or grimace of satisfaction effortlessly recalls the master."

Despite the generally positive reviews, the homage *Fist of Legend* allowed him to pay to Bruce Lee, and the movie's substantial themes (including the romance between a Japanese and a Chinese that surmounted racial pressures), Jet did *not* consider the picture a successful production. "I had done my best to make a movie with a fresh twist. But the Asian audience didn't embrace it. After this setback, I closed my production company and decided to focus on acting only. I wanted to give myself time to find projects that I really wanted to work on."

On the other hand, *Fist of Legend* remains a solid favorite among Jet Li enthusiasts. As Stefan Hammond elaborated in *Hollywood East: Hong Kong Movies and the People Who Make Them* (2000), this film "is most revered as a virtual clinic on the martial arts, with Jet demonstrating a mastery of nearly every imaginable fighting style in the world. . . . " Regarding the movie's dynamic finale, Hammond offers, "Here's where *Fist of Legend* attains the status of legend. The towering, knock-down-drag-out brawl between Chen and General Fujita is marked by nearly 15 minutes of combative physical abuse. . . . [T]here are no fancy props, no clever visual gimmicks, no furniture gags—just two outstanding martial artists [and a team of expert choreographers] working at the peak of their abilities to create what still stands as one of the most blisteringly visceral hand-to-hand confrontations ever recorded."

Rebounding from *Fist of Legend*, Jet's next screen showcase was 1995's *My Father Is a Hero* [Kap Ang Ang Dik San], for which Jet's past collaborator Wong Jing served as its producer. An element of the picture that must have intrigued Li was one of the film's plot points. In particular, it was the twist of having the undercover cop hero suffering from guilt over (1) being away from his family so much, and (2) for his infiltration assignments which made it seem—to the public at large and his household in particular—that he was a reprehensible, dishonorable soul. Adding further interest to the star was that this entry provided him with a rare on-screen opportunity to portray a loving family man, both to his wife and his adoring but often perplexed young son. To play the boy, Tze Miu (Xie Miao), who shined in *The New Legend of Shaolin* (1994) as the hero's offspring, repeated a similar assignment here, and the new project offered great opportunities for the young actor to show his naturalness in front of the camera and to display his ever-improving martial arts skills. As the leading lady, pop singer/actress Anita Mui Yin-fong (known as the "Madonna of Hong Kong") was cast as Li's leading lady. She was assigned to be the tough, respected police officer with strong maternal yearnings.

It is a rudiment of show business that working with young (scene-stealing) actors can be tough on the star. On this matter, Jet had his own method of approaching the situation: "With child actors I find that one must develop a comfortable relationship with them first. At such a young age, mood swings are frequent—and there may be many things on the set to confuse or even scare a child. Developing a firm trust with the child is essential to let him know you are a human being, that you can be approached."

Made on an expansive budget, director Corey Yuen (Yuen Kwai) was a past master at providing his action pictures with fast pacing and memorable visual action—as he had already done with Li's contemporary-set *The Bodyguard From Beijing* (1994) and a trio of Jet's costume action entries. Jet Li's Kung Wei is a

Jet Li: A Biography

Beijing undercover police officer dispatched to Hong Kong to infiltrate the ring of a high-powered gangland boss. While Kung is away on assignment, his ailing wife dies and his young son is left bereft. As the mob leader and his thugs (which includes Wei) plan an elaborate shipboard heist, the lawman struggles between honoring his duty (not to reveal his identity and to remain on the case) and taking charge of his motherless boy. Meanwhile, Hong Kong police Inspector Fong Yat Wah has been following Kung's trail to Beijing, not realizing at first that he is an undercover cop. Circumstances lead her to taking care of Wei's adrift son. When she and the boy return to Hong Kong, the youngster soon becomes a pawn in the mobsters' robbery scheme. However, the boy, a natural-born sleuth, high-tech maven, and disciple of martial arts, helps his dad to outmaneuver the villains. By story's end, the two cops have acknowledged their growing romantic attachment for one another. It is a development which pleases Wei's offspring.

Jet Li and young co-lead Tze Miu in action poses for *My Father Is a Hero* (1995).

Despite the clumsiness on camera of some of the supporting players, there is much to recommend within *My Father Is a Hero*. In particular, this production allows Li to display paternal instincts and warmth as he devotedly watches over his boy and, later, teams with him to outsmart the Hong Kong triad members, headed by Po Kwong. An especially evocative moment occurs in the narrative when the undercover cop is preparing for his workday at home in Beijing. One daily task is to teach his son skills that might come in handy in the future. An exercise they do together is to dunk their heads into basins of water to improve their capacities to breathe underwater. After several seconds of the routine, the young boy squirms, but his father (without bringing his own head out of the water) gently keeps his boy's head submerged with a light, loving tap, and the youngster proudly obliges. It is one of such several effective interchanges in the picture between the adult star and child performer and gives viewers a rare insight into the off-camera star as to how he relates to his own children.

Released in Hong Kong in March 1995, *My Father Is a Hero* garnered $15.530 million (in Hong Kong dollars). For the 1995 Hong Kong Film Awards, it was nominated for Best Action Choreography. When the feature played at the NuArt art house cinema in Los Angeles in December 1995, Andy Klein (*LA Reader*) endorsed, "*Father* is simultaneously touching and action-packed. This one's a keeper." When this entry was screened at Festival Hong Kong '96 at the Cinema Village Theater in New York City in August 1996, Gary Dauphin (*Village Voice*) wrote, "Li's action sequences are as crisp and pumped up as you'd expect, and when Li starts fighting off thugs using nothing but a small child and a long piece of rope, *Hero* becomes about perfect."

In retrospect, Thomas Weisser assessed in *Asian Cult Cinema* (1997), "Celebrated action director Corey Yuen has done something very unusual here. He's created a film that contains more character development than action. . . . But *My Father Is a Hero* is a three-dimensional study of an undercover cop." On the down side, Weisser pointed out, "The movie also suffers from some unfortunate scenes of slapstick and stupid sight gags. . . . At least Corey Yuen's tight direction has kept those lapses to a minimum." Stefan Hammond in *Hollywood East: Hong Kong Movies and the People Who Make Them* (2000) concluded, "Despite a higher action quotient than *The Bodyguard from Beijing*, *My Father Is a Hero* is actually the dramatically riskier of the two, a mix of sentimental melodrama and action that relies heavily on the abilities of Jet [Li] and Corey Yuen to work within the confines of more serious material. Thanks to their versatility—and the smart casting of Anita Mui—many of the film's most memorable scenes involved neither action or comedy."

Jet Li: A Biography

• • •

Although leading Hong Kong movie personalities Jet Li and Jackie Chan had both played the same character on screen (the folk hero Wong Fei Hung), each martial arts star had focused the major thrust of his screen activity in the specialty in which each excelled: Chan in comedic action entries filled with impressive stunts, Li in purer martial arts action stories (both historical and, more recently, contemporary). Off screen the two were said to be friends and hoped one day to team in a screen project. That said, in 1995, Jet starred in *High Risk* [Sue Daam Lung Wai], a bigger budget actioner which was a satirical takeoff on Bruce Willis's *Die Hard* (1988), its several sequels, as well as such as other thrillers as *Speed* (1994). More important, Jacky Cheung Hok-yau was signed for *High Risk* to play a movie star very much like Jackie Chan, one who leaves dangerous on-screen stunt work to others and proves to be as timid and cowardly off camera as he is aggressive and brave on the sound stage. It was, admitted Jet, "a savage parody of Jackie Chan, accurate in all its minor details. Hopefully inaccurate in its portrayal of his personality."

As produced, scripted, and directed by Wong Jing, with Corey Yuen (Yuen Kwai) serving as co-action director, *High Risk* took care to ensure that Jet Li's modern-day hero would be suffering once again from a turbulent moral dilemma. (In prior Wong Jing-Jet Li big-screen excursions there had been similar plot premises. In their *The Kung Fu Cult Master* [1993] the hero's parents were killed; in *The New Legend of Shaolin* [1994] the lead's wife was butchered.) In *High Risk*, Li's Kit Li was a law enforcer who had been on site when his schoolteacher wife and their son were among those killed when a dynamited bus exploded. The mayhem had been engineered by a mysterious criminal named the Doctor as part of his plot to kidnap rich students. Haunted by the brutal deaths of his loved ones, Kit becomes emotionally unreachable. He abandons his law enforcer profession and now, two years later, has become a bodyguard and secret stunt double who risks his life mindlessly for martial arts movie star Frankie Lone. The latter is a self-involved, woman-chasing individual, a hard-drinking, hammy celebrity whom no one in his inner circle respects.

The narrative heats up when the Doctor arranges to rob priceless Russian royal jewelry to be exhibited for celebrity invitees at a gala being held at a high-rise Hong Kong Hotel. Unwittingly, Frankie (along with his father) and Kit are among those in the targeted building when the daring heist (and slaughter of many of the swank guests) occurs. Both Frankie and Kit rise to the occasion as they play cat-and-mouse with the cunning criminal mastermind and his underlings (which includes one thug—played in venal yet comical fashion by Billy Chow Bei-lei—whose biggest ambition is to go one-on-one in kung fu with his screen idol, Frankie Lone).

By the finale, many characters have met an unpleasant death, including the Doctor who has been poisoned thanks to Kit. Meanwhile, Lone has become a real-life hero. As for publicity-shy Kit, who really engineered much of the out-matching of the gangsters, he has redeemed himself for not having saved his wife and son's lives in the earlier tragedy. Now his emotions are unfrozen sufficiently so that he can respond to an attractive, high-powered TV reporter played by Chingmy Yau Suk-ching. (In true Jet Li movie formula, the newscaster must take the initiative with the reticent bodyguard.)

This feature is resplendent with spectacular action peaks, especially when Jet's hero rams a car into the hotel. He careens the vehicle across the lobby and into an elevator which takes him and the auto to the scene of the crime. When the elevator doors open he recklessly zooms out in the ballroom filled with gang members and the battle zips into high gear. This ferocious sequence is outdone when the lead character, with his mousse-styled hair, takes charge of a helicopter demanded by the robbers. He pilots the craft into the side of the hotel, many stories above the ground, and the machinery wrecks havoc. As in other Jet Li thrillers set in modern times, the plot finds reasons for Li's Kit (who fires many rounds of bullets) to frequently abandon using firearms in exchange for rousing displays of good, old-fashioned creative martial arts skills.

High Risk opened in Hong Kong in July 1995 where it grossed $11.403 million (in Hong Kong dollars). Needless to say the movie proved to be controversial among Jackie Chan devotees who took this send-up of their idol too seriously (as supposedly did Chan himself). When the feature played in Los Angeles that same month, Andy Klein (*LA Reader*) alerted, "The more you know about Hong Kong cinema the funnier *High Risk* is, but there's enough silliness and excitement to please even the uninitiated." Klein did fault filmmaker Wong Jing for his "irritating, anything-for-a-laugh-no-matter-how-inappropriate style" but conceded "the over-the-top action scenes are great . . . and much of the humor is hilarious." Gary Dauphin (*Village Voice*) advised, "Fans interested in high body count pleasures will find plenty to scream and kick the seats about. . . . The hyped-up *High Risk* is chock full of catty, Hong Kong industry in-jokes, but since its plot and setting are nearly identical to the first *Die Hard*, it could as easily be skewing the Bruce Willis franchise as it is Jackie Chan's (alleged) off-screen habits."

When dubbed into English for television and home entertainment presentation, *High Risk* was retitled *Meltdown*.

Jet Li: A Biography

• • •

Jet Li began reformulating his screen image in 1993/1994 into a more contemporary character in order to attract a wider audience. He had been most successful in this process when he played an emotionally and verbally repressed man who, initially, seems out of his element, but who quickly adapts to the on-screen challenges and emerges bruised but victorious. On the other hand, the powers behind Dr. Wai in the *Scripture With No Words* [Mak Him Wong] really went far afield when they fashioned this elaborately conceived and expensively produced feature presentation. It attempted to have the tongue-in-cheek flavor of Harrison Ford's *Indiana Jones* movie franchise. At the same time, however, it mixed up the "light-hearted" on-camera adventure and oversized satirical action interludes with a misguided conceit: namely the old *Rashomon* (1954) gambit of having a plot situation told from different points of view. To further compound the problem it didn't offer a narrator to keep the complex threads together and to get at the truth behind any situation within the picture. Worst of all, it offers Li as a bespectacled writer of romantic action literature who is woefully henpecked by a shrewish wife. Playing a timid soul was not a posture that served Jet well. His co-star in this lumbering movie project was his *Once Upon a Time in China* series co-lead, Rosamund Kwan Chi-lam, cast as his wife, a woman of too many contrasting emotions.

In scattershot fashion and without sufficient tongue-in-cheek levity, the expensively mounted feature produced by the China Film Co-Production Corporation, relates a dual story, that of a temporarily burned-out fiction writer who has difficulties meeting his publisher's deadlines because of ongoing battles with his temperamental spouse who is demanding a divorce. Meanwhile, associates and friends try to help him with his unfulfilled writing quotas. The narrative switches back and forth from present-day Hong Kong, where the frustrated tale-spinner is overwhelmed by matrimonial woes, to his period-set, over-the-top action fiction which comes to life (with the film's cast members in dual roles in both the Hong Kong and the adventures sequences).

As the frustrated on-camera author imagines himself the key figures in his tales, he has "heroic" encounters in the African desert with a mad scientist and his steamroller of destruction, deals with Japanese spies in pre-World War II, searches for the legendary *Scripture With No Words* (a Tibetan scroll that can foretell the future), etc. During the course of these escapades, in which he becomes his fictional archaeologist Dr. Wai, known as the King of Adventurers, the harried writer thrusts himself vicariously into his fictitious situations. In these fantasies, he and his trusty assistant combat enemies with each party using flaming swords (a nod to the *Star Wars* adventures and the light sabers its Jedi knights used), wrestle with an oversized wolf-cum-rat, meet head-on rampaging sumo wrestlers, match blows with a deadly ninja squad, etc. In one sequence, Jet's screen alter ego dresses in drag to carry on espionage activity. The mishmash was directed by Ching Siu-tung who had helmed Jet Li's far superior *Swordsman II* (1992) as well as such other films as the popular series of *Chinese Ghost Story* movies.

Dr. Wai in the Scripture With No Words opened in Hong Kong in March 1996, pulling in $13.847 million (in Hong Kong dollars). At the 1996 Golden Horse Film Festival (in Taiwan) it won a prize for Best Visual Effects. The next year at the Hong Kong Film Awards, the picture was nominated for Best Action Choreography. The troubled vehicle ended by being released in two versions. The domestic/Hong Kong edition presented the dual stories, while the international version deleted the modern story line and filled out the running time (to the same length) with additional period footage.

Abroad the feature received mixed reviews. Derek Elley (*Weekly Variety*) thought the recut version had "a self-deprecating sense of fun that's very engaging." As to the "wooden" star, he detailed, "The humorless Li, whose martial arts skills are woven into the set pieces rather than stand out on their own, is cleverly played off against [the other characters] . . . to consistently entertaining effect, . . . " For Andy Klein (*New Times Los Angeles*), he judged it "a disappointing comic-book romp. . . . It has a great concept . . . but the execution just isn't as exciting as it ought to be."

In retrospect, *Dr. Wai* had some champions. For example, Thomas Weisser in *Asian Cult Cinema* (1997) decided the film was "an intelligent, great-looking, effects-laden actioner filled with an impressive array of endearing characters." Weisser noted, "this is the most impressive collection of special effects ever amassed for one movie. . . . " He also lauded Li's performance because here he was "very likable. He actually smiles a number of times in the film."

For some stars the misstep of *Dr. Wai in the Scripture With No Words* might have been severely damaging professionally. However, Jet Li had too much career momentum for even this misconceived saga to permanently affect his industry and public standing. By now he was already involved in two bigger budget vehicles: One would seek to place him in a comic book hero franchise of his own, the other was a much anticipated return to his signature movie role of Wong Fei Hung in a new adventure in the ongoing *Once Upon a Time in China* series.

13
A Hong Kong Farewell

In 1996, champs at the Hong Kong box office included Jackie Chan, Chow Yun-fat, Jet Li, Stephen Chow, and Leslie Cheung Kwok-wing, with Chan's *Rumble in the Bronx* [Hung Faan Au] being the number one hit with local moviegoers. By now the Hong Kong film industry was in a state of great flux. The long-awaited, but much-feared, return of Hong Kong from British control to that of mainland China was now only a year away. No one could predict accurately what the changeover would mean to the once thriving Hong Kong movie industry, an arena already besieged by local film pirates who were mass producing illegal copies—of even the newest movies—to be sold on the black market to home entertainment enthusiasts. For example, would coming under the supervision of the People's Republic of China in July 1997 create insurmountable bureaucratic and censorship roadblocks? No one knew for sure, but everyone—as in most every Hong Kong-based industry—was panicked and led to a great many (potential) financial backers dropping out of the local motion picture scene for the time being. (Among those abandoning the film business were many of the triads which had been heavy investors/controllers of Hong Kong filmmaking in the early 1990s.)

Filmmaker Gordon Chan Ka-seung (who had helmed Jet Li's *Fist of Legend* in 1994) described to *Time* magazine for its international edition of January 29, 1996, another factor that was crumbling the Hong Kong movie industry: "It's like a landslide. Our audience is going to see Hollywood films the way they used to come to see us. I feel as if I'm in Moscow during World War II and under attack from the Third Reich." To meet the increased competition of American films and to grab whatever profits there might be left currently, many of the surviving Hong

James Robert Parish

Kong moviemakers were jumping hastily onto the latest box-office fads and rushing out imitation products. (Some of the local moviemakers and stars were rushing off to Hollywood hoping to rebuild their careers there.)

Now filmmakers could not count on the once lucrative Hong Kong box office to recoup their production costs. (Ticket receipts for local product was tumbling both from the competition of American pictures and because of the general recession encompassing Hong Kong as the turnover to mainland China grew imminent.) Thus when planning new projects, these filmmakers had a growing desire to export their pictures on a far greater basis to mainland China. As such, it meant tailoring the contents of their product to, as Raymond Chow Man-wai, head of Golden Harvest Films described, "a region with different political systems, different cultures and religions." What would be successfully received by the Chinese mainland (its government and its filmgoers) was anyone's guess.

In this confused film industry climate, Jet Li was giving fresh thought to trying his luck again in Hollywood. (Several of his contemporary features were already being dubbed into English for airing on American TV and for home entertainment versions. Thus, he was an increasingly known commodity beyond the Chinese-language movie theaters and the film festival circuit. As such, Li was already receiving feelers from Tinseltown about making Hollywood movies, but nothing that was definite yet.) In addition, there now were less ties to keep him in the Far East. His companion, former actress Nina Li Chi, had abandoned her investment business which was tottering under the economic perils of the time. Now retired from her enterprises, she was available to be with Li wherever he chose to work.

With two such prolific Hong Kong film figures as superstar Jet Li and filmmaker Tsui Hark, it was almost inevitable that their paths should cross professionally again. It had been three years since they had teamed for *Once Upon a Time in China III*. Now the occasion arose for Tsui's Film Workshop to join forces with Win's Film Entertainment (a production company involved with Jet's *My Father Is a Hero,* 1995, and *High Risk,* 1996) to make *Black Mask* [Hak Hap]. A deal was negotiated for Jet to star in this production as part of the existing six-picture deal he had with Win's.

The sophisticated screen vehicle was to be based on a popular Hong Kong comic book of the same name. The adaptation was following in the wake of the well-received *Young and Dangerous* [Goo Waak Chai Ji Yan Joi Kong Woo], a 1996 feature that also derived from a comic book and which was generating a

126

series of follow-up pictures. Jet's new screen outing was to be produced and cowritten by Tsui Hark (who had a great passion for comic book literature), but was *not* to be directed by him. Rather it was to be helmed by Daniel Lee Yan-gong, a former TV producer, movie art director, and scripter who had made his film directing debut with a 1994 martial arts entry, *What Price Survival* [Duk Bei Diy Ji Ching]. Yuen Woo-ping was to return in his familiar capacity on Jet Li movies, as co-action director.

It was envisioned that *Black Mask*, which placed the original comic book character into a new adventure, could be the cornerstone of a movie franchise. It could be one that would provide Li with an ongoing and lucrative showcase for his well-honed martial arts skills in contemporary settings. With its blend of science fiction, the gothic, and old-fashioned chapterplays, the upcoming project was perceived as a high-energy adventure in which the swordplay of past times was replaced by high-tech weaponry and gadgets and filled with the three b's—bodies, bombs, and bondage—all geared to appeal to young filmgoers at home and abroad.

Black Mask was budgeted at $45 million (in Hong Kong dollars), making it one of the most expensive productions to be produced there, ranking in cost with some of Jackie Chan's most elaborate and expensive Hong Kong screen vehicles. In Jet's new showcase, Karen Mok Man-wai was cast as Tracy, the ditzy heroine who has a crush on the hero Tsui Chik, while Francois Yip Fong-wa played the high-kicking villainess. Patrick Lung Kong was the chief nemesis, and Anthony Wong Chau-sang was hired to appear as a sleazy drug lord. Lau Ching-wan, who usually specialized in comedy, had a change-of-pace role here as the stern police inspector who has an enduring friendship with the hero. Later, when the rough cut of *Black Mask* was assembled and Win's Film Entertainment's chief executive, Charles Heung, saw the completed footage, he was so impressed that he approved another $20 million (in Hong Kong dollars) to expand upon the movie's high-tech special effects.

Within *Black Mask*, Tsui Chik is a former member of an elite crew (squad 701) of government-trained assassins. As part of the preparation for duty, they had been surgically enhanced (by severing their nerve centers) to withstand pain in order to maximize their usefulness on the job. Also, chemicals were introduced into their systems to give them super powers. Later, when it was discovered that these medical alterations caused the individual to go berserk eventually—and thereafter die—the unorthodox program was halted. Before they could be exterminated by government forces, several of the 701 group, including Tsui, had escaped. He went undercover in Hong Kong, posing as a meek individual and working in a public library. His only friend is the tough-as-nail police Inspector Shek. Unknown to Tsui's workplace associates or to Shek (at first), Chik moonlights as the Black Mask, a powerful crime fighter devoted to righting wrongs in the metropolis.

Meanwhile, other surviving members of the elite 701 commando unit under the leadership of deranged Hung Guk are eliminating the city's crime lords, planning to take over the local underworld and eventually spread their power throughout Asia. Their aim is to acquire enough money and clout to blackmail the government into providing them with a serum antidote to their prior surgery. Now Tsui must battle his former comrades, including cosquad member and ex-lady love Yeuk Laan (who saves him at the cost of her own life). Events lead to a showdown between the Black Mask and the deranged Commander Hung. After eliminating Hung, Tsui/Black Mask reunites with Tracy (from the library) and Inspector Shek. At the finale plans are made to search for a remedy to restore his medical condition to normalcy.

With its amalgam of plot concepts, there are similarities within *Black Mask* to such classic comic book superheroes as Batman and Superman. In true comic book fashion, the hero—a geek by day and a masterful super crime fighter by night—is masked. Many critics and viewers would note the similarities between the corrugated black mask that Jet's hero wears when on his crusade to the masked Kato of another comic book/film/TV property—the Green Hornet. (Bruce Lee had played Kato in the American TV series of 1966–67.) Also, as favored by comic book arch villains, the mega-baddie in *Black Mask* resides in a dank subterranean hideout (here the subbasement of police headquarters!). To provide the movie's quotient of lowbrow humor, the librarian heroine is played as a scattered, hyperactive young woman who dreams of having great romantic adventures, but is always bumbling through real-life situations. Giving the production its dark tone is the deranged mastermind criminal who is almost matched in colorful eccentricity by one of the only surviving crime kingpins. (The latter is a particularly grizzled, twisted soul. He lovingly keeps a collection of relatives' body parts returned to him by the 701 squad who are trying to frighten him out of his underworld rule.)

In standard Jet Li fashion, his screen alter ego in *Black Mask* is again a repressed man which the plot contrives to explain its origin. Then too, in this excursion Li's celluloid persona is pursued by aggressive women: the librarian Tracy and his former 701 team member, Yeuk Laan. A nerdy librarian by day, the seemingly mild-mannered hero (like Clark Kent/Superman) turns into a super figure when he dons his mask and dark clothing. However, in contrast to Batman, the Green Hornet, et al., this mighty crusader is not above meting out gruesome finales to his adversaries (e.g., a favorite method of his is to launch—Frisbee style—blade-sharp CD discs to finish off his opponents). Another twist to the leading man's movie character is the underplayed suggestion that the relationship between Tsui Chik and Inspector Shek—neither of whom have girlfriends—may go beyond the platonic.

Within this film action scenes arrive in bursts ranging from the opening salvo, as the Black Mask attacks a battery of opponents, to a deadly confrontation on a high scaffolding above a tall building to the finale battle in the murky underground cavern. Again, the plot forces the Black Mask not to always use high-tech weaponry and to sometimes rely on his superior martial arts skills.

Released in Hong Kong on November 9, 1996, *Black Mask* grossed $13.286 million (in Hong Kong dollars), making it the twenty-ninth most popular picture in the territory for that year. For the 1997 Hong Kong Film Awards, the picture received three nominations: Best Action Choreography, Best Art Direction, and Best Makeup/Costume Design.

Evaluating this feature, Derek Elley (*Weekly Variety*) concluded that the production would "appeal to genre buffs and should prove a smart video item in the West." But the reporter predicted, "wider breakout looks unlikely because, as with so much of Li's work, the thesp's cool personality militates against much emotional involvement." He explained further, "The pic is less successful overall than other recent Li vehicles . . . which put his icy qualities to positive (and often very funny) dramatic use."

As with others of Jet Li's Hong Kong-made movies acquired for American release (now in theaters as well as home entertainment format), *Black Mask* received more than just a redubbing into English. A gangsta rap soundtrack was substituted for the original score, scenes here and there were reedited, and a new campaign was devised to add Hollywood glitz to the end product. When *Black Mask* showed up in U.S. distribution in 1999 (after 1998's *Lethal Weapon 4* had made Jet an American name), Owen Gleiberman (*Entertainment Weekly*) labeled the import "an excruciatingly garish and inept sci-fi schlocker." He reasoned, "The plot makes almost no sense, and instead of the high-flying, dancerly stunt work that is Li's specialty, the movie features endless badly edited scenes of machine-gun mayhem and surgical gore. This is fun? Maybe in Hong Kong."

Frank Scheck (*Hollywood Reporter*) found the Jet Li new showcase "almost completely lacking in coherence." He detailed, "*Black Mask* is an particularly gruesome entry in the action genre, more closely resembling a horror film in its slavish attention to decapitations, severed limbs and bloodletting. The fight sequences are photographed and edited in the kind of hyper-stylized, quicksilver fashion that can produce seizures, and the results—though at times impressive—are more jumbled than exhilarating." According to Eric Harrison (*Los Angeles Times*), "Much of *Black Mask's* plot and a good deal of its rapidly cut action sequences are mystifying." Regarding Jet Li, the reviewer acknowledged, "He is a magnetic presence—and his balletic stunts are amazing." Harrison also pointed out, "Most of the humor is supplied by Karen Mok, who plays the equivalent of Lois Lane. . . . [H]er rubbery face and comic timing give the movie the familiar feel of an American TV sitcom."

Even with *Black Mask's* mixed reviews, the slam-bang gore fest grossed $12.491 million (in U.S. dollars) at the American box office. There would be later adaptations of the *Black Mask* character to the screen in 2001, but they did not boast Jet Li in the lead role.

After Jet Li and filmmaker Tsui Hark went in different career directions after *Once Upon a Time in China III* (1993), Hark had made installments *IV* (1993) and *V* (1994) of the series with the role of Wong Fei Hung assumed by Vincent Zhao Wen-zhuo (Chiu Man-cheuk). The Hong Kong box-office take on each of these lesser offerings showed a fast diminishing return: $11.189 million in Hong Kong dollars for *IV* and $4.902 in Hong Kong dollars for *V*. In the interim, Li had played the legendary Wong Fei Hung in *Last Hero in China* (1993). Now, under the banner of Win's Film Entertainment, Li and Hark reunited for a much anticipated sequel, *Once Upon a Time in China and America* [Wong Fei Hung Ji Sia Wik Hung Shut] (1997). The most recent *China* installment had revolved around Wong Fei Hung and Aunt Yee's interaction with pirates. The new episode would bring the beloved screen characters to the American West, where the strangers in a strange land now would not be foreigners in mainland China, but the Chinese arriving on the U.S. frontier. Actor/action choreographer/director Sammo Hung Kam-bo, who had appeared in Jet's *The Kung Fu Cult Master* (1993), was contracted to both direct and provide the action choreography. Tsui Hark served only in a producer's and coscripter's capacity on this new project.

Later there would be suggestions that some plot ideas that Jackie Chan thought of using on a future picture (2000's American-made movie *Shanghai Noon*) might have been (inadvertently) discussed with one or more members of the *China VI* team when the latter film was in the scripting stages. Be that as it may, as of late October 1996, Li, Rosamund Kwan Chi-lam (as Aunt Yee), Chan Kwok-bong (as "Buck Teeth" Sol), and Xiong Xin-xin (Hung Yan-yan) (playing Club Foot, but now called Seven) were in Brackettville, Texas, near San Antonio for twelve weeks of filming. There were rumors that Hollywood filmmaker Quentin Tarantino, a great advocate of Hong Kong cinema, might join the cast in the role of the good-natured outlaw, Billy. However, it was Jeff Wolfe (who had appeared in 1996's *Bloodsport 2*) who took on that assignment. Much of the supporting cast of townsfolk, members of the Chinese community, and the Native Americans were drawn from regional talent. Reportedly there were problems during the making of *China VI* in blending the work habits and techniques of the Chinese and American film crews.

Within the narrative, Wong Fei Hung, Aunt Yee, and Wong's trusty helper Seven are on the final lap of their arduous trip from China to the American West to visit another of Fei Hung's students, "Buck Teeth" Sol. The latter has opened a branch of Fei Hung's Po Chi Lam herbal/medicine clinic in a Texas frontier town. As their stagecoach nears its destination, the Chinese trio encounter a down-on-his-luck stranger named Billy whom they befriend. Later, after holding off warring braves who attack the group, Fei Hung is injured, loses his memory, and is separated from the others. He is nursed back to health by Native Americans who regard this yellow-skinned stranger as an interesting oddity. Meanwhile, Yee and Seven reach their journey's end where they reunite with Sol and where Billy rescues them from the bigoted white townspeople.

Eventually Wong reencounters Yee and, after a tense period of not recognizing her or recalling his past, she helps him to regain his bearings. Thereafter, the corrupt mayor and other villains in town arrange a bank holdup and, with the help of a duplicitous Chinese man, place the blame on the Chinese and Billy. Just as they are about to be hanged the actual robbers return to town and, in a shootout, the outlaws and the dishonest locals are killed and/or arrested. Billy becomes mayor and proclaims the Chinese neighborhood to be known now as Chinatown.

With its nod to such comic approaches to the Western as Mel Brooks's *Blazing Saddles* (1974), *Once Upon a Time in China and America* focuses on the Chinese emigrants and their perspective of the Old West where, like the Native Americans, they are considered lowly outsiders by the racist locals. As such the Chinese exist in depressing, makeshift quarters. Interestingly in this not so politically correct feature, Wong Fei Hung comes to accept the white Americans and their strange ways (which is a tremendous step forward for him since the first episodes of *Once*

In 1997's *Once Upon a Time in China and America,* the star returns to his famous characterization of Wong Fei Hung.

Upon a Time in China series). However, once his memory is restored (except for his interlude in the tribal village), he displays little respect for the warrior braves and maidens who helped him to regain his health. In his full-bodied characterization of the complex Wong Fei Hung, Li is a mixture of a proud Chinese, a humorous greenhorn in the Old West (even to wearing a cowboy hat), as well as the perpetual preacher of Chinese pride and virtue (who bores his listeners, sending them to sleep).

Expectedly, there are many on-screen opportunities for the great warrior from the Far East to display his virtuosity against the rampaging redskins (and to prove his superiority to the white locals). In typical Wong Fei Hung fashion, Li's hero uses any weapon at his immediate reach, including tomahawks, lances, knives, and, of course, his trusty flying hands and feet. These battles to the death between cultures is well-staged by Sammo Hung Kam-bo. Unfortunately, the actors (seemingly all Caucasians) playing the Native Americans in this Wild West exercise are not dramatically up to their assignments and look/act as phony as possible (especially in their postbattle interactions with Fei Hung).

Once Upon a Time in China and America, made for $12 million (U.S. dollars), opened in Hong Kong on February 1, 1997 where it grossed a whopping $30.268 million (in Hong Kong dollars), making it the fifth most popular film released in Hong Kong that year. At the 1998 Hong Kong Film Awards, Sammo Hung Kam-bo earned a nomination for Best Action Choreography.

The picture received mixed reactions from the English-language press. Derek Elley (*Weekly Variety*) suggested, "This sixth outing could turn a few silver dollars in specialized distribution on novelty value alone, with some recutting and a new soundtrack." Elley allowed that "when Li is onscreen and the stunts are in full flow, the movie is an enjoyable ride, . . . " For Andy Klein (*New Times Los Angeles*), "While this chapter doesn't have the majesty of the first or the thematic interest of the second and third [installments], it is a consistently amusing romp. Sammo knows how to stage action and comedy as well as anyone in the world—his old comrade Jackie Chan not excluded—and *Once Upon a Time in China* and *America* is basically a nonstop action/comedy fest."

From the viewpoint of Mick LaSalle (*San Francisco Chronicle*), "For about half of its 90 minutes . . . [it] is the funniest Western since *Blazing Saddles*. It probably wasn't intended to be." He explained, "Everything's right, yet everything's wrong. Someone forgot to budget a technical adviser, as the film has some nagging authenticity problems. For example, several of the Texas bandits are not just handy with a six-gun—they're experts in kung fu." LaSalle pointed out that, in this picture, "By far the best, funniest, wildest, looniest touch is that the Indians are played here by white guys. Big, strapping white guys, with California accents that they try to modify by speak-ing-in-mea-sured-ca-den-ces." Pointing out another flaw with which this author wholeheartedly agrees, LaSalle detailed that the seasoned stars "play alongside English-speaking actors who look incredibly amateurish, as though they were plucked from some nearby campus and handed a script." In the estimation of the *San Francisco Chronicle* reviewer, "In a year or so, Jet Li . . . may prove to have the crossover appeal of Jackie Chan. But it won't be the result of any movie like this one."

Jet Li completed his multipicture movie pact with Win's Film Entertainment with *Hitman* [Saai Sau Ji Wong] filmed in 1997 but not released until the next year. For this Hong Kong-made action vehicle, Li broke with his working tradition and did his own dubbing on the soundtrack of his character's dialogue. It was an indication that, with this screen venture, he wanted to readjust his movie image yet again for the Hong Kong film market by personalizing his visual characterization with his own voice. Moreover, in this contemporary gun fu actioner, he no longer plays a good guy forced into seemingly bad actions (as was the case in his 1995's *My Father Is a Hero*). Instead, Li's screen character is a novice contract killer (with an exceedingly bad hair day) intent on fulfilling a murderous mission for the much-needed cash payment. (The action picture was directed by actor/action choreographer/director Stephen Tung Wai—his first teaming with Li—and was produced by Gordon Chan Ka-seung, a staple of recent Jet movie productions.)

Jet's hero now is a congenial young man living in cramped Hong Kong quarters. He is a novice member of a murder-for-hire organization, having been signed up due to his reputed background as a seasoned soldier/killer from his military service days. However, in his new post he has yet to carry out a hit assignment successfully, always finding some meager excuse to renege on the job. Things have reached an impasse and he is about to be fired as a killer for hire. At this juncture he begs his superior to let him represent the organization for a new hit assignment. The job, which is being touted about town, concerns a recently murdered, mega-rich, unscrupulous Japanese businessman. The deceased, who had predicted his fate, had established a huge revenge fund ($100 million—in Hong Kong dollars) as a reward for the man who uncovers his killer, tracks him down, and then eliminates him. When Li's boss won't take seriously his wish to be a candidate for this multimillion dollar assignment, the underling sneaks into the interview process at the Japanese corporation and eventually maneuvers a way to be considered for this manhunt.

As the young man displays both ingenuity and mettle—he badly needs money to help his mother—he gains assistance from an unexpected source. The helper is an onlooker (played in quasi-humorous, quasi-dramatic fashion by Eric Tsang Chi-wai) who assumes initially that Li's character is a seasoned gunman. He offers to be the hit man's agent, finance his hefty entrance fee into the bizarre competition, and

One of Jet Li's contemporary action thrillers, *Hitman* (1998).

even to buy him a new wardrobe, so he will impress the event's administrator. Things quickly go awry, especially when the agent's lawyer daughter (performed by Gigi Leung Wing-kei) enters the scene. She has long been disgusted by her disreputable father because of his shady past and his prison stays, but still has deep-down respect for him. Meanwhile, she falls in love with the rookie killer. By the finale, not only have a host of rivals, suspects, and complicit parties been eliminated permanently, but the picture also ends with a bittersweet twist for Jet's bounty hunter who finds a whole new career has opened up for him.

Released in Hong Kong in April 1998, *Hitman* grossed a relatively tame $10.296 million (in Hong Kong dollars). For the 1999 Hong Kong Film Awards the picture received a prize nomination in the category of Best Action Choreography.

With Jet Li having an increased international reputation thanks to his body of work since 1982 and his announced upcoming projects, *Hitman* received more screenings in the United States than many past Li entries. It showed, for example, in Boston in August 1998 as part of the Hong Kong Film Festival at the Museum of Fine Art. In addition, more reviewing sources took occasion to assess this latest Li offering.

Wade Major (*Boxoffice*) observed, "As with most Hong Kong action films of this type, *Hitman* walks a precarious moral tightrope, frequently forcing its audience to root for individuals of questionable character only because everyone else around them is so much worse. Where the film transcends its genre is in its surprisingly well-wrought script . . . Beyond the usual array of eye-popping set pieces, including a stunning fight sequence in an elevator shaft, *Hitman* features more than a few very clever twists—so clever, in fact, that even in the film's climactic moments a clear resolution is far from evident. That the actual resolution is so satisfying makes the accomplishment even more impressive."

In the estimation of *Variety*'s Derek Elley, "Jet Li is showcased to good effect in *The Hitman*, an above-average blend of comedy and action. . . . Cast in a role he's honed to perfection—the seemingly dumb mainlander manipulated by wiseacre Hongkies—Li plays well against local comic Eric Tsang and is given a range of opportunities to show his action smarts under helmer Tung Wai, an experienced stunt coordinator." On the downside, Elley recorded, "Pic veers in all directions and the script often does somersaults to reconcile some of its loose ends. The cute [Gigi] Leung [Wing-kei] is underemployed as the daughter, and Simon Yam [Tatwah], a star in his own right, often seems to be in a different movie, as a cop in charge of a *Rising Sun*-like investigation into the magnate's death."

Ironically, having fashioned a somewhat new screen image in Hitman, Jet Li was about to abandon the Hong Kong filmmaking scene. He had finally received a professional offer from the West that he liked, one to go to Hollywood to co-star in *Lethal Weapon 4* (1998) with that franchise's regulars Mel Gibson and Danny Glover.

14

Hollywood and
Lethal Weapon 4

By July 1, 1997, when the control of Hong Kong switched from the British to mainland China, several Hong Kong talents (both in front of and behind the camera) had already migrated Westward—some on a full-time basis—to participate in American-made (or -produced) film and TV projects. They ranged from film directors like John Woo, Tsui Hark, and Ringo Lam Ling-tung to actors like Jackie Chan, Michelle Yeoh, Chow Yun-fat, and Sammo Hung Kam-bo. Already Columbia Pictures had made overtures to Jet Li, suggesting that they coproduce a picture with Win's Film Entertainment after Li completed 1997's *Once Upon a Time in China and America*. (That did not happen at the time.) In the same period, Miramax Pictures, after acquiring the worldwide rights to six of Jet's Hong Kong–made features to be redubbed and edited for the English-language market, expressed real interest in working with Jet on new projects. (That would occur eventually.)

One of the recurrent stumbling blocks to Jet making his debut in an American-made vehicle had been his lack, so far, in mastering the speaking of the English language. Another problem was that after years of arduous, often hazardous filmmaking in China and Hong Kong, Li was feeling professionally burned out. While the Hong Kong film industry was sinking into the doldrums, he even considered retiring. As he viewed the situation, he did not need more material wealth or popularity in order to "do right by my mother, my family and my children—to provide for them."

Part of his current thought process had to do with his growing (re)interest in Buddhism, a religion which, over the course of his life, many had told him would play an important role in later years. In (re)exploring this ancient and traditional religion he appreciated that the original, pure teachings of Buddha (contained in the holy scriptures called sutras) taught that the individual should abandon his/her ego as much as possible, and that base desires—in their many outlets—were extremely detrimental to a person. Realizing that, with his movie star lifestyle—albeit modest compared to Tinseltown celebrities—it would be difficult for him to practice Buddhism in its purest form, Jet gravitated to Tibetan Buddhism. Li was drawn to this version of Buddhism because, as he interpreted on his Internet website, it "doesn't reject desire or ignore the ego altogether. Instead, it aims to purify our primal urges by using them to help attain spiritual development. Work with what we have, with what we are faced. This is an alternative way to enlightenment."

In was in this period of questioning his life and again exploring religion that Jet came into contact with Lho Kunsang. The latter had been born in the holy province in Tibet and was believed by many Buddhists to be the eighth reincarnation in a highly respected Tibetan lineage. Judged a Rinpoche (the equivalent in Catholicism to an abbot), it was viewed that, in the years to come, Lho Kunsang was meant to preside over the lives of monks. The holy man's devout study of Buddhism as well as the fields of astrology, poetry, etc., was interrupted by the Cultural Revolution of the People's Republic of China. During this time of great hardship, he had to study his religion in secret. Meanwhile, determined to preserve Buddhist relics, he made it his mission to rescue as many sacred scrolls, statues, and so forth as he possibly could. As the Cultural Revolution ended, he came out of hiding and began several tasks—teaching Buddhist monks, visiting other countries to spread the tenets of his religion, and crusading to restore the Rinpoche monastery.

It was Lho Kunsang who suggested to Li that his course in life was *not* to abandon moviemaking and retreat, for example, to a monastery or elsewhere to study the holy words. Instead, Jet must return to his work and use his fame to bring the teachings of Buddhism to others. With the guidance of his newfound teacher, the actor determined a new mission in his life: "I just want to do my part to promote the Buddhist philosophy of loving-kindness and unconditional love, so that some can understand, even just a little, how to make the most of this human opportunity, this lifetime. I'm not trying to convert my audiences; I just want to offer information—to expose them to ideas they might not otherwise encounter. If they're not interested in the message, they may not even notice it. If they're ready to listen, they will."

Jet Li: A Biography

• • •

By mid-July 1997 Jet Li was in New York City to participate in the promotion for the American debut of his *Black Mask* (1996) which was to be screened at the Twentieth Asian American International Festival at the Sony Lincoln Square Theater. When cornered by the press, Jet acknowledged that yes, he was studying English, so he could communicate better to American audiences in the future. He talked on a variety of topics. He told the *Village Voice*'s Edmund Lee about the current state of his genre of action movies: "For me, they have become too violent. I want to give a smart and positive image to martial arts, not this bloody, fight-for-no-reason image." As to his status in the picture business: "I'm not really an actor or movie star. I'm on a crusade to show the whole world the goodness of this [martial] art." Regarding Hong Kong returning to mainland control: "I feel great. In fact, I look forward to Macao, which goes back in 1999 [to Chinese jurisdiction]—and even, hopefully, Taiwan. I'm proud of a unified China." But he added, a China that is "with human rights, with a democratic government . . . "

When queried about rumors that he would soon be making his Hollywood sound stage debut, Jet cautioned, "Before I choose something I want to make sure that everything is top-notch." (At this juncture Li had already been approached about projects by filmmakers Oliver Stone, Francis Ford Coppola, and Quentin Tarantino, and he had turned down a recent offer to co-star on screen with Jean-Claude Van Damme. There was also talk of teaming Jet with Jackie Chan, Chow Yun-fat, and Michelle Yeoh in a remake of the 1966 Hollywood western, *The Professionals*, but this did not develop into a reality.)

Describing the Asian movie star of this period, the *Village Voice*'s Edmund Lee reported, "Throughout the interview, Jet Li sits upright in his chair at a hotel café, never showing emotion. He calls the waiter and orders tea in the middle of the conversation, never missing a beat. The stoic aura of Wong Fei Hung comes through. But at one point, this façade crumbles and a big smile breaks across his face as he starts to wave his hands. 'Come here!' he yells out. A woman rushes over, pen and paper in hand. He signs his name. She hesitates, then kisses him on the cheek. As she leaves, his face reverts back to the sober look of a martial arts master."

Back in 1987, a Hollywood cop movie entitled *Lethal Weapon* had grossed $65.207 million at the box office. Part of its sleeper success was due to the teaming of white Mel Gibson with black Danny Glover as two contrasting types of law enforcers who bond together while combating deadly villains amidst a high quotient of action and lots of explosions. Its success led to *Lethal Weapon 2* (1989) also directed by Richard Donner and also coteaming Gibson and Glover, with the addition of Joe Pesci as a grating but humorous sidekick. The results were a domestic box-office gross of $147.253 million. This prompted Warner Bros. to make its third entry in the franchise, *Lethal Weapon 3* (1992). Again Donner directed Gibson, Glover, and Pesci, this time adding Rene Russo to the roster as Gibson's on-screen girlfriend and a fellow member of the police department. This production grossed "only" $144.731 million domestically, but the worldwide gross had increased from *LW2*'s $227.3 million to *LW3*'s $319.7 million. While many critics said the film series was creatively wearing out its welcome, all the major players involved knew that one day *Lethal Weapon 4* would be made.

It took over five years for *Lethal Weapon 4* to be announced as a forthcoming reality—partly because of the conflicting work schedules of the key actors and director, and to some extent, because a viable script had yet to evolve. Then came word that Mel Gibson would be available from January 1998 until the spring of 1998 to shoot the picture. After that, the superstar was locked into other projects for an unbroken stretch of time. So, after years of leisurely mapping out the fourth installment, everything suddenly had to be rushed for the fast-approaching 1998 start-up date and then pushed through to a rapid completion so that with a speedy postproduction phase the picture could be premiered in early July 1998 (the peak of the summer season when action blockbusters did best).

Among the critics' complaints about *LW3* had been that its formula was running dry and that the primary cast members were too middle-aged. It was agreed that fresh blood was needed to reinvigorate the on-screen proceedings. Determining that the addition of a young African-American character to the cast mix would be strategically sound, the filmmakers sought a young Eddie Murphy—type to play a *Beverly Hills Cop* (1984) sort of law enforcer role. It was hoped that such a talent would draw in hip, young filmgoers. In short order, sharp and sassy comedian Chris Rock was hired to join the star lineup of Mel Gibson, Danny Glover, Joe Pesci, and Rene Russo. This left one additional key role to be cast in this latest sequel to the *Lethal Weapon* series—that of a youngish Chinese villain. With an eye on the international box office and wanting a name personality to fill the pivotal assignment, overtures were made to, among others, Jet. The potential offer came at just the right time for the Hong Kong–based superstar.

In the most diplomatic fashion, the Hollywood powers inquired if Jet, despite his impressive track record in the business, would be agreeable to auditioning for this film assignment. He said yes. Li reasoned, "I don't mind having to audition because that is the way they do things there; they are all used to that method . . . I feel that as an actor, one should not have those feelings of arrogance. It's not like they are purposely making life difficult for us, they have their way of doing things. It's just the difference between the two cultures."

Li flew to Los Angeles where the crucial test for *Lethal Weapon 4* was to take place. As he would recall the event: "It was very informal. My audition was with Mel Gibson and we had to do a short scene together. We just did it for a while and after that we started chatting and got to know each other. . . . It was nothing really special but we got along really well." During this getting-to-know-each-other period, series' director Richard Donner explained to Li why he wanted him for the picture: "I saw all of your movies. You are baby-faced and your youth is very nice, but when you change your face, the feel is very serious, very dangerous."

At one point in this consideration concerning Jet for the production, a studio executive questioned Joel Silver (the film's veteran producer) about the wisdom of hiring Li because of his pronounced accent. The executive asked Silver to list one Hollywood action star who spoke with such a heavy accent. Silver replied "Arnold Schwarzenegger." (He might also have added Jean-Claude Van Damme, not to mention the heavily New York–accented Sylvester Stallone.)

Eventually, it was agreed that Jet was suitable for the *LW4* role if the price was right. Negotiations got underway between the studio/film's producers and Jet's people (by now he had Hollywood handlers). There was no possibility that Li would receive anywhere near the enormous salaries (and percentage deals) afforded the series' mainstays. Nor, at present, was the China-born celebrity in the same league (according to Hollywood guidelines) as Chris Rock. The latter, after all, had an established TV following from his TV series (*Saturday Night Live, In Living Color*, and *The Chris Rock Show*), and already had been in such American-made feature films as *New Jack City* (1991), *Panther* (1995), and *Beverly Hills Ninja* (1997). As such, Jet was signed to *LW4* at a salary closer to $1 million than to the rumored $3 million. For Jet, the most important aspect of this production was that it would introduce him to Hollywood filmmaking and to the American moviegoing public.

Unlike such peers as Jackie Chan or Chow Yun-fat, Li had no qualms about playing a screen villain for the first time. (In his Asian-produced movies, he'd always been the hero, even in such recently made entries as his 1997 film *Hitman*, in which he portrayed a quasi-bad man.) He explained, "The audience is more mature these days and they know it is just a film role. Besides, a lot of famous actors, like Robert De Niro, play villains all the time. I am not worried about it."

With co-star Danny Glover at the July 1998 Los Angeles premiere of *Lethal Weapon 4.*

As to having his screen character in *LW4* die, the performer insisted, "It's in the story. If he [Gibson's lawman] kills me, it's nothing!"

With his participation agreed upon, Jet began preparing for the early January 1998 shoot date. As he detailed, "Other than practicing my kung fu for eight hours a day, I also needed to take English lessons. I just started with the simple things and slowly started learning from there." He amplified about his role and the Hollywood moviemaking process: "In the film I play one of the snakeheads [i.e., gangsters] who smuggle in illegal immigrants from China for a fee. So, I also have some dialogue in putonghua. The character is a very cool one so he does not speak too much. It's not like in Hong Kong where you write a bit of the script and then start shooting and have to wrap up the whole movie in twenty days or something." Although he did not have a big lead part in *LW4*, Li, ever the perfectionist, made a concentrated effort in his prepping for this Hollywood debut. Not only was this his normal work style, but he wanted to insure that this assignment went very well and that he absorbed as much as he could, as quickly as possible, about American filmmaking. This drive was part of his lifelong belief that he must always do his best and, in doing so, bring honor to his family, whom he continued to support and help out financially. "This," said Lee, "is why I train very hard."

By late 1997 Jet, along with Nina Li Chi, had moved to a rented home in Los Angeles. He was studying English (partly through a tutor, and by watching American movies and TV shows as well). He was soon sucked into the regimen of meetings which are a ritualistic prelude to Hollywood filmmaking of today. As an important cast member, he was present for those conferences which dealt with his role and his on-camera tussles with the script's good guys (especially Mel Gibson). As Jet detailed, "Whenever we had meetings, the director would always say to me, 'You have a voice. You can say anything you like. If you don't agree with anything all you have to do is say so.' I hadn't worked with other Hollywood people before so I didn't know what it would be like. But they were really very good to me."

As for the on-camera interaction in which his character employed martial arts, Jet "asked Richard Donner if he wanted me to fight in the U.S. way or the Hong Kong way. . . . I told him it was very different and that if he wanted my kind of action then he had to give me freedom to work. He said, 'We just want your style.' So it was great because I could bring some of my people in to help choreograph the scenes." One thing Donner made Jet promise was to "never, ever hurt Mel Gibson [in their on-camera work together]." The jovial Jet, who had struck up a solid rapport with Gibson, reassured the director that the request was no problem. Meanwhile, the film's producer, Joel Silver, assured the extremely cooperative Jet that when they next worked together, Li would play a good guy on screen.

On January 16, 1998, filming on *LW4* began at Warner Bros. Studio in Burbank, California (and at other locales in and around Los Angeles, such as L.A.'s

Chinatown and a vintage warehouse down in Carson City, south of Los Angeles).
Jet was already choreographing his martial arts sequences (which would not use
wire fu). He was guided in this process by his frequent action collaborator, Corey
Yuen (Yuen Kwai), as well as by others of the Hong Kong action team brought by
Li to Hollywood for this project. Meanwhile, Jet worked on his characterization.
Throwing himself into the bad guy role, he analyzed the character's motivation.
His guideline was, "I never think that a villain thinks, 'I am the villain.' In real
life, the bad guy never things he's the bad guy. He just thinks, 'I need to do that.
It's my job.'" This helped Jet to build his role as Wah Sing Ku.

As preparation continued with the fierce on-camera encounters between Li and
Gibson's characters, Jet kept sight of his goal in his three fight scenes with the picture's star: "They aren't just martial arts fights. We tried to bring the Hong Kong
style of kung fu and American fighting styles together, to do something different."
(Already Gibson had informed Li: "I saw your pictures, I like your fights; just
decide how to beat me up.") This led to a good deal of improvisation on the set.

There was also much playfulness among the cast and crew during the making
of *LW4*—it helped to dissipate the tension of the relatively tight shooting schedule
on this big-budgeted project. According to Jet, "Everyone told me to watch out
for Mel and his practical jokes. So every day I was on my guard, but nothing ever
happened." It led the Hollywood newcomer to take the initiative. "I bought this
trick ring that gives you a shock, and I walked over and did it to Mel. Mel jumped
and said, 'Hey! Wait a minute. I never did anything to you!' I got him good."

As to Li's on-set demeanor, the film's executive producer, Jim Van Wyck,
observed, "Jet was playing a really tough guy; then you'd cut the camera, and he'd
have the most wonderful smile. He's so charismatic." The picture's top honchos
quickly realized that Li had a lot of valuable input to offer. This soon led to Jet
convincing his employers to add more scenes of him to the proceedings which
would give his character more continuity in the plot and, of course, increase Li's
visibility in the final product. (One of Jet's few spoken lines in the release print
would be, "In Hong Kong, you'd already be dead.")

When it actually came time to film the crucial battles between Jet and Mel's
characters, Li had already agreed to tone down the deliberately exaggerated moves
that, in his Asian-made movies, had so brilliantly showcased his skill and grace.
He also had to slow down his moves a bit so that, despite the reality of his quick-
ness, they would not seem to be computer-manipulated special effects on the part
of the action star. Even with these alterations on Jet's part, Gibson, no newcomer
to handling on-camera brawls, could not match the swiftness with which Jet

144

executed hand jabs, leg kicks, or body twists. (Li detailed, "When I worked with Mel Gibson, if I punched seven times, he saw maybe two.") Eventually it was agreed that Mel would memorize the intricate movements in his fight scenes with Jet. Everything went relatively smoothly thereafter.

What amazed Jet during the shooting of *LW4* was the luxurious manner—in contrast to Hong Kong picturemaking—in which the process was accomplished, from the on-set accommodations for the lead players to the shooting schedule itself. Back home Li was accustomed to working sixteen hours a day, seven days a week when a new film was in production. On this Hollywood project, he actually had Saturdays and Sundays free. He was very impressed by that perk.

As concocted by four scriptwriters, in *LW4*, Los Angeles Police Department Sgt. Roger Murtaugh (played by Danny Glover) and his partner, Sgt. Martin Riggs (played by Mel Gibson), and their weasellike friend Leo Getz (played by Joe Pesci), the ex-con artist who is now a private investigator, are fishing in the Los Angeles Harbor aboard Murtaugh's boat. Before long they are sideswiped by a huge freighter which leads to a shootout against several Asian men who are aboard the freighter. It is soon discovered that the vessel is full of illegal Chinese immigrants.

Murtaugh is distracted from brooding over his smashed yacht when he discovers at the scene of the mishap a Chinese immigrant family and their patriarch, Mr. Hong. Roger decides to take them into his home. Meanwhile, at the precinct, it is the consensus that Los Angeles Chinatown crime boss "Uncle Benny" Chan is behind the smuggling ring, and the law enforcers (with Leo Getz in tow) go into action. Sgt. Lorna Cole (played by Rene Russo), of the Internal Affairs Department, is unable to help out on this latest case because she is pregnant with Riggs's baby. (Meanwhile Murtaugh's daughter Rianne is also pregnant.) Helping Martin, Roger, and Leo in their investigation is young Sgt. Lee Butters (played by Chris Rock), secretly the father of Rianne's baby.

Wah Sing Ku (played by Jet Li), a leader in the Chinese Triads, is very annoyed that the Hongs have vanished, and he (and his thugs) track the family to Murtaugh's home. They grab the Hongs and set the house ablaze, with incapacitated Riggs and Lorna, as well as Murtaugh, his wife, and their three children caught in the trap. Fortuitously, the youngest Hong family member was overlooked by rampaging Wah Sing Ku. The boy helps Riggs to break loose and he, in turn, frees the others. Later, after it is discovered that Wah Sing Ku has killed Mr. Hong, the latter's uncle, and Uncle Benny Chan, Roger takes the deaths of the Hong family members quite personally. He and Martin chase down Wah Sing Ku and, in a free-for-all between the Chinese gangster and Riggs which ends in an underwater showdown, Wah Sing Ku is killed and the two cops can now focus on domestic matters. (A prerelease test version of *LW4* had Jet's character not dying from a volley of bullets from Riggs's firearm, but being only injured and thereafter fighting further with his opponent. However, preview audiences did not buy this anticlimax and the above-stated alternate version was spliced into the picture.)

Throughout the story line, there are several politically incorrect remarks made about Chinese people, including Riggs quipping to Jet's character as he arrives on the scene, "Hey Bruce [Lee]. Nice pajamas." (A later joke, involving another Asian character, riffs on the old "flied lice" joke about Asians' mispronunciation of the phrase.) As the smirky kickboxing psychopath, Li adeptly displayed his martial arts prowess, whether fighting opponents one-handed (with the other hand fingering his prayer beads) or taking on the two lead cops in a brutal encounter.

As *LW4* prepared for its release, neither the movie's official Internet website nor the film's initial advertising campaign thought to include Jet Li among the illustrated grouping of the five other key players. This oversight was noticed quickly by Li's fan base and they made their feelings known to the studio. In short order, Li was placed prominently in the revised promotional materials for the film. He also was asked to promote the feature and, as such, gave press interviews, appeared on TV talk shows, etc. (When Jet was a guest on television's *The Tonight Show With Jay Leno* he came across as boyish, a bit nervous, but charming. He made a hit with the host when he offered to show Leno martial arts moves geared for "older" stars. An amused Jay immediately asked Li if he knew the Chinese word for "smartass." Then Jet proceeded to exhibit some gentle tai chi moves for Leno to try. On another occasion, on Howie Mandel's TV program, Li gave a martial arts demonstration. In the process he—accidentally?—broke the host's on-set desk with a quick kick.)

Of the demanding and exhausting promotion process for the picture, Jet described, "One day, we met with seventy reporters. I used my poor English, just talk, talk, talk. I used my heart. I do my best, to explain, explain, to them." Finally, on Tuesday, July 7, 1998, *LW4* premiered at Mann's Chinese Theater in Hollywood. The film's main players were all in attendance. For the occasion, two blocks of Hollywood Boulevard was closed off, with stadium-size video screens installed strategically to show all the VIP arrivals. To add flavor to the proceeding, a dozen acrobatic wushu exponents battled with swords and spears, while ceremonial drummers provided music. Some 1,500 invitees attended the opening which was followed by a postpremiere party for 850 celebrity guests. (At a later date, Li, along with Gibson and others, embarked on an international promotional tour for the picture, with Jet receiving great attention by the Asian media.)

Only the kindest critics had anything positive to say about *LW4*'s tired premise and weak story line, or even the picture's two main stars who coasted through the proceedings. Amy Taubin (*Village Voice*) observed that co-stars Gibson and Glover, as well as director Richard Donner, are "so determined to get their last licks and leave us feeling satisfied and well-disposed toward them and whatever they think they and the franchise represents that they deluge us with as much bonhomie as shattered glass and crushed steel. It's a veritable firestorm of good feeling."

In contrast to the mild praise reviewers offered the series regulars and even to the franchise's newcomer, Chris Rock, the critics were much impressed by Li. "The charismatic Jet Li adds some much needed luster and impressive martial arts fighting," said Mike Goodridge (*Screen International*). Steven Rosen (*Denver Post*) enthused that what saved the picture is "a mesmerizing, terrifying villain. Chinese martial arts star Jet Li. . . . His presence gives *Lethal Weapon*'s best, most brutally sensational confrontations a Hong Kong action-movie flavor." Kenneth Turan noted in the *Los Angeles Times*: "Chinese action star Jet Li, playing a villain for the first time, not surprisingly benefits from having almost no dialogue in English. His nifty Hong Kong martial arts moves add a welcome intensity to the picture, but even Bruce Lee couldn't bring this baby back from the dead."

One of the few critics to fault aspects of Jet's invigorating presence in *LW4* was Leonard Klady (*Weekly Variety*). In his assessment of the release, he judged, "As the chief villain, Li is a mixed bag: His physical prowess is nonpareil, but his limited command of English inadvertently casts him as the sort of Asian devil that borders on caricature."

Made on a budget estimated to be around $140 million, *LW4* grossed $129.734 million in domestic distribution, with an additional $138.4 million grossed abroad. All this intake did not include the ancillary sales to pay, cable, satellite, and regular TV, the home entertainment editions, nor merchandizing rights, etc.

With his first true Hollywood film production now a reality, Li (re)assessed the value of *LW4* to his career battle plan for the immediate future: "I always play the hero in Asian movies. I always tell reporters and the audience that I'm not a hero, I'm an actor. As an actor, I want to do something new to challenge my career. I want to do something that's more than action; I also want to act, that's why I picked *LW4*. Also, three years ago, a lot of people in the States know who Jet Li is, but the studios don't trust you until you play by the rules. If a movie comes out and the audience likes your character, then the studio realizes, 'Oh, maybe we can make a movie with him and he can play the good guy.' So I think that opened the door. Let the audience know you first, then prove you can [make money] for the studio. It's step by step."

15

Making *Romeo Must Die*

In 1998, four of Hong Kong's most famous movie stars were in American-made movies or TV series. Jackie Chan had a huge hit with *Rush Hour* (which led to a 2001 sequel), while Chow Yun-fat was stuck in the unsatisfactory *The Replacement Killers* (but would do better with his releases in the following year: *The Corruptor* and *Anna and the King*). Sammo Hung Kam-bo was headlining the U.S.A. network TV comedy/drama *Martial Law*, which would last a few seasons. As for Jet Li, his appearance in and his promotion of the high-profile and quite successful *Lethal Weapon 4* had done a great deal to make him better known to a wide range of American moviegoers. (Li would describe, "After *Lethal Weapon 4* people on the street would say, 'Jet, Jet, you're so cool! But you're so mean.' I would say, 'That's a character, not Jet Li.'") Li gained further visibility for his *LW4* role when he was nominated for a 1999 MTV Movie Award in the category of Best Villain. Then too, in November 1998, *People* magazine published its "The Sexiest Man Alive '98" issue. The publication rated Jet Li as a hot contender in the ranking, describing him as one of "the handsome globe-trotters" who "made it a very good year for foreign affairs."

Even before *LW4* was in distribution, Li had won the strong interest of the Hollywood entertainment industry. Test screenings of *LW4* had shown that women filmgoers loved him in that picture. Immediately, that had prompted Warner Bros. and producer Joel Silver to option Jet's services for a forthcoming release to be determined. In the meantime, Universal Pictures wanted Li to star in their upcoming action vehicle, *The Art of War*, and were offering a reported seven-figure salary for Jet's services. This led Warner Bros. and Silver to exercise their option on Jet, and they scurried to find a showcase for the hot Hong Kong star. (As for *The Art of War*, which Li now had to reject, it would eventually be made at Warner Bros. for a 2000 release with Wesley Snipes and Cary-Hiroyuki Tagawa in lead roles.)

While action producer Joel Silver was putting together the Jet Li vehicle, Li and his companion Nina Li Chi returned to Hong Kong. When asked if he minded shifting headquarters back and forth around the globe, Li allowed, "I have been traveling since an early age because I was with the national wushu team in Beijing. We traveled all over the world and quickly became used to being in different places. I'm not too picky about food too." (On the subject of cuisine, he noted about the fast-food American culture: "Simple! Easy! Straight! [When the] Chinese have lunch we have maybe thirty different kinds of food on the table. It's very complicated. What's that? What's that? American culture is so easy: Go there [to fast-food restaurant]. Hamburger. Pay your money. Go back. Eat. Go back.")

On both sides of the globe he was asked repeatedly to contrast the differences between making motion pictures in Asia and in Hollywood. "Making movies in Hong Kong is like a small family business. There are two brothers in the Hong Kong movie family. One says, 'I want to make a movie.' The other replies, 'Why make this one?' The first brother replies, 'Because this type of movie popular now.' And the other brother says, 'OK.' After two weeks, they begin to make the movie. In America, the family's huge. If you want to make a movie, you first ask if mother agrees, then father, then uncle, then grandmother, then grandfather, then brother-in-law, then siblings—you have to get everyone's consent. The preparation takes two years before you can actually start. In a big family you have to please everyone before you can do the things you want."

On a technical level, Jet found many intriguing differences between the American and the Hong Kong ways of shooting a picture. "Over the years, Hong Kong has amassed its own set of rules about how to shoot movies, based on budgets of a certain size and equipment limitations. America has its own set of traditions, involving union workers and set schedules and so on. Hong Kong directors not only used to have two cameras at the most, whereas in America, five or seven camera may be set up to film a single shot. They [in Hollywood] like to shoot an entire scene straight through from beginning to end, whereas in Hong Kong, they shoot it in little bits and pieces. The method of using the camera is different, as well as the pace and the procedure of work."

When asked to pinpoint his style of martial arts, the star responded, "I think it's wushu. For sure, it change, change, change. Because with time it grew up. You cannot keep the old style still very old. This time, you need to learn this. Later, you need to learn that. Martial arts grew up. In the beginning, it was your head behind your hands. But it's not good-looking. The camera cannot see you! So we change. Anything changes, because the world continues. When the world moves, we need to change."

As to the frequently dangerous stunts his characters did in his films, Jet acknowledged freely that he did not perform *all* of his own stunt work on camera: "I do [all the] martial arts in my movies, but I'm not trained to jump off buildings or that kind of stuff. Every actor in the world needs a stunt man to help. I'm a normal guy. I only play the hero."

By April 1999 it was announced that, with Joel Silver producing, Warner. Bros. would make *Romeo Must Die* (2000) as the new Jet Li Hollywood movie. For economy sake, the $25 million production was to be lensed in Vancouver, British Columbia, Canada, and the star would receive an approximately $3 million salary.

The property, as scripted initially by Mitchell Kapner, had been on the studio's project shelf for nearly a decade. Originally it was conceived to feature a Caucasian star and involved an Italian mob war against members of Japan's Yakuza. One of the reasons for selecting this city-set project for Jet was that the studio's market research had indicated that Li most appealed to an urban audience. With this in mind, the powers-that-be determined the picture would benefit by combining Jet's martial arts skills with a hip-hop music ambiance. To play his co-star, the filmmakers selected African-American Aaliyah (pronounced Ah-LEE-yah), the twenty-year-old Brooklyn-born R & B singer who had already enjoyed several hit albums. This was to be her feature film debut. Also in the cast were to be such African-American talent as respected character actor Delroy Lindo, music producer/performer DMX, and rising young actor Isaiah Washington. Other Asian (-American) talent included in the lineup were Russell Wong, Henry O, and Jon Kit Lee.

When advised of the characters' ethnic mix and the casting choices, Li said, "I was concerned about the subject matter. It's an Asian and black film. I said to the studio, 'What about white people, what will they think, will they watch the film, what will the American audience think?' The studio kept telling me that wasn't a problem, so I thought, 'O.K.' " (Similar blending of Asian- and African-American cultures on screen had worked earlier in 1985's *The Last Dragon*. In 1998's hugely popular *Rush Hour* Jackie Chan had teamed with black comedian Chris Tucker. On Sammo Hung Kam-bo's then current TV series, *Martial Law*, he was partnered in the cop show with African-American comedian Arsenio Hall.)

Jet Li with his leading lady Aaliyah at the Los Angeles premiere of *Romeo Must Die* in March 2000.

Originally Stuart Baird was to direct *Romeo Must Die*, but he dropped out and Andrzej Bartkowiak (who had been the cinematographer on *Lethal Weapon 4*) was signed to make his feature film directing debut. (Several key members of the cast and crew—including Bartkowiak, Li, and Isaiah Washington, were all represented in negotiations for this picture by their powerful talent agency, ICM.) Corey Yuen

(Yuen Kwai) and his action choreography team were made part of the project. (It had been decided this time to utilize wire work in the martial arts sequences because *The Matrix*, released in March 1999, had done so well financially, and that sci-fi entry had employed wire fu in its presentation.)

When preparing his action routines for the start date of *Romeo Must Die*, Jet took into account of the fact that, "In Hong Kong, audiences like to watch the fighting sequences for up to five minutes. They like to study the movements and the style. In American culture, as with boxing, audiences want to see who wins. If one guy can knock somebody out in thirty seconds, that's great with them." Producer Joel Silver was in full agreement with this theory and urged Li to make his on-camera fight scenes "shorter and tighter, so American audiences will enjoy them more."

If tailoring his fight sequences to American tastes was relatively easy for Jet, it was another matter when it came to the story's romantic interludes. Said Li, "I can feel very brave through all the action scenes in front of the people who are on the set but when a girl comes close to me my face turns red because I'm so shy." (As it would turn out, the one on-camera kiss between Jet and co-star Aaliyah would be cut from the release print of *Romeo Must Die*. The producer would insist this was done because he wanted to keep the relationship between the two figures platonic and more in line with Jet's past screen image. Others claimed that the fear of possible adverse reaction to an overt interracial romance kept the locking of lips from the studio's final cut.)

As filming of *Romeo Must Die* got underway, producer Silver could boast, "Traditionally in the west, action sequences have been essentially assembled in the editing room. The stunt people who do the actual fighting are shot from various angles, and the lead actor's close-ups are subsequently inserted. The eastern film style has revolutionized the action sequences by using actors like Jet, who are the real thing and can do all the fighting themselves, and shooting them from head to foot. So, Jet has enabled us to make all of the action in this film completely authentic, without fooling the audience. All the fighting, all the stunts and wire work—it's all Jet."

Whereas in *Lethal Weapon 4*, there had been four staged fights, in *Romeo Must Die* the number was doubled. The filmmakers reasoned, "We wanted to make each one different, with a variety of moves and styles for the various characters involved. In different situations, you need different kinds of martial arts. If you want to hurt people, or you want to stop people, or you want to kill people—that involves all different types of fighting."

In working with Corey Yuen to prepare the film's action showcase, Jet had a particular philosophy: "First, we need to know the characters and the actors involved, and then we can create the fight scenes. . . . I don't like movies that are just fights. That's a demonstration, not a movie. The story is the most important thing to consider when planning the fight sequences."

During production, there was a plot point where Jet's hero must deal with a female opponent (played by Françoise Yip Fong-wa, who was Li's nemesis in 1996's *Black Mask*). It was Jet's idea that rather than be ungentlemanly and fight her one on one, that he pick up co-star Aaliyah and guide her fists as his "weapon" against the woman in this confrontation. Another gimmick used in the fight scenes of *Romeo Must Die* was a carryover from *The Matrix* (which Silver had produced). In those moments where characters are being bone crunched, the visuals switch to a computer-enhanced X ray of the disabled (or murdered) crunchee being pulverized.

Being the focal center of *Romeo Must Die* was a further learning experience for Jet about the ways of Hollywood moviemaking. For example, he noted, "In Hong Kong, we work on the martial arts scenes for two months and the drama for only one month. In Vancouver we worked for two months on the drama and only one month on the fighting."

Production on *Romeo Must Die* was completed by September 1999. During the period when the elaborate postproduction special effects were engineered, the soundtrack album was prepared, one which featured songs (including "Try Again") by Aaliyah. Jet joined the singer on the sound stage in Hollywood to play a role in one of her music videos for the numbers.

The movie had its premiere on March 20, 2000, at Mann's Chinese Theatre in Westwood, California, adjacent to Los Angeles. Among those in attendance were the film's co-stars Jet, Aaliyah, and Russell Wong, movie star Keanu Reeves, the music world's Kenny "Babyface" Edmonds, and sports figure Magic Johnson. Bruce Lee's widow, Linda, who came to the event with her daughter, told the media there, "I think Bruce would be very proud and happy that this occasion is taking place twenty-seven years after he passed away, because he really did create a genre of action film. And I think he's given the opportunity to many young, talented Chinese martial artists and a chance to display their talents, and to show the beauty of Chinese culture to the world. I think he'd be real happy and proud of Jet."

In *Romeo Must Die* Jet Li plays Han Sing, an ex-policeman who takes the rap for his criminal father and his spoiled younger brother. Thus, he is now serving a prison sentence in Hong Kong. When he learns that his sibling has been murdered in Oakland, California—where the father has reestablished his shady enterprises—Han escapes from the jail and flies to California to investigate the killing. There he meets and falls in love with Trish O'Day (played by Aaliyah) the independent-minded daughter of Isaac O'Day (played by Delroy Lindo), an African-American crime boss. The latter is involved in a business combine scheming to build a new pro football stadium in Oakland. To do so, however, they must acquire an expanse of waterfront property. Some of the Asian(-American) owners of this turf have been reluctant to sell out, resulting in several of them suffering damage to their present establishments or losing their lives. Another holdout has been Silk (played by DMX), the black owner of a wharf-side club, who likewise doesn't want to give up his valuable property. Also involved in the see-sawing battle for power is Mac (played by Isaiah Washington), O'Day's greedy, right-hand man, and, in addition, several unscrupulous Caucasian businessmen. After a shootout which sees O'Day gunned down, Han discovers that his own father, along with the latter's duplistic bodyguard Kai (played by Russell Wong) had arranged for the murder of Han's brother. In the finale, Han eliminates Kai and Han's disgraced father commits suicide.

With Jet as the film's focal point, three of the movie's highlights concern the use of martial arts and/or great physical agility. Near the picture's opening, there is a jaw-dropping scene as Li's hero, being punished for having gone berserk when he learned of his brother's death, is hanging by one foot in a Hong Kong prison cell. Bent on escaping and doing as much damage as possible in the process to his guards/tormentors, Jet's character executes some amazing moves as he swivels at warp speed around the room. Still dangling perilously from the rope he knocks each of his assailants down for the final count. The gracefulness of his lethal moves in this contest of one against several armed men is so adroitly executed that it remains long in the viewer's mind.

Later in the story, in Oakland, the newcomer to America gets embroiled in a roughly played football game. With his balletic nimbleness—bolstered by wire work—Jet's Han Sing quickly makes mincemeat of his very surprised opponents. While there are other fight sequences, the longest contest is saved for the finale as Li and Russell Wong's characters battle it out to the finish. Here, what should have been the last and best encounter seems a bit of a letdown as if each performer— both of whom were well-trained in martial arts—were holding back in the intensity of their moves out of respect for the other. Nevertheless, the sequence, set in the garden of a house, boasts a very imaginative and unusual moment in the canon of Jet Li's on-camera battles—he cries with pain. This occurs as the two men vie to finish off the other. At one point, Li's on-screen opponent takes advantage of his rival's proximity to a flaming object (set ablaze by the outdoor grill during the ongoing fight). Jet's Han screams out (very believably!) in pain as the fire sears his hands and temporarily disables him from combat. But not to fear, the macho man wraps torn strips of cloth around his injured body parts and soon is back in the heat of battle, ready to pulverize Wong's Kai.

In reviewing this modern, loose adaptation of Shakespeare's *Romeo and Juliet*, Susan Wloszczyna (*USA Today*) conceded, "It isn't necessarily a bad idea to mix Shakespeare, hip-hop and kung fu in a pop-culture cocktail. But the hangover isn't entirely worth the effort. . . . [What we get is] a plodding, play-it-safe rendition of [the TV game show] *The Family Feud*." On the other hand, the reviewer allowed, "Li never embarrasses himself, not even when reduced to tugging down his pants to look more street or using a fire hose as a weapon. In his hands, it's a cobra." Tom Maurstad (*Dallas Morning News*) was also disappointed by the final results on screen: "Nothing ever makes much sense, a lot of stuff is hinted at with no follow-through whatsoever and when the inevitable double-crosses come, they are executed with all the surprise and spontaneity of someone checking off items on a things-to-do list." For Maurstad, "The big problem with this action picture is that there's isn't nearly enough action in it. With Jet Li, the Gene Kelly of martial arts, as the star, this is an almost criminal waste. The fight scenes that are here range from just fine to borderline brilliant."

Maitland McDonagh, writing for *TV Guide*'s online *Movie Guide*, complained, "If you didn't know Li was a world-class WuShu champion, you'd never guess it— all his action scenes are edited within an inch of their lives." Roger Ebert (*Chicago Sun Times*) was also disgruntled. He wrote, "Much is made of the presence of Jet Li, the Hong Kong martial arts star. . . . but his scenes are so clearly computer-aided that his moves are about as impressive as Bugs Bunny doing the same things."

On the more positive side—at least as far as Jet's participation in this action feature film was concerned, Michael Rechshaffen (*Hollywood Reporter*) described Li as "an entertaining adrenaline blast." He pointed out, "Li, a highly magnetic screen presence, has obviously worked on his English during the past few years. He also proves quite adept at handling the light, comedic tone in between doing what he does best . . . " Michael Tunison (*Entertainment Today*) judged, "In the time allotted to him, the star makes an impression every bit as powerful as his Hong Kong contemporaries Jackie Chan and Chow Yun-Fat did in their recent

Holywood solo debuts. Equally adept at taking out enemies with a flailing fire hose, engaging in light romantic-comic banter with his leading lady or putting a hilarious kung-fu spin on tackle football, Li would seem to be the most likely candidate to pick up Bruce Lee's crown as Hollywood's all-purpose Asian action superstar. To do so, however, he'll need to find a more effective venue than *Romeo Must Die*."

Weighing in on the plus side for Jet Li's presence in *Romeo Must Die*, Bob Graham (*San Francisco Chronicle*) wrote, "Li is a phenomenon. His flying feet figure in all the action sequences, strategically spread throughout the movie—and there are several surprises as well—but my favorite stunt occurs when Li hangs by a necktie out a window several stories up. The necktie is still attached to the throat of a loudmouth Li had warned he would get."

When all was said and done, *Romeo Must Die* grossed a respectable $55.973 million in domestic distribution and took in over $100 million worldwide. While its revenue flow was not in the same league as *Lethal Weapon 4*, neither was its production costs. Besides Jet's kinetic martial arts demonstration, the picture's most noteworthy ingredients were its hip-hop score and (in retrospect) the fact that its young colead, Aaliyah, would make only one more movie (2002's *The Queen of the Damned*) before dying in an airplane crash in the Bahamas in August 2001.

As for Jet, the relatively modest *Romeo Must Die* was the successful next step in his transition into an American/international motion picture star. At the time the movie was ready to be released, he had said, "I hope the audiences like the movie. If they like it and the movie becomes successful, I'll have another opportunity to work in the future and make another good action movie." His wishes were soon to come true.

16
Life Changes and Making
Kiss of the Dragon

When Jet Li met China-born actress Nina Li Chi while they were making *Dragon Fight* in California in the late 1980s, the couple had fallen quickly in love. He was married at the time and had two little daughters. While his first marriage was already falling apart, he and Nina made a promise to each other. As he suggested, "Let's not rush into anything. What I mean is, if we still feel this way about each other ten years from now, I think we should get married then." Thereafter they had remained constant companions while each pursued a film career. She had retired from movies in 1992 and, four years later, had abandoned her financial enterprises.

Now it was September 1999, over a decade after the duo had first met. Jet had completed principal photography on *Romeo Must Die* (2000). He and Nina decided it was time to wed. On Tuesday, September 14, in Los Angeles, Jet, age thirty-six, and Nina, age thirty-eight, married in a private ceremony. The following Sunday, the newlyweds hosted a traditional Chinese wedding banquet for family and close friends at their (rented) home in the Pasadena, California, area.

With his moviemaking career again on an upswing, Jet was now receiving many film offers. One of them was from Taiwan-born director Ang Lee. The project was *Crouching Tiger, Hidden Dragon* (2000). It was a property which the moviemaker and Jet had been discussing off-and-on for years, exchanging ideas on how this elaborate production could best be shaped and executed. Now it had come time for the picture to be made. However, not only had Jet been involved with making *Romeo Must Die* at the time, but Nina was pregnant. Back in 1989 he had promised her that whenever she should become pregnant with their child, he would put his career on hold to be with her throughout the pregnancy. Thus, intent on keeping his word to her, he turned down the male lead role in *Crouching Tiger, Hidden Dragon* which went to Chow Yun-fat. (The costume action movie would become a blockbuster hit in the United States and elsewhere, and it earned four Academy Awards.) On April 19, 2000, Nina gave birth to a six-pound, thirteen-ounce baby girl whom they named Jane. To this day Jet expresses no (public) regret about losing out on participating in the celebrated *Crouching Tiger, Hidden Dragon*. He reasons, "I made thirty movies, but I can't have thirty babies. Life is not just working. You need to keep the balance."

If Jet did not wish to be away from Nina during her pregnancy, there were other career activities which he could pursue. One such item was agreeing with actor/producer Mel Gibson—with whom he became friendly when they had made *Lethal Weapon 4* (1998) together—to produce a TV venture (a syndicated television series in which they would *not* star) in the near future. Another matter was establishing and constantly refining his own elaborate Internet website. The latter allowed Li to communicate better with his fans in all parts of the world and also provided a forum in which he could express his views on many subjects including martial arts and Buddhism. Jet also found time to do limited promotional work for some of his Hong Kong–made movies, such as 1996's *Black Mask*, which were receiving U.S. distribution in dubbed, reedited versions. In February 2000, Li attended the Los Angeles Comic Book Convention to promote *Romeo Must Die*, his first lead role in a Hollywood-made feature.

Jet was also continuing his studies to improve his command of English, a necessary chore but one that he found tedious. He exclaimed, "I use sentences one hundred, two hundred, even three hundred times and still can't get them right. I'm too old for this. I never want to study again. . . . Even when I use a word in the wrong order in a sentence I get mad. It's very stressful."

By now the star was very content to remain in the United States. Jet explained, "I don't see any reason to go back [to Hong Kong]. Besides, the world feels so small now. Technology is changing that and I think being in the U.S. is my big opening. I don't want to give that up. Anyway, I can watch CNN on television or the Internet to find out what happened in Hong Kong ten minutes ago. After all it doesn't matter where something is made, we're all part of the same big family now."

Most of all he wanted to continue making Hollywood pictures: "In America, productions are bigger and better than in Hong Kong, so if I have a chance, I want to work here. Because you have more help and more money, you can tell a story a little bit better than in Asia."

Jet Li: A Biography

• • •

As *Romeo Must Die* was about to be released in late March 2000, the film's producer Joel Silver was in negotiation, with his associates, to have Jet take on a key role in the two sequels to 1999's *The Matrix*, which were going into preproduction in order to meet their planned release in 2002 and 2003. The original movie's trio of leading players (Keanu Reeves, Laurence Fishburne, and Carrie-Anne Moss) were signed for the two follow-ups as was Li's *Romeo Must Die* co-star Aaliyah (who would later have to be replaced when she died in a plane crash in 2001). Many reasons were given at the time and later for Li declining the two-film offer, but it basically came down to money. Reportedly Jet was being offered $3 million for his participation in both features, and he felt for the time that these complex projects would demand, and compared to the hefty salaries and percentage deals that Reeves, Fishburne, et al., were commanding for participating in them, it was not a worthwhile commitment for him.

Another cinematic adventure to which he did say yes was Universal Pictures' offer that he play Kato in their projected big-screen version of *The Green Hornet*. Not only was the salary appealing ($5.2 million against five percent of the film's gross), but it also would give Jet another opportunity to follow in the footsteps of the revered Bruce Lee. Jet's movie *Fist of Legend* (1994) had been a homage to Bruce's *Fist of Fury* (1972), and now Li would have the opportunity to succeed Bruce Lee in *The Green Hornet*, recreating the role of the hero's servant/helper that Bruce had played on the 1966–67 TV series. The project had been long in development, and Universal was still revamping the script about the comic book hero and his sidekick. The studio hoped for a production start date in early 2001.

By early May 2000 Jet was on a brief promotional trek for *Romeo Must Die,* which included a stopover in Japan. While there, he pursued his favorite hobby—collecting antique prayer beads.

As *Romeo Must Die* completed its first-run engagements around the world, Jet, now a new father, spent a good deal of time at home monitoring his website to gain feedback from his fans regarding his latest movie. One matter of constant discussion on the Internet was why his character in *Romeo Must Die* did not have any kissing scenes with co-star Aaliyah. As the star posted on the Internet, "[When] the entire film was put together, with all the drama and tension in that last scene with Han's father, we thought it might be somewhat strange and awkward for Han to have just witnessed Chou's [i.e., the parent's] suicide, then to come out and kiss Trish. Thus it was decided that Han should take it slowly with Trish. . . . do a hug first and maybe leading into a 'real' relationship later. So it was not really a decision by the powers that be to prevent an inter-racial relationship from happening on screen. It just did not feel right for that moment." (On another occasion, Li would tell a reporter regarding the film's lack of love scenes: "The script was not romantic to start with and the feeling was that with a Jet Li action film, you couldn't start putting in romance, that would be too slow. The producers wanted more energy.")

Regarding his enthusiasts on the Internet, the star determined, "I have two kinds of audience. One is the hardcore Jet Li fans. They watched all my older films so they say they don't like the action sequences in *Romeo Must Die* because they're too choppy, not as good as my older films. But the new audience [formed] since *Lethal Weapon 4*, they know who is Jet Li. And they like it."

However, Li was very concerned that there was a significant portion of his loyal audience around the world who were disappointed by the fight sequences in *Romeo Must Die*. These filmgoers felt that the action scenes were too Hollywoodlike (with their wire work and computer-generated effects) and not sufficiently realistic and hardcore. Lee vowed that this would not be the situation with his next movie.

In June 2000 Jet was still waiting for *The Green Hornet* script to be finalized so that he could plan accordingly. Now Universal had moved the start date of the project up to late winter 2001 as the script kept being revamped and the studio was still weighing options about the Caucasian actor who would play the title role. Meanwhile, through a mutual friend, Jet was introduced to French-born filmmaker Luc Bresson who was visiting in Los Angeles.

A director/writer/producer, Bresson was best known to American moviegoers for his pictures *La Femme Nikita* (1991) and *The Professional* (1994), each of which had combined an action drama with a gritty, downbeat ambiance and memorable *film noir*-type characters. Not too long into their conversation, Jet and Luc determined they'd like to work together on a project, one that would combine European, Asian, and American talent (and financing). In short order, a deal was struck and not long after Luc returned to Paris, a draft script (by Besson and Robert Mark Kamen) was sent to Los Angeles for Li to review. After studying the screenplay, Jet had many questions about his character and the overall plot. These concerns were presented to Bresson who made adjustments to the dialogue and plot line. In the revised version Li (who would be credited for the screen story on this production) was cast as a duty-first type of government agent from China who is sent on a delicate mission to France. Bridget Fonda (who had starred in 1993's *Point of No Return*, the Hollywood remake of Besson's *La Femme Nikita*) was contracted as Jet's colead. She was to play a hooker/single mother. (Her profession as a prostitute was deliberately chosen in order to create an emotional roadblock between her and the very chaste hero.) Turkish-born Tchéky Karyo, who had grown up in Paris, was hired to portray the film's nemesis, the corrupt police inspector. Britisher Burt Kwouk (famous as Peter Sellers's manservant Cato in the old *Pink Panther* movie series) was given a featured part as the elderly Asian who is the hero's Parisian contact.

Newcomer Chris Nahon, who had previously directed French TV commercials, was hired to direct the vehicle. As one of the film's producers (the picture was a coproduction between Besson and Li's movie companies), Jet insured that his long-time associate, Corey Yuen (Yuen Kwai), and his action choreography team were brought aboard the project. In deference to those among his fans who had not been enthralled by the high-tech martial arts interludes in *Romeo Must Die*, Li insisted that in this new picture, the fight scenes must more closely resemble those of his *Fist of Legend*. As such, wire work was not to be an ingredient of the new undertaking. According to Jet, "The action had to be very realistic. But it also had to fit the uniqueness of the Parisian setting. I put a lot of pressure on my team—Corey Yuen and my stunt guys from Hong Kong—to be creative and innovative."

Far more so than in *Romeo Must Die*, Jet wanted "the martial arts to build the character and help the story. If people don't like the story and aren't interested by the characters, it doesn't much matter that you are good or not in the sequences of fight, they make fun of it." As such, before the film actually started shooting, he was preparing both his character's motivations (which he termed "the mental and spiritual part of the script") and the figure's action moves.

What appealed to Jet most about the new project, now called *Kiss of the Dragon* (2001), was the simplicity and honesty of the narrative. "This story focuses on a normal man, trying to do his job, he doesn't know how to deal with the girl. He gives the promise to the girl. Later on the character develops, because he has to do something to keep his word. Even if that something is against his job, his country. But he still needs to keep his word." He explained further, "In my personal life I'm a very traditional Chinese person, and when you promise a girl something you need to do it. Also, in a lot of Asian audiences, and probably American too, the man wants to see the action movie, he's begging the girl to go see an action movie. This time, I really want the girl to say, come on man, let's go see the movie.

Because, remember your promise. I think the man needs to be honest, take a little responsibility. Whatever you do that's my personal thought."

Overall, Jet appreciated the fact that in this drama "everything has a reason to develop in the story, the character. . . . " The fact that his newest screen alter ego was not a super hero was just what Li wanted.

During the compacted six weeks of filming of *Kiss of the Dragon*, Jet was joined in Paris by his wife and infant daughter. Since he was one of the production forces behind the project, this movie was far more reflective of Li than had been either *Lethal Weapon 4* or *Romeo Must Die*. It also revealed that the Jet Li of the year 2000 was still a bit of a traditionalist in his viewpoint of female coplayers. This crept into his discussion of the picture's structure with the press. He told one journalist, "Usually, for an action movie, the actress plays a beautiful flower [i.e., the heroine]. There's fight-fight-fight, then bring in the flower for some rest in between. But in this film, Bridget [Fonda]'s character is the key between the good guy and bad guy. She makes the whole situation change, and, also, my character learns a lot of things from her. . . . " This description led the same journalist to comment in his published interview with Jet: "Li's 'beautiful flower' metaphor, while certainly true of a lot of Asian action cinema, seems rather retro after a good decade's worth of Hong Kong fighting girl flicks and the female-centric swordplay of the international hit *Crouching Tiger, Hidden Dragon*."

The action-heavy plot of *Kiss of the Dragon* required a large number of martial arts stunt people. Li explained, "We found around one hundred fighters from . . . Germany, London, all of Europe. We flew them in, we saw their physical ability and then we said, 'This guy knows how to do this.' And then we'd use this part for that scene. We really took their physical abilities to decide how to use them in the film." With such a diverse crew of on-camera opponents, Jet acknowledged, "It was hard fighting with all the fighters." Yet, he admitted later, "I feel very comfortable with the whole tone of the movie, the character, and the changing situations. When the situation changes, the fighting changes. The feeling is real. That's what we aimed for."

When the scripters came up with the title *Kiss of the Dragon* for the project, it was envisioned that the words referred to a martial arts move involving acupuncture that would somehow fit into the story line. Thus, according to the star, "When I was working two months later, in the middle of the shooting, I was thinking about this name. I thought maybe it was a good idea in the end to use your mouth with the needle to stop the bad guy, maybe that was a kiss of the dragon! You always want something creative, something the audience hasn't seen before." Within the narrative, Li's character has acupuncture needles attached by Velcro to his wrists—a foresight which comes in handy in his final showdown with the chief villain.

The picture's acupuncture gimmick sparked Lee's creative energies: "I always focus on the reason to fight. If you don't want to fight, how do you stop them? They have guns, so I created acupuncture to stop people. That's it. I don't want to hurt you. I don't want you to hurt me. You also want to use it for healing people. To help people, also I think it's a nice thing. In real life, acupuncture can help physical ailments. I used it a lot of times, the doctor used it on me. But not a kiss of the dragon . . . it really doesn't go to that powerful a level. That's movie magic."

The filming of *Kiss of the Dragon* began in Paris in September 2000 and was completed by early November 2000. Unlike his recent Hollywood-produced features which utilized enormous crews, this French-shot action feature had a condensed number of behind-the-camera workers. This fit in with Bresson's filmmaking style and the movie's budget of about $25 million. Actual Parisian locales, including the Bridge Alexandre III and a deserted subway station, were employed to flavor the narrative.

So that he would have ample opportunity to display his martial arts talents, Jet's character relies very little on firearms in the brutal action sequences. Rather he uses anything that is handy, whether it be chopsticks, laundry irons, or a flagpole—not to mention the finale's acupuncture needles—to outmaneuver the onslaught of adversaries. One of the few computer-enhanced action moments within the picture occurs after the extended opening rumble at the Parisian hotel. In this respite from tough battling, the fleeing hero takes refuge in a pool hall. While playing a game and to divert his assailants, he takes a pool ball and, with a deadly flick (thanks to computerized special effects), shoots the ball at his human target. While halfway through the six days allocated to shooting the complexly structured finale, Jet and his associates rethought the choreography of the interaction and reshot it.

Regarding working with Jet Li on *Kiss of the Dragon*, co-star Bridget Fonda would say, "He's pretty fascinating to watch. He's also incredibly charming and has a mischievous sense of humor."

Within the butt-kicking, bone-crunching *Kiss of the Dragon*, Liu Jian (played by Jet Li), a government agent, is sent by China from Shanghai to Paris on a top-secret mission. The taciturn single man (who favors double-breasted black jackets

Co-stars Jet Li and Bridget Fonda smile for the media at the debut of *Kiss of the Dragon* (2001) in Los Angeles.

like the outfit worn by Kato in *The Green Hornet*) is in Paris on a delicate matter. He is to assist gruff Inspector Jean-Pierre Richard (played by Tchéky Karyo, a very unorthodox French police official, in dealing with a Chinese heroin smuggler. Unknown to Liu at first, Richard is an extremely corrupt official who maintains a private army of thugs within the police department and enjoys a steady income from his prostitution ring, drug trafficking, and other nefarious activities. The cunning Richard decides to make Liu (whom he dismissively calls "Johnny boy") the fall guy in the murder of this wanted drug dealer (actually a rival to Richard in the drug trade) at a Paris hotel. Before long, the French lawman has convinced the entire Paris police bureau that Liu is a psychotic killer.

The only one who can prove Jian's innocence is the American Jessica (played by Bridget Fonda), one of Richard's hookers. She had witnessed the murder and had also fled the scene of the crime. Circumstances soon bring Liu and Jessica together. In order to get her to help him clear himself in the case, he agrees to rescue her young daughter who is being held hostage by the ruthless police inspector. It is a difficult promise to execute, but he does so.

As constructed, filmed, and edited, the plot is not always logical or coherent. However, it allows Jet Li as the implacable hero an ample showcase for his skills. Besides the skirmishes aboard a tourist boat and a free-for-all inside a shop, two great action sequences bookend this movie. The opening salvo occurs at the French hotel where Jet's hero battles his way out of the hotel using every available object at hand to defend himself against and/or to attack the inspector's goon squad. Near the finale, Li's Chinese law enforcer arrives at the police precinct to confront Richard. However, first, he must pass through the obstacle of a martial arts class made up of the inspector's underlings. Thereafter, in the gory finale, Liu uses the deadly "kiss of the dragon" acupuncture move on Richard.

Kiss of the Dragon, which had its U.S. premiere on June 25, 2001, debuted in North America as a Twentieth Century-Fox release on July 6, 2001. This time, Roger Ebert (*Chicago Sun Times*) was much more in tune with Jet's on-screen performance. After noting, "In a movie where the physical actions border on the impossible, why expect the story to be reasonable?" Ebert judged, "Li is the right star for the material, not too cocksure, not too flashy. His character isn't given a lot of motivation, but one key element is that he's never been in Paris before. . . . He's a stranger in a strange land. . . . "

Weekly Variety's Joe Leydon assessed, "Boldly kicking ass like no ass has been kicked before, *Kiss of the Dragon* is a slick, straight-ahead action-thriller that marks a small step back and two bounding leaps forward for toplined Jet Li. Pic overall seems rather conventional, even retrograde, when compared with the genre-scrambling, crossover-appealing *Romeo Must Die*. . . . But *Dragon* is more consistently exciting as a rock-the-house, shoot-the-works adventure opus, loaded with fight scenes that rank with the classic rough stuff of *Enter the Dragon*, *The Legend of Drunken Master* and Li's own *Fist of Legend*. Just as important, the French-U.S. coproduction underscores Li's increasing ease and confidence working in English . . . "

In evaluating Jet's screen appeal, Joe Morgenstern (*Wall Street Journal*) decided, "More amazingly still, he keeps us focused on dialogue scenes that would not otherwise pass muster on TV. How? By banishing all expression from his face so we can project on it what we want. Mr. Li is a master not only of martial arts, but of composure; no one does nothing better."

Elvis Mitchell (*New York Times*), no great champion of the overall movie, found positive qualities in the action footage which were "a relief from the onslaught of clichés." He explained, "In each fight scene, the other players circle him, their heads lowered as if they're about to choose him as a tango partner. Mr. Besson makes existentialism into a set of flash cards: the men in *Kiss of the Dragon* all have sallow complexions, pockmarked waxen faces that look like the skin of an orange and are rendered in wide screen." As to how the star meets the challenge of so many on-screen opponents: "It's his burden that he has to fight to live, but he lives to fight. His worried intensity means he doesn't have a lot of range as an actor, but his physical confidence carries a lot of weight." The *Times* reviewer concluded, "Mr. Li will come out of *Kiss of the Dragon* smelling like a rose; the combat couldn't be better. But next time around he should leave the script to more capable hands."

When the movie played in England, John Patterson of the (Manchester) *Guardian* reacted with: "*Kiss of the Dragon* isn't by any stretch of the imagination a great movie—nor perhaps even a particularly good one—but somehow its inter-

Jet Li with his wife Nina (left) and Hong Kong actress/singer Karen Wok Man-wai (right) at the Hong Kong premiere of *Kiss of the Dragon* in July 2001.

nal mechanics are so pleasing to something lurking at the base of the brain that it is one of the best pure moviegoing experiences of the hitherto scarcely endurable summer of 2001."

As for Andy Klein (*New Times Los Angeles*), he rated that "*Kiss of the Dragon* will probably please hard-core action fans who have become inured to plot idiocies, but it remains a terrible waste of talent." Regarding the film's raison d'être—the martial arts displays—Klein decided, "There is enough cleverness on display to keep these scenes enjoyable, but there is also the frustration of how much better they could have been."

After commenting on the deliberately sparse amount of dialogue given to Jet's character in *Kiss of the Dragon*, *Screen International*'s Emanuel Levy suggested, "What should be developed by producers of Li's future action films are the seeds of an appealing screen image based on a set of contradictory traits: he can appear shy and strong, low-key yet dangerous, all at the same time."

Before his newest picture (R-rated for its violence) debuted, Jet, himself a new father and, thus, very concerned about the type of movies youngsters attended, placed a warning about the film on his Internet website: "*Kiss of the Dragon* is an adult movie and deals with adult themes of a man keeping his promise and understanding his responsibilities. The action scene are also directed toward an adult audience and as such the movie is rate R. I ask that you please do not take your young children to see *Kiss of the Dragon*." It was an unusual gesture for a star to make such a potentially box-office-damaging statement. In any event, the tightly budgeted feature grossed a respectable $36.833 million in the domestic marketplace, with other revenue materializing from its release in the rest of the world. At the annual Ammy Awards (sponsored by *aMagazine*) which saluted Asian (-American) talent, both Jet Li and *Kiss of the Dragon* were nominated for awards. However, it was Chow Yun-fat and the movie (*Crouching Tiger, Hidden Dragon*) in which he replaced Jet that won, respectively, in the Best Actor and Best Hollywood Picture categories.

Largely happy with his creative participation in *Kiss of the Dragon*, Li had little opportunity to ponder the box-office pros and cons of this release. Already, he'd completed his next picture. The star, full of marketing savvy, when cautioning parents on his website about not taking their young children to see *Kiss of the Dragon*, had announced proudly, "If you would like a movie to share with your children please wait a few more months. On November 2 my film *The One* will be released. This is a PG-13 film and more appropriate for younger children to view."

17

Being *The One*

In the history of Hollywood filmmaking, it was not a novel concept to have an action actor play multiple roles in the same screen production. Jean-Claude Van Damme, for example, had accomplished that in *Double Impact* (1991) and *Replicant* (2001). Nor was it unique for a martial arts star to headline a science fiction entry. Again, Van Damme had done that in *Cyborg* (1989), *Universal Soldier* (1992), and other vehicles; Arnold Schwarzenegger had appeared—among other such offerings—in *The Terminator* (1984) and *Total Recall* (1990); Sylvester Stallone in *Demolition Man* (1993); etc. But Tinseltown was proficient at recycling old screen ideas. In this mode, Revolution Studios optioned a sci-fi property about parallel universes in which an individual's duplicate exists in many other separate worlds. The script was entitled *The One* (2001).

To play the lead in *The One*, Revolution wanted Dwayne "The Rock" Johnson, the colorful and popular, six-feet, five-inch wrestler who weighed 275 pounds. While the decision-makers were finalizing this casting, Johnson scored well playing the Scorpion King in Universal Pictures' big-budgeted *The Mummy Returns* (2001). Excited by that movie's over $202 million gross domestically, Universal wanted to spin off Johnson's character into his own elaborate feature, *The Scorpion King* (2002). The Rock agreed to accept this starring vehicle and to pass on headlining *The One*.

Now needing a new leading man for *The One*, its distributor (Columbia/Sony), which a few years earlier had hoped to contract Jet Li, agreed to the possibility of his taking over this part. At the time Li was still optioned for Universal's forthcoming *The Green Hornet*, but a satisfactory script still had not been achieved.

Thus, one day after his commitment to *The Great Hornet* expired in October 2000, Jet was contracted for *The One* at a reported $7.5 million fee.

On this project (conservatively budgeted at under $70 million), Jet was not one of the producers, but he was allowed to provide input. Director/coscreenwriter James Wong (a Chinese-American TV series writer and the director of the popular thriller, *Final Destination*, 2000) and his frequent collaborator Glen Morgan restructured the script of *The One* to suit Jet. Among the changes, they accepted Li's suggestion to add the flavoring of Eastern philosophies in refining the plot. In tailoring the role to fit Jet's usual screen persona, the two main characters he would portray became serious, intense men of few words. (Li's command of English had improved but he was still not highly fluent in the language.) Also, the hero (as well as his alternative universe other selves) were redesigned to be martial arts whizzes.

As *The One* was reshaped, Jet met repeatedly with coscripter Glen Morgan (whom he already knew) and scripter/director James Wong to further blend martial arts into the story line and to reshape the characters accordingly. Li reasoned, "Like I've said before, with an action movie, the most important thing is how you describe the character. And [to] use martial arts to make this more clear. What are they thinking, what are they fighting? So I play two characters in this film, one is good, one is bad." It was soon decided by Jet and the film's other creative forces—which now included veteran action choreographer/director Corey Yuen (Yuen Kwai)—that, "The bad guy, he uses xingyi [version of martial arts]. Not exactly 100 percent xingyi. But straightforward. Because he wants to destroy everything. He wants to kill all of himself in different universes. So he tries to reach that goal. He wants to become the One. If you know xingyi it uses a very straight line. . . . But the other character is the good guy, Gabe, he doesn't know what's going on. But suddenly the power is going through his body. His philosophy is more circular. He has a wonderful family, a beautiful wife, sweet dog, so he just wants to make a circle. Everything is balance. That's what I always talk about in my philosophy that life needs to be balanced. . . . So, it's why he tries to protect his family. He believes in the circle. Bagua [another form of martial arts] is the circle."

Having refashioned the plot with this infusion of Eastern thought and the integration of martial arts to further explicate the characters, Jet was excited about the evolving project in which one of his selves would battle another on camera. "It's unique, we've never seen it in an American film. Maybe a little bit in the HK [Hong Kong] films. Because, that kind of fight I think is three times harder than normal martial arts movement." He was excited by the physical challenges of the production: "This kind of martial art, xingyi and bagua, you really need to learn, a few years, maybe ten years, then you can control your body. Not just making your arm move straight forward, you really need your whole body, from inside to outside. Everything is working together." Jet emphasized, "I really want to talk to the audience through each of my films. Life is about balance. It is the Earth view. It's about trying to understand people, to walk in another man's shoes. It's also about focusing on today and not worrying about the future."

While the screenplay was being finalized, Jet continued to work closely with Glen Morgan. The latter recalled of this team process: "He'd go, 'That word I will say. That word I won't.' But he's also got a great sense of humor. Once, I joked, 'You know, I really wanted [martial arts film star] Steven Seagal for this movie.' He looked at me like he was going to beat me up—and then just laughed." As the shooting script was refined, director James Wong enthused, "I think the audience, when they watch this movie, will really get it: get the concept of these different worlds by (seeing) similar things happen, but they don't happen the same way, and things veer off from there."

By now, others cast for *The One* included Delroy Lindo (who had worked with Jet in *Romeo Must Die*) and Britisher Jason Statham (2000's *Snatch*, 2001's *Ghosts of Mars*). They were to play the Multiverse government agents dispatched to track down the arch villain. (Lindo would also appear briefly in the narrative as his other self, a humble gas station attendant in a different parallel universe.) Carla Gugino (who had rated well in the sleeper hit *Spy Kids*, 2001) was hired for the dual role of the hero's wife and the villain's flinty girlfriend.

The One was made in and around Los Angeles, including lensing at the Sybil Brand Institute in Monterey Park, location work in Glendale, Torrance, Valley Village (in the San Fernando Valley), and in sections of downtown Los Angeles. The Universe of Hades attraction at Universal Studios was rented and adapted to provide the Stygian Penal Colony locale in the movie (with heavy-duty lavender lighting gels employed to provide an intense, futuristic feel). Much of the principal photography was accomplished on sound stages in Playa Vista, not too far from LAX airport. As such, during the filming of *The One*, Jet had the luxury of commuting home nightly to be with his family.

One of the bigger on-location sites for this futuristic narrative was in Redondo Beach, twenty-two miles southwest of Los Angeles. There the production rented the use of a large Southern California Edison generating station. It was a perfect site to stage the climactic clash between the hero and villain because the facility had few shooting restrictions compared to other alternate private locales. Soon, under the guidance of production designer David Snyder, the building expanse was repainted and turned into a factory site with working pumps, compressors, orange scaffolding, etc. A two-story catwalk was constructed for the two opponents to clamber on during their big fight. Much of this lengthy finale sequence was shot at nighttime using huge lighting arcs which were beamed through the plant's twenty-foot high windows and aimed at the deliberately sterile, utilitarian expanse. Director James Wong explained, "We wanted to be able to control the amount of light even though these scenes take place in the day. We decided that a night shoot with artificial light would be easier, other than the hours."

In this intricately conceived and executed final battle, Jet would be fighting himself. To make use of high-tech computer special effects, stuntmen were employed in long shots to stand in for one or the other of Li's on-screen persona. Each such stunt person, besides wearing a duplicate of the costume that Jet's character used, also wore a green life mask of Jet Li. This mask was applied to the stunt man's face and tracking points were marked on it for the camera to pick up during the shoot. Then, in postproduction, the FX team prepared a digital version of Li's face in assorted expressions. By using the tracking points on the stuntman's green mask, the special effects squad could then paste the digital face onto the screen image of the stunt double. In this way, Jet could engage in an on-screen battle with his Multiverse duplicate

Describing the four weeks it required to complete this on-camera struggle, Li said, "We have one part [of the narrative done in] traditional action movie style, when the good character becomes angry, loses control, and wants to kill the bad guy. He loses his form. So, then he must calm down, relax, because he knows he can't win if he's so angry . . . So then the internal martial art comes out." He acknowledged, "I've made a lot of films, but this is the hardest. Usually I play the good guy, and I fight, with the bad guy. Now, I need to fight with the stuntman, and when I finish my part I have to turn back to be the bad guy, and fight the stuntman again. Sometimes you hit the bad guy, and the stuntman turns around and hits you. So, it's quite hard . . . to do everything."

There were other technical matters to consider in staging the big encounter, in which the sinister lead character, endowed with super powers, is sixty pounds heavier and moves much faster than normal people. According to action choreographer Corey Yuen: "He [i.e., the "bad Jet"] can hit people into the air and because he moves so fast, it looks like they're dropping to the ground in slow motion. This is difficult to film as a practical effect because you can't use real

Jet Li the celebrity interacting with the public.

stuntmen going fast and slow in the same shot. So we film Jet doing it with the hanging objects and then later he will do the stuff with real stuntmen so we know the real movements. . . . He's so fast that even after he has finished fighting these guys, they're still floating in the air and falling to the ground. It's quite a challenge."

In this and other action/fight segments within the picture, there was a return to the use of wire work for the martial arts scenes. This was done because the creative forces controlling *The One* felt that audience expectations after 1999's *The Matrix* and 2000's *Crouching Tiger, Hidden Dragon* demanded such gravity-defying techniques. Moreover, because *The One* was a sci-fi tale, the high-flying/bounding activity would lend an eerie, futuristic tone to the proceedings. Regarding the required wire work, stunt coordinator/second unit director Gary Hymes noted, "Whenever we fly people through the air, we use a lot of pneumatic devices and hydraulics. Rehearsals are essential not only for the best possible performance, but also to fine-tune the stunts. This was probably the most rigging-intensive film I've done since *Hook* [the 1991 version of *Peter Pan* starring Robin Williams and Julia Roberts], in which we had quite a few people flying on wires and rigs."

All in all, Jet dealt well with the especially heavily physical demands of making this picture, particularly in the intricate procedures required to capture the final clash to the death. As for working with Li, fellow cast member Jason Statham allowed, "He's the best fun, really. He's always messing around and cracking jokes and he's got a great sense of humor, which a lot of people fail to keep these days. Especially big stars. You meet them and some of them are very serious . . . But he's great."

When his work on *The One* was over, a reporter asked Jet how it felt to play *both* the good and bad guy in the same picture and which role had been more artistically satisfying for him. "Both have their character," he said. "You need to love both. If you don't love both characters it doesn't work. Everything comes from your heart. If you don't like the character, you can't play the character. You must enjoy what the character is thinking. I just, in a few months, try to become that person. Even the bad guy. He thought everything was clear, where he wants to go, what he wants to do. Very clear.

"Then you need to forget the bad guy. The good guy's philosophy, you need to believe that, you need to love the character, then you can become the character. If it's not from here [i.e., the heart] it doesn't stick."

According to the futuristic premise of *The One*, there are at least 125 universes within the Multiverse. Thus, everyone on Earth has duplicates living on these parallel universes. When a person dies in one universe, his powers/energy is divvied up among his opposite numbers within the other universes. (In this manner, the balance is kept through the Multiverse.) However, an escaped criminal, Yulaw (played by Jet Li), has discovered an exception to this rule of nature. He realizes that if he destroys all 124 other versions of himself, he will become an invincible person, so powerful in strength that no one will be a match for him. Before long the megalomaniac Yulaw has eliminated 122 of his counterparts, and soon he claims Lawless (also played by Jet Li) as his latest victim. By now he is being hotly pursued by Multiverse agents (played by Delroy Lindo and Jason Statham) who must stop this super killer from becoming the Only One. To set the cosmos right, they must both bring Yulaw back dead or alive and also not let Gabe (also played by Jet Li) merge into a super survivor.

The maverick Yulaw arrives on Earth searching for his last alter ego, Gabe. The latter is a Los Angeles lawman who has a sweet-natured wife (played by Carla Gugino). Gabe has been puzzled why he is experiencing a remarkable increase in his physical abilities and feeling such strange psychic emanations. Before long, as Yulaw closes in on Gabe, the perplexed cop finds himself not only being chased by his deadly doppelganger, but also by Los Angeles police officers. The latter think that Gabe has committed the local killing actually done by the rampaging Yulaw. Of course, all this leads to the final showdown between Gabe and Yulaw.

Because of the September 11, 2001, tragedy at New York City's World Trade Center and fears of other forthcoming terrorist activity, most Hollywood movie studios temporarily suspended having star-studded premieres to promote their new product. However, the publicity mechanism for *The One* charged full steam ahead along other lines. For example, to promote the November 2, 2001, debut of *The One*, Jet appeared on, among others, *The Tonight Show With Jay Leno*. In his chat with the host, Li came across as being far more relaxed and playful than on his past guest stints on this network TV talk show. (Jet had returned only recently to Los Angeles from China, where he'd been working for several weeks on his next film, 2002's *Hero*. His wife and daughter, who had accompanied him abroad, were still in the Far East as Li was concerned about their flying back to the United States during such uncertain and dangerous times.)

Besides publicizing *The One* on its official website, the studio created a free game for hand-held PDAs, basing the computer-generated diversion on concepts within the picture. The game could be downloaded from several appointed Internet sites. There were also special screenings of the trailer and/or the feature at the San Diego and Los Angeles Comic Book Conventions, with Jet featured in a special taped introduction for his fans. Later, when Li returned to China to complete his new picture, he stopped over at key cities en route to promote this science fiction entry.

The reviews for *The One*—released with a relatively short running time of eighty-seven minutes—proved to be a mixed bag. Jeffrey M. Anderson (*San Francisco Examiner*) announced, "I'm happy to report that Jet Li's fourth American film crosses the finish line as far and away the best of them. It's still no masterpiece, and still a good distance from *Swordsman II* [1992] and *Once Upon a Time in China* [1991], but at least we're making progress." Jan Stuart (*Los Angeles Times*) reported, "It's hard to work up extreme passions for or against the martial arts star. He's cool, cocky and effortlessly nice-looking in the way that male teenage moviegoers aspire to be, and he can crush a cop between two motorcycles the way one might snuff a candle with one's fingers. But he's far too unthreatening a presence to cause much of a stir amid the din of hard rock music and the pall left by fight choreography that has had every last bit of life digitally drained away." As to the movie's much-touted tussle between the two Jets, Stuart commented, "Whatever agility and grace there are to be gleaned from Jet Li's climactic pas de deux with himself are all but eviscerated by computerized hoo-ha that mechanizes a martial arts ballet into a herky-jerky bunny hop."

Kirk Honeycutt (*Hollywood Reporter*) found Li's new movie to be a "disappointing step backward for the martial arts star into lackluster genre gimmickry." Regarding the two Jets in the picture, he judged, "the film's raison d'être is its division of Li into both predator and prey. It's a gimmick too clever for its own good: At times highly confusing, these identical twins dissipate audience involvement. Which Li do you root for?"

Jack Garner (Gannett News Service) summed up PG-13-rated *The One* as "a confusing, action-packed sci-fi romp that puts *The Matrix* through a blender and tosses in a bit of *Star Trek*." For Joe Williams (*St. Louis Post-Dispatch*) *The One* was "preposterous" and "so reliant on camera tricks that it has almost no value as a martial-arts flick." He editorialized, "Li is one martial artist who doesn't need gimmicks to prove his athleticism, and between the high-wire kicks and the choppy ending, the net effect is so unconvincing that it's inadvertently cartoonish."

Stephen Holden (*New York Times*) acknowledged that, "The taut choreography of sound (in which techno music segues to rap to heavy metal) and image (the movie's comic-book gadgetry is as fetishistic as in any James Bond film) lends an illusion of order and discipline to a movie whose story is largely impenetrable." He also observed, "Beyond the sci-fi concept, what's of interest are the fighting sequences, which occasionally attain an elegant severity, and the special effects. The most spectacular effects show the characters whooshing from one alternate universe to the next through 'black holes' that appear at regular intervals. The figures digitally decompose while being sucked into the sky. When they reconfigure, they look as though they have had an especially rough patch of turbulence while inside a 'Star Trek' transporter."

Regarding the picture's final battle, *The New York Times* critic decided, "Elaborately punctuated with electronic beats and by explosions that produce alternating showers of sparks and rain, the sequence has the look and sound of a pop 'ballet mechanique.' At moments it even suggests an aerialist 'Singin' in the Rain' for the kickboxing set."

Holden was less charitable about the cast: "Even by the grunting and grimacing standards of comic-book action films, the performances in *The One* are undernourished, with Mr. Li's Yulaw and Gabe one-note opposites. (One looks blankly cheery, the other demonically charged up.) Vocally, Mr. Li tends to speak his lines in a flat, uninflected monotone."

Hazel-Dawn Dumpert (*LA Weekly*) aptly summed up the film's chief failing: "What would be better than one delicious Jet Li [on camera]? . . . That would be two delicious Jet Lis. . . . Yet, director Wong . . . never lets the movie catch its breath, and, rather than enhancing Li's silken physicality, the all-consuming effects rob it of its organic flow. There's nothing like a feature-length video game to make you feel you're being played."

The One, considered one of those action movies that was supposed to be critic-proof, grossed a respectable but still tame $43.905 million in domestic distribution, with foreign revenue still to be charted as it was released around the globe, ending with a spring 2002 debut in the United Kingdom.

18

Hero and Beyond

On November 18, 2001, a few weeks after *The One* went into release, Jet Li was represented on screen—this time on television—with a new entertainment venture. Through his Qian Yang International production firm, he was one of the several producers, along with actor/filmmaker Mel Gibson (his co-star on 1998's *Lethal Weapon 4*) of a new cable TV movie. Entitled *Invincible*, this science-fiction project was geared both as a two-hour made-for-cable entry and as the pilot for a projected syndicated series. Originally, when the deal was put together with the TBS Superstation and Alliance Atlantis Communications, Inc., it was envisioned that the finished project would be ready to air in late 2000 or early 2001.

Jet described the history of *Invincible*: "After [*Lethal Weapon*] 4 Mel [Gibson] came to me, he's such a great guy. He's honest, funny, has a lot of energy. He says, Jet, if you want to do something, I support you. I say I want to do television because with TV, every week, you have more time to talk about some philosophy, not just physical moves. So, we developed the whole TV series. We did a two-hour pilot." Li envisioned that "*Invincible* will feature awesome action sequences that go beyond the light-headed, bang-bang action often found on television. There will be a healthy underlying moral theme, emphasizing control, discipline and the balance of good and evil."

Made for $8 million on sound stages in Australia, *Invincible* featured Billy Zane (of *Titanic* fame) as the mystical leader Os, a 2,000-year-old dark angel who has a sudden revelation. It leads him to abandon his evil ways and become a good soul. His current mission is to battle those sinister forces which are threatening the

Jet Li offers fans a traditional Chinese greeting.

extinction of mankind. To help with his task, Os recruits four modern-day war-riors (Byron Mann, Stacy Oversier, Tory Kittes, and Dominic Purcell), each of whose predestined martial arts fighting style reflects the essential elements of the universe: air, fire, water, and metal. Their goal is to vanquish the Shadowmen who aim to destroy all the good in the world.

Following suggestions of Jet Li about the way Hong Kong martial arts action movies were filmed (i.e., the efficiency of utilizing two directors, one of whom choreographs/directs the fight sequences), *Invincible* was churned out on an economical twenty-three-day schedule. In the production's martial art scenes there was frequent use of wire work. Thereafter, Calibre, a Canadian-based special effects studio, created the 150 special effects shots required for the narrative.

Heavily promoted by TBS, *Invincible* received less than enthusiastic reviews from the critics. For example, David Kronke (*Los Angeles Daily News*) reported, "Like the old *Kung Fu* TV series and the *Billy Jack* movies, *Invincible* rather dubiously preaches love through butt-kicking." He detailed, "What follows is lots of cribbing from action sequences from *The Matrix* and *Crouching Tiger, Hidden Dragon*, pseudo-spiritual mumbo jumbo and production design apparently inspired by too many peyote buttons." Kevin McDonough (*Newsday*) decided that the cable feature was "short on action and long on platitudes." He rated it "mind-numbing banality" while acknowledging "Not that some of this doesn't look good." According to Steven Oxman (*Daily Variety*), "The martial arts actioner *Invincible* starts strongly, promises much and delivers little. It's a movie that markets itself as a kung-fu pic, but is so determined to be spiritually meaningful, and is so puerile in its sensibility, that lead Billy Zane is more self-help guru Tony Robbins than Bruce Lee. If the ensemble would just shut up and fight, pic would be bearable, but even when they do battle at the end it's pretty underwhelming."

Despite the generally unfavorable response of media reviewers to *Invincible*, the program did very well in attracting home viewers to watch it. As such, the next steps were taken to turn the property into a weekly cable TV series.

While Jet's two 2001 features (*Kiss of the Dragon* and *The One*) moved into theatrical release, the star was busy fielding industry offers for new starring vehicles. In early 2001, there were rumors that he'd star in a new Oliver Stone–produced project in which Li would portray an eleventh-century Chinese general. He was to have substituted for Asian singer/dancer/actor Aaron Kowk in this venture which Anthony Minghella (*The Talented Mr. Ripley*) might direct. The project, however, soon cooled.

In June 2001, Jet attended the Cannes Film Festival to promote his new releases and to network with filmmaking powers. At the Festival's Hong Kong night, he and Jackie Chan posed together for the press and paparazzi. The two reminisced about old times when they both had worked for Hong Kong's Golden Harvest film company and had frequently taken meals together. In the same month there was industry buzz that Li would star for Columbia/TriStar in the studio's latest Asian-theme picture, *Angel's Dust,* to be coproduced with the star's own production company. Using a premise similar to *Charlie's Angels* (2000), it was to feature Cecilia Cheung Pak-chi, Cathy Tsui Chi-kei, and Vicky Zhao Wei as a trio of crime fighters and be helmed by Jet's long-time collaborator, action director Corey Yuen (Yuen Kwai). It was to shoot in Thailand or Hong Kong. Weeks later, it was announced that Li was no longer involved in the project. Another touted possible venture was the suggested screen union of Jet Li and Chow Yun-fat in a picture devised by producer John Strong. Set in the eighteenth century, *White Dragon,* budgeted at $45 million, would deal with rival warriors from China, Japan, and Korea. That potentiality soon faded from trade paper news.

One proposed picture that actually led to a contractual commitment was for Li to star in the future in a new Miramax Pictures offering. It was to be an action comedy in which he would play a Tibetan monk who wins a trip to Manhattan and brings harmony to a tough neighborhood. Meanwhile, in July 2001 the veteran actor embarked on a promotional jaunt to, among other destinations, France and Japan to promote *Kiss of the Dragon.* By midmonth, he was in Tibet with Robert Mark Kamen (the coscripter of *Kiss of the Dragon*) researching the upcoming Miramax venture now called *A Tibetan Monk in New York.* (Meanwhile, one of Jet's "rivals," Chow Yun-fat, was preparing to shoot his own religious-man tale, *Bulletproof Monk,* at MGM in early 2002. That property was based on a cult comic book of the same title.) While in Tibet, Li was also joined by Lho Kunsang, his spiritual guide.

Having moved into the ranks of a Hollywood star, it certainly must have been a strange situation for Jet to make promotional treks to Hong Kong where he had been one of the territory's box-office kings in the 1990s. Now such stars as Donnie Yen Ji-dan and Vincent Zhao Wen-zhuo (Chiu Man-cheuk) had replaced Li as top cinema favorites in the arena of martial arts action flicks. (There were some in Hong Kong who felt that Jet had sold out by relocating to Hollywood and abandoning his Asian fan base.) Then, of course, there was superstar Jackie Chan, who bounced back and forth between making popular Hong Kong and well-liked American features. He was still very popular with filmgoers in Asia and was enjoying a new triumph with *Rush Hour 2,* which grossed $225.307 million just in North American distribution. Then too, a great legend from Hong Kong's past was about to be revived on screen. In 2002, Bruce Lee's image was to be digitally resurrected in a $50 million martial arts feature entitled *Dragon Warrior.* It was being produced by a Korean film production company which had gained the necessary clearance from Lee's estate.

Whatever his popularity ranking with Hong Kong moviegoers, Jet's high-profile celebrity image was on the rise in many other sectors, especially in Hollywood. As such, he was coping with the same types of problems that superstars before him had endured. Regarding life in Tinseltown, he elaborated, "A lot of people around me, they're very polite. They say, 'You're great. You're fantastic. You're wonderful.' . . . Everybody tell you: 'Jet, you're fantastic, you're WON-derful, you're a-MAZ-ing!' . . . In the beginning, of course, you're happy because you don't know the culture. But later on you figure: 'Come on. Wait a minute. Who tells me the truth? I can't be perfect. Nobody can be perfect.'" On the other hand, he found his fans to be more honest (especially in their feedback on his Internet website). "The audience, they don't care. They say, 'I don't like this. I like this. Do something. Show me something!' I think it was very nice thing to hear their opinion."

Learning to cope with the ways and demands of Hollywood moviemaking had not been easy for Jet. Frequently he relied on his renewed interest in Buddhism to place him in a calming mode when maneuvering through the film industry's power games. Rick Lyman (*New York Times*) described the new, calm Jet Li during the course of a mid-2001 interview at the plush Ritz-Carlton Hotel in Pasadena, California, not far from where Jet, his wife, and their baby girl resided. Seated at a corner table in the hotel restaurant, Li had only a glass of tap water in front of him. Lyman detailed that the celebrity "slowly fingered the Buddhist prayer beads coiled around his wrist. Several times, waiters came by offering something to eat, something to drink, something, anything. But Mr. Li just shook his head. Plain water would do."

By fall 2001, after four feature films and over three years since he'd left Hong Kong for the United States, Jet was back in China to work. After its script had been revised according to his suggestions, he was joining Maggie Cheung Man-yuk and Tony Leung Chiu-wai to make the historical epic *Hero* (2002). It was to be directed by Zhang Yimou, a two-time Golden Bear Award winner (at the Berlin Film Festival). Li agreed to a pay cut to play the psychological and tragic role of a professional bodyguard to the ruler who became China's First Emperor in the third century B.C. The protector's task within *Hero* is to stop assassins from killing the exalted one, a man who has fought to unite China into a major empire. (This saga overlaps historical facts presented in director Chen Kaige's 1999 feature

The Emperor and the Assassin [Ging Nyn Chi Chun Wong].) *Hero* was being produced by Bill Kong who had done similar chores on 2000's *Crouching Tiger, Hidden Dragon*.

Production began in mid-August 2001 in Dunhuang in the province of Gansu located in northwest central China between Mongolia and Tibet. Filming also took place in a small village in the province of Sichuan in west central China. There, at a specially constructed lakeside pavilion, a key sequence was lensed in which Wu Ming (played by Jet Li) battles Broken Sword (played by Tony Leung Chiu-wai) around, in, and above the picturesque lake. Meanwhile the seriously wounded Flying Snow (played by Maggie Cheung Man-yuk) lies in a perilous condition nearby. This elaborately staged sequence required three days to capture, using extensive wire work to bring the scene dramatically to life. Later, the cast and crew relocated to the Hengdian Studio in the mountainous Zhejiang province in east China. Because of the director's meticulous demands for having the right (real and/or electrical) lighting to showcase properly the colorfully costumed cast, cinematographer Christopher Doyle (who had shot the new *Psycho, Liberty Heights*, etc.) had to prepare much more laboriously for each shot setup. During the shoot, action director Ching Siu-tung (who had done similar chores for such Jet Li vehicles as 1992's *Swordsman II* and 1996's *Dr. Wai in the Scripture With No Words*) was brought in to replace another action choreographer who had not meshed with those in charge of the project.

Talking about his return to China for this much-anticipated screen project Jet said cautiously, "A man should not expect too much. Expecting too much will bring you pain. Higher the expectation more the disappointments. Cherishing every single opportunity and doing my best are my rules of selecting projects." He also noted of *Hero*: "This script is very special, which explores the definition of 'hero.'" The big-screen costume action drama was projected for release at the end of 2002 in both Asia and the West.

As 2001 ended Jet was completing *Hero* in China. By now, after a decade of pre-production, Universal had dropped interest in filming *The Green Hornet* feature itself. Instead, the project had moved over to Miramax Pictures (with Universal having the option to coproduce the venture if it so chose). Because of the transition, Jet was no longer attached to the vehicle. If *The Green Hornet* now seemed unlikely to be in Jet's future, he had other pictures to replace that. For example, after he finished *Hero*, he would begin work in winter 2002 on *Cradle 2 the Grave* for Warner Bros. For this relatively modest-budgeted action entry he reunited with director Andrzej Bartkowiak, actor/rapper DMX, and producer Joel Silver—all from Jet's *Romeo Must Die* (2000). Based on a script by John O'Brien and Channing Gibson, *Cradle* dealt with a government agent (played by Jet Li) forced to work with a crime lord (played by DMX) due to unique circumstances. (The picture was planned for a late 2002 release.) Thereafter, Li would take the next steps on *A Tibetan Monk in New York*. In addition, there was *First King*, another production to be made in conjunction with producer Joel Silver. *First King* was based on an idea provided by Li and would combine elements of action, suspense, and the thriller genre. Also, besides working to bring *Invincible* to the small screen as a weekly series, Jet was involved in a TV project entitled *Number One Son*.

While Jet was contracting for these several new screen assignments, his fans were still hoping that he would fulfill their long-cherished dream of uniting with Jackie Chan for a picture. (Not long ago, this screen teaming concept led to such a potential vehicle being scripted by Robert Mark Kamen, who had written *Kiss of the Dragon*.) Of this much-anticipated pairing with Jackie, Jet has said, "When is the right time to make that film? My fans say Jet Li can beat Jackie Chan. Jackie Chan's fans say, 'Oh, Jackie will beat Jet Li.' Jackie is a friend of mine. We just do our job. He does his. I do mine. I think an audience knows what's Jet Li's style for the action sequences and what is Jackie Chan's style. In Asia, it's crystal clear. This is a Jet Li film, this is a Jackie Chan film where it's comedy action."

When Jet was asked not long ago if he'd ever direct another movie after his long-ago experience on 1986's *Born to Defence*, Li informed *DVD* magazine: "I realized that I was not enough endowed (laughs)! I prefer to produce, to find good directors and good scriptwriters to develop my ideas. In this way, I can better concentrate on the story and on my way of acting."

Meanwhile, back in the United States, *aMagazine*, in its December 2001/January 2002 issue, featured an article on "The Twenty-Five Most Noteworthy Asians in America in 2001." Among the top ranking of the selected group were Jet, actress Zhang Ziyi (of *Crouching Tiger, Hidden Dragon*), director Ang Lee, and pro athlete Ichiro Suzuki of the Seattle Mariners. (Meanwhile at E! Entertainment Television's online site, they had picked Jet as among the top Sexiest Men in Entertainment.)

As Jet Li looks to the future, he has many ambitions and plans which include, but also extends beyond, filmmaking. For example, regarding the 2008 Olympics he says, "I've found out that if China hosts the Olympics in 2008, there is a possibility that wushu will be a category." But he does not envision participating in any way in that sports event. "No. I don't want to be the one who collects the flowers; I want to be the one who plants the seeds. When they bloom, others can reap the harvest."

Instead, as Jet told *Playboy* magazine profiler Mathew Polly in August 2001, "I feel my next step is to share a message with everybody, through movies and TV, about how to live on the earth with other human beings, how to reduce the sufferings of life, how to understand the reality of the world. This is what motivates me the most right now; otherwise, I would have retired already. . . . On my website . . . I talk about yin and yang and how to help people understand one another. If the Chinese people try to understand American culture and American history, for example, there will be better communications. If Americans work to understand how the Chinese people think, they will realize that the Chinese are not a people looking to start fights with other countries."

Regarding his renewed religious beliefs in the tenets of Buddhism, Li appreciates that "Buddhism is not the only means. There are many other religions and they all have the same idea. I believe religions are like several famous universities. Although they use different methods to teach, they have the same goal: to tell you how to become a kind person, a loving person, how to use your selfless mind to care about others. Whether the end is heaven, hell or reincarnation is not the issue."

Now attuned to Hollywood's filmmaking ways, Li has the perspective to appreciate it. "The outside always changes, the studios, the producers. But you have to think about it. You have to think about the situation outside your body. You think they're tough, they're tough. If you think it's easy, it's easy. It really depends on what's your point of view. What you want to get. You want to get famous? You want to become rich? What do you want to get? If I think, I only want to work, do my best, that's it. You give me more money, more fame, it's OK. You don't give it to me, I go home. That's very easy. Just relax. Enjoy life. Do your best."

Li hopes to be involved increasingly in filmmaking in a producer's capacity. "I like to dream! I think a movie is a dream. I want to become a producer because you can bring some good ideas, and then find a good, talented director and choreographer and writer to finish our dream. To make your dream become truth! That way is very interesting to me."

Whatever his capacity might be in making a picture, he has applied to this entire process the knowledge he has gained from his religious studies: "In Buddhism, nothing is permanent. This flower is very beautiful now . . . but a few months later, no flower. Now martial arts movie is popular all over the world, but how long? You don't know. One year, two years, maybe gone. You hope your

A beaming Jet Li in the late 1990s.

movie becomes successful, but all you can do is your best and keep your responsibility to yourself." If the widespread interest in the martial arts film genre should decline, Li says he is prepared because, "if you're always challenging yourself, do your best, then you can move around to different things."

At present Jet is still primarily an action star so that requires him to remain prepared for the heavy physical demands of his on-screen work. Because he has studied and trained in wushu for over thirty years, "most of the movements have been permanently ingrained, so to speak, in my mind. I do not have to spend much time to relearn these movements; they have become more than just second nature. What is essential is that I work to regain that endurance needed to perform these movements. After a period of respite, the muscles, the whole condition of the body will naturally idle and call for restoration. To get my body in shape, playing badminton, Ping Pong, swimming, bicycling, or just good old stretching always helps."

As a result of being in the limelight for such a long time, Li has a large coterie of fans from the world of martial arts and motion pictures. These enthusiasts have often placed him on a lofty pedestal. Contrary to many celebrities, Jet still finds the situation very uncomfortable. "I've never had an idol, and I don't really encourage that kind of behavior. When you idolize somebody, you only see the successful face and fail to see the bad side. It's an imbalanced perspective. There's nothing wrong with looking to successful people to see what it takes, and then using that knowledge to plan your own path. But I don't believe in encouraging people to model their lives after somebody else's as in: 'I want to become him.' No matter how faithfully you imitate somebody else you will never be able to duplicate their life. It's impossible. Out of the billions of people living on the planet, no two lives are exactly the same."

Rather, the star views himself as "just a boy from China, a guy who has had special opportunities in the martial arts. Now I play in the action movies because I have special background. . . . I watch movies, meet with friends, talk business, read the newspaper, have some dinner, read a lot of books. . . . I'm just a normal guy, but my background is a little bit different."

Most of all, Jet Li believes in living fully in the present. His guideline remains, "Don't think too much about the future. Don't think too much about past tense. Not good?"

Filmography

• Character names, wherever possible, have been replicated in the format utilized for the production's on-screen credits.
• Alternate names are provided in brackets

FEATURE FILMS

The Shaolin Temple (Chung Yuen Motion Pictures/SYS Entertainment, 1982) Color, 94 minutes.

Executive producers: Lau Fong and Fu Chi. Producer: Yuen Liu-yet. Associate producer: Chan Man. Director: Zhang Xinyan [Cheung Yam-yim]. Screenplay: Lu Shau-chang and Shih Hou. Art director: Wong Hok-sun. Costumes: Wong Kwai-ping and Fung Tong-yuet. Music: Wang Li-pin. Action sequence coordinators: Ma Xian-da, Hai Yue, Fu Pan-qing, and Wang Chang-kai. Sound: Wong Kwan-sai. Camera: Ling Chau-pak and Lau Fung-lam. Editors: Chang Hsin-yen, Wong Ting, Wai Ku-chi, and Wai Li-yuk.

Cast: Jet Li (Jue Yuan), Ding Laam (Bai Wu Xia), Hai Yue (Shi fu), Qiang Hu-jian (Wu Kong), Ku Sun-jian (Se Kong), Liang Liu-huai (Liao Kong), Wang Jue (Ban Kong), Yang Du-chuan (Wei Kong), Qiang Chi-zhi (Xuan Kong), Xuan Feng (Dao Kong), Guang Pan-han (Zhi Cao), Fang Ping (Hui Neng), Tong Shan Qui Bo (Hui Yang), Zhang Jian-wen (Fang Zhang), Yang Di-hua (Seng Zhi), Wang Guang-kuan (Li Shi Min), Yu Cheng Hui (Wang Ren Ze), Hua Ji-chun (Tu Ying), Fu Pan-qing, Su Fei, Chen Guo-an, Chang Bian-li, Wang Guo-yi, Kong Fan-yan, and Sun Sheng-jun (generals), and Gai Chun-wa (guard of chained prisoners).

Alternate titles: *Shao Lin Chi*; *Siu Lam Si*.

Kids from Shaolin (Chung Yuen Motion Pictures, 1984) Color, 98 minutes.

Executive producer: Fu Chi. Producer, Yuen Liu-yet. Director: Zhang Xinyan

[Cheung Yam-yim]. Screenplay: Leung Chi-keung and Ho Shu-wa. Music: Yu Feng. Action director: Hu Jian-qiang Sound: Chang Mong. Camera: Ling Chau-pak. Editors: Wai Li-yuk and Wai Ku-chi.

Cast: Jet Li (San Lung), Yue Hai (sifu), Gai Chun-wa (One Eye), and: Wong Chiu-yin, Dim Nam, Chang Ho-chen, Yu Chen-wei, Zhang Jien-hwu, and Huang Qiuyan.

Alternate titles: *Kids of Shaolin*; *Shaolin Boys*; *Shaolin Kids*; *Shaolin Temple 2: Kids from Shaolin*; *Shao Lin Xiao Zi*; *Siu Lam Siu Ji*.

Martial Arts of Shaolin (Pearl River Film Productions, 1986) Color, 80 minutes.

Executive producer: Fu Chi. Producers, Ann Tse Kai, Yuen Liu-yet, Kwan Lam-ping, and Pei Lu-yin. Director: Liu Chia-liang [Lau Kar-liang]. Screenplay: Si Yeung-ping. Action director: Qiang Hu-jian. Music: Law Dik. Camera: Cho On-sun. Editor: Chiu Bo-lin.

Cast: Jet Li (Zhi Ming), Wong Chau-yin (Miss Si Ma Yin), Yue Sing-wai (Lord He Suo), Woo Gin-keung (Zhao Wei), Gai Chun-wa (bald villain), Yue Hoi (Instructor Zhi Ren), and: Huang Qiuyan, Suen Gin-fooi, and Lau Waai-leung.

Alternate titles: *Arahan*; *Naam Bak Siu Lam*; *Nan Bei Shao Lin*; *North and South Shaolin*; *Shaolin Temple 3: Martial Arts of Shaolin*.

Born to Defence (Sil-Metropole, 1986) Color, 90 minutes.

Producer: Fu Chi. Directors: Jet Li and Chui Siu-ming. Screenplay: Si Yeung-boon and Chit Yi-gwoh. Music: Hau Tak-Chiu and Chui Siu-chung. Action director: Chui Siu-ming. Camera: Cho Him.

Cast: Jet Li, Kurt Roland Peterson, Sung Gaai, Jia Song, Paula H. P. Tocha, Erkang Zhao, Chui Siu-ming, and Biu Law-do.

Alternate titles: *Born to Defend*; *Chung Wa Ying Hung*; *Zhong Hua Ying Xiong*.

Dragon Fight (Maan Lee Din Ying Yau Haan Gung Shut, 1989) Color, 96 minutes.

Executive producer: Henry Fong-ping. Producer: Henrick Wong. U.S. line producer: Michael Chu. Director: Billy Tang Hin-shing. Screenplay: James Yuen Sai-sang. Production designer: Aric Kam. Art director: Ma Chi-ming. Digital music: Violet Lam Man-yee. Action director: Dick Wei. Action instructor: C. L. Tu. Camera: Lam A-do. Editor: Siu Laam.

Cast: Jet Li (Ah Lap), Nina Li Chi (Ah Kuen), C. L. Tu (Wai), Stephen Chow Sing-chi (Ah Yao), Henry Fong-ping (Marco), Dick Wei (Tiger Wong), Marc D. Williams (Ray, Marco's bodyguard), Victor Chow (Ah Ping), Michael McFall

(Tong), Tom Spinoza (big boss), George Chung and Ernie Reyes (big boss's killers), Adam Noah and Wong Wai-tong (Wai's bodyguards), Fong Chuk-ming (ambassador of China), Lynn McCree (flight attendant), Terry Chan (Coach), Aileen Heimes (Marco's girlfriend), Christopher Notley, Jeff Finder, Byron Carmichael, and Barry Wong (drug dealers).

Alternate titles: *Dragon Kickboxer*; *Long Zai Tian Ya*; *Lung Joi Tin Aai*.

Once Upon a Time in China (Golden Harvest, 1991) Color, 134 minutes.

Executive producer: Raymond Chow Man-wai. Producer/Director, Tsui Hark. Screenplay: Tsui Hark, Yuen Gai-chi, Leung Yiu-ming, and Elsa Tang Bik-yin. Production designer: Lau Man-hung. Art director: Hai Chung-man. Costumes: Yu Ka-on. Music: James Wong Jim. Action directors: Lau Kar-wing, Yuen Shun-yi, Yuen Cheung-yan, and Yuen Woo-ping. Camera: David Chung Chi-man, Bill Wong Chung-piu, Arthur Wong Ngok-tai, Ardy Lam Kwok-wah, Chan Dung-chuen, and Chan Pui-ka. Editor: Marco Mak Chi-sin.

Cast: Jet Li (Wong Fei Hung), Yuen Biano (Leung Foon), Jacky Cheung Hok-yau ("Buck Teeth" Sol), Rosamund Kwan Chi-lam (Aunt Yee), Kent Cheng Jak-Si ("Porky" [Lam Sai Wing]), Yen Shi-kwan ("Iron Robe" Yim), Yuen Cheung-yan (Yim's opponent), Karel Wong Chi-yeung (governor), Jonathan Isgar (Jackson), Lau Shun (naval commander), Wong Chi-yeung (naval officer), Wu Ma (old man), Yuen Gam-fai (Kai), Yuen Shun-yi (honorable Manchu soldier), and Jimmy Wang Yu (slave from America).

Alternate titles: *Huang Fei Hong*; *Wong Fei Hung*.

Once Upon a Time in China II (Golden Harvest, 1992) Color, 106 minutes.

Executive producer: Raymond Chow Man-wai. Producers: Tsui Hark and Ng See-yuen. Director, Tsui Hark. Screenplay: Tsui Hark, Charcoal Chan, and Chan Tin-suen. Production designer: Eddie Ma. Costumes: Chiu Gwok-san. Music: Richard Yuen Cheuk-fan and Johnny Njo. Action director: Yuen Woo-ping. Camera: Arthur Wong Ngok-tai. Editor: Marco Mak chi-sin.

Cast: Jet Li (Wong Fei Hung), Rosamund Kwan Chi-lam (Aunt Yee), Donnie Yen Ji-dan (Lan), David Chiang (Luke), Max Mok Siu-chung (Leung Foon), Xiong Xin-xin [Hung Yan-yan] (priest Kung), Paul Fonoroff (British consul), Kwan Yan-yee (Chung), Ho Ka-kui (Mak), and Cheung Tit-lam (Dr. Sun Yat-sen).

Alternate titles: *Huang Fei Hong Zhi Er: Nam Er Dang Zi Jiang*; *Wong Fei Hung Ji Yee: Laam Ngai Dong Chi Keung*.

The Master (Golden Harvest, 1992) Color, 92 minutes [made in 1989].

Executive producers: Anthony Chow Deng-au and Michael Lai Siu-tin. Producer: Tsui Hark. Coproducer: David Lo. Director/Story: Tsui Hark. Screenplay: Lau Daai-muk and Lam Kee-to. Production designer: Peter Cheung. Art director: Lynn Christopher. Music: Lam Yee-tat. Action directors: Brandy Yuen Jan-yeung and Yuen Wah. Camera: Henry Chan Jun-git and Paul A. Edwards. Editors: Peter Cheung and Ma Kam.

Cast: Jet Li (Chuck), Yuen Wah (Uncle Tak), Crystal Kwok Gam-yan (May), Jerry Trimble (Johnny), Anne Rickets (Anna), Rubén González (Cito), Guy Fadallone (Ruben), Derek Annunciation (Mouse), Michael Reilly Burke (Oscar), Camille Carrigan (Jeannie), Wayne Post (Jimmy), Pamela J. Anderson (coach), George Cheung (Paul), Steve Ho, Kevin Cole, Chris Carnel, David Wald, and Stefanos Miltsakakis (Johnny's Students), Mark Williams, Erwin Villegon, Spencer Platerns, Ray Wizard, Alfred Bonilla, John Kreng (members of the Hawks), Billy Blanks (thug), and Corey Yuen [Yuen Kwai].

Alternate titles: *Huang Fei Hong '92; Ji Lung Hang Tin Gwong; Wong Fei Hung '92: Zhi Long Hang Tiani Xia.*

Swordsman II (Golden Harvest, 1992) Color, 110 minutes.

Producer: Tsui Hark. Director: Ching Siu-tung. Based on the novel *The Proud and Laughing Warrior* by Louis Cha. Screenplay: Tsui Hark, Chan Tin-suen, and Elsa Tang Bik-yin. Costumes: William Chang Suk-ping and Bruce Yu Ka-on. Music: Richard Yuen Cheuk-faan. Action directors: Ching Siu-tung, Yuen Bun, Ma Yuk-sing, and Cheung Yiu-sing. Camera: Tom Lau Moon-tong. Editor: Marco Mak Chi-sin.

Cast: Jet Li (Ling Woo Chung), Brigitte Lin Ching-hsia (Asia the Invincible [Dong Fang Bu Bai]), Michelle Reis [Lee Kar-yan] (Kiddo), Waise Lee Chi-hung (Hattori), Rosamund Kwan Chi-lam (Ren Ying Ying), Fennie Yuen Kit-ying (Blue Phoenix), Yan Yee-kwan (Wu), Cheung Kwok-leung (Eunuch Hong), Lau Shun (Zen), Wong Chi-yeung (interpreter), Yu On-on (Cici), and Candice Yu (Chin Ka-lok).

Alternate titles: *Siu Ngo Kong Woo Ii: Dung Fong Bat Baai; Xiao Ao Jiang Hu Ii: Dong Fang Bu Bai.*

Once Upon a Time in China III (Golden Harvest, 1993) Color, 103 minutes.

Executive producer: Raymond Chow Man-wai. Producers: Tsui Hark and Ng See-yuen. Director: Tsui Hark. Screenplay: Tsui Hark and Charcoal Tan. Art director: Timothy Yip Gam-tim. Costumes: Win Ching. Music: William Hu Wei-li. Action director: Yuen Tak. Camera: Andrew Lau Wai-keung. Editor: Marco Mak Chi-sin.

Cast: Jet Li (Wong Fei Hung), Rosamund Kwan Chi-lam (Aunt Yee), Lau Shun (Wong Kay Ying), Max Mok Siu-chung (Leung Foon), John Wakefield (Tomanovsky), and Xiong Xin-xin [Hung Yan-yan] (Club Foot).

Alternate titles: *Huang Fei Hong Zhi San: Shi Wang Zheng Ba*; *Wong Fei Hung Ji Saam: Shut Wong Chang Ba.*

Fong Sai Yuk (Golden Harvest, 1993) Color, 97 minutes.

Executive producer: Lee Yeung Chung. Producer: Jet Li. Director: Corey Yuen [Yuen Kwai]. Screenplay: John Chan Kin-chung, Kay On, Choi Hong-wing. Production designer: Ann Hui On-wah.Art director: Lau Man-hung. Costumes: Shirley Chan Goo-fong. Music: James Wong Jim, Romeo Diaz, and Mark Lui Chung-tak. Action directors: Corey Yuen and Yuen Tak. Camera: Jingle Ma Choh-shing. Editor: Peter Cheung Yiu-chung.

Cast: Jet Li (Fong Sai Yuk), Michelle Reis [Lee Kar-yan] (Ting Ting), Josephine Siao Fong-fong (Mother Fong), Paul Chu Kong (Father Fong), Chan Chung-yun (Tiger Lu), Vincent˅20Zhao˅20Wen-zhuo [Chiu Man-cheuk], Adam Cheng (Chan Ka Lok), and Sibelle Hu-Hui-zhong (Ting Ting's mother).

Alternate titles: *Fang Shi Yu; Fong Sai Yuk; The Legend; The Legend of Fong Sai Yuk.*

Last Hero in China (Golden Harvest, 1993) Color, 108 minutes.

Executive producer: Lee Yeung Chung. Presenters: Charles Heung Wah-keung and Jimmy Heung Wa-sing. Producers: Jet Li, and Stephen Shiu Yeuk-yuen. Associate producer: Lo Kwok. Director/Screenplay: Wong Jing. Art director: Jason Mok Siu-kei. Costumes: Tony Au Ting-ping. Music: Lui Tsung-tak and James Wong Jim. Action directors: Yuen Woo-ping and Yuen Cheung-yan. Sound: Tsu Tsi-ha. Camera: Jingle Ma and Lau Mun-tong. Editor: Poon Hung Yiu.

Cast: Jet Li (Wong Fei Hung), Nat Chan Pak-cheung (Mr. Pimp [Mass Tar Wong]), Dicky Cheung Wai-kin ("Buck Teeth" Sol), Sharla Cheung-man (Yin-er/Yan Lei), Alan Chui Chung-san (Lui Yat Siu), Chu Chung-shun (Ching Wa), Chung Faat (Yuen Long), Chu Tee-Wor (Chow Hung), Leung Kar-yan (Leung Fu), Liu Chia-hui (Master Liu Heung), Anita Yuen Wing-yee (Miss Nine), Yuen King-tan (the madam), and Julie Lee Wa-yuet (hooker).

Alternate titles: *Claws of Steel; Deadly China Hero; Huang Fei Hong Zhi Tie Ji Dou Wu Gong; Iron Rooster vs. the Centipede; Wong Fei Hung Ji Tit Gai Dau Ng Gung.*

195

Fong Sai Yuk II (Golden Harvest, 1993) Color, 97 minutes.

Producer: Jet Li. Director: Corey Yuen [Yuen Kwai]. Screenplay: Kay On and John Chan Kin-chung. Production designer: James Leung Wah-Sing. Costumes: Cheung Sai-wang. Music: Lowell Lo Koon-ting. Action directors: Corey Yuen and Yuen Tak. Camera: Mark Lee Ping-bin. Editor: Angie Lam On-yee.

Cast: Jet Li (Fong Sai Yuk), Josephine Siao Fong-fong (Mother Fong), Adam Cheng Siu-chow (Chan Ka Lok), Michelle Reis [Lee Kar-yan] (Ting Ting), Amy Kwok Oi-ming (Man Yin), Corey Yuen (Li Kwok Bon), Chan Lung (Macu), and Gai Chun Wa (bald villain).

Alternate titles: *Fang Shi Yu Xu Ji*; *Fong Sai Yuk Chuk Chap*; *The Legend of Fon Sai Yuk II*; *The Legend II*.

The Tai-Chi Master (Golden Harvest, 1993) Color, 92 minutes.

Executive producer: Lee Yeung Chung. Coproducer: Chui Po-chiu. Associate producer: Julia Chu. Director: Yuen Woo-ping. Screenplay: Kim Yip Kwong-kim. Art directors: Raymond Lee King-man and Fu Delin. Music: William Hu Wei-li. Action directors: Yuen Woo-ping and Yuen Cheung-yan. Camera: Tom Lau Moon-tong. Editor. Angie Lam On-yee.

Cast: Jet Li (Zhang Junbao), Michelle Yeoh (Siu Lin), Chin Siu-ho (Chin Bo), Fennie Yuen Kit-ying (Miss Li), Yuen Cheung-yan (Reverend Ling), Lau Shun (Master Jueyuan), and Yue Hoi.

Alternate titles: *Taai Gik Cheung Saam Fung*; *Tai Ji Zhang San Feng*, *Twin Warriors*.

The Kung Fu Cult Master (Newport Entertainment, 1993) Color, 115 minutes.

Executive producer: Lee Yeung Chung. Presenters: Charles Heung Wah-keung and Jimmy Heung Wa-sing. Producers: Jet Li and Wong Jing. Director/Screenplay: Wong Jing. Art director: Jason Mok Siu-kei. Music: Goo Ga-fai. Action director: Sammo Hung Kam-bo. Camera: Bill Wong Chung-piu. Editor: Poon Hung-yiu.

Cast: Jet Li (Chang Mo Kei), Chingmy Yau Suk-ching (Siu Chiu), Cheung Man (Yan So-So/Royal Princess), Sammo Hung Kam-bo (Chang San Fung), Francis Ng (Chang Tsui San), Richard Ng Yil-hon (King of Green Bat [Wai Yat Siu]), Leung Kar-yan (Sung Yuen Kin), Ngai Sing (Sung Ching Su), Cho Wing (Shaolin monk), Gigi Lai Chi (Chow Chi Yu), and Chun-yu, Dior cheng, John Ching, Paul Chu, Lam Ching-ying, and Tsui Kam-kong.

Alternate titles: *The Evil Cult*; *Kung Fu Cult Master*; *Kung Fu Master*; *Kei Tin Tiu Lung Gei Ji Moh Gaau Gaau Chu*; *Lord of the Wu Tang*; *Yi Tian Tu Long Ji Zhi Mo Jiao Jiao Zhu*.

The New Legend of Shaolin (Newport Entertainment, 1994) Color, 88 minutes.
Executive producer: Yang Teng-kuei. Producer: Jet Li. Associate producers: Helen Li Yangzhong and Pei Hsiang-chuan. Director/Screenplay: Wong Jing. Art directors: Raymond Lee King-man and Fu Delin. Costumes: Shirley Chan Goo-fong. Music: Jonathan Wong Bong. Action director: Corey Yuen [Yuen Kwai]. Camera: Tom Lau Moon-tong. Editor: Angie Lam On-yee.

Cast: Jet Li (Hung Hei Goon), Chingmy Yau Suk-ching (Red Bean), Deannie Yip Tak-han (Red Bean's mother), Chan Chun-yung (Ma Kai Sin), Damian Lau Chung-yan (Chan Kan Nam), Tze Miu [Xie Miao] (Hung Man Ting), Johnny Wang Lung-wei (commander), Gai Chun-wa (poison juice monster), and Adam Cheng Siu-chow, and Wong Jing.

Alternate titles: *Hong Xi Guan Zhi Shaolin Wu Zu*; *Hung Hei Goon*; *Legend of the Future Shaolin*; *Legends of Shaolin*; *Shaolin's Five Founders*.

The Bodyguard from Beijing (Golden Harvest, 1994) Color, 95 minutes.
Producer: Jet Li. Director: Corey Yuen [Yuen Kwai]. Screenplay: Gordon Chan Ka-seung and John Chan Kin-chung. Art director: Jason Mok Siu-kei. Costumes: Shirley Chan Goo-fong. Music: William Hu Wei-li. Action directors: Corey Yuen and Yuen Tak. Camera: Tom Lau Moon-tong. Editor: Angie Lam On-yee.

Cast: Jet Li (John Chang), Christy Chung Lai-tai (Michelle Yeung), Ken[t] Cheng Jak-si (Sgt. Charlie Leung Kam-po), Ngai Sing (Wang Wen-jun), Leung Wing-chung (Ken), Ng Wai-kwok (James Shong Sai-cheung), William Chu Wai-lim (Billy Yeung), Corey Yuen (passerby in mall), and Wong Kam-kong (Chiu Kwok-man).

Alternate titles: *Chung Naam Hoi Biu Biu*; *The Defender*; *Zhong Nan Hai Bao Biao*.

Fist of Legend (Newport Entertainment, 1994) Color, 103 minutes.
Producer: Jet Li. Director/Screenplay: Gordon Chan Ka-seung. Art director: Horace Ma Gwong-wing. Costumes: Chan Kei-hop. Music: Jonathan Wong Bong. Action directors: Yuen Woo-pin, Yuen Shun-yi, and Yuen Cheung-yan. Camera: Derek Wan Man-git. Editor: Chan Kei-hop.

Cast: Jet Li (Chen Zhen), Chin Siu-ho (Huo Ting-en), Ada Choi Siu-fan (Xian-hong [So Lan]), Billy Chow Bei-lei (Fujita), Paul Chun Pui (Nong), Yasuaki Kurata (Fumio Funakoshi), Jackson Lau Hok-yin (Akutagawa), Shinobu Nakayama (Mitsuko Yamada), Yuen Cheung-yan (Captain Jie), Yuen Shun-yee (Ngai), and Toshimichi Takahashi.

Alternate title: *Cheng Miu Ying Hung*; *Jing Wu Ying Xiong*.

My Father Is a Hero (Upland Films, 1995) Color, 102 minutes.

Producers: Wong Jing and Tiffany Chen Lan. Presenters: Charles Heung Wah-keung and Jimmy Heung Wa-sing. Director: Corey Yuen [Yuen Kwai]. Screenplay: Sandy Shaw and Chung Wai-hung. Art director: Ben Lau Man-hung. Costumes: Shirley Chan Goo-fong. Music: James Wong Jim and Mark Lui Chung-tak. Action directors: Corey Yuen and Yuen Tak. Camera: Tom Lau Moon-tong. Editor: Skip Williams.

Cast: Jet Li (Kung Wei), Anita Mui Yim-fong (Fong Yat Wah), Tze Miu [Xie Miao] (Kung Ku), Yu Rong Guang (Po Kwong), Ngai Sing, and Low Houi-Kang (thugs), Damian Lau (Yat Wah's boss), Henry Fong-ping (auction bidder), Blacky Ko Sau-leung (Darkie), Corey Yuen (bartender), Thorsten Nickel (Russian arms dealer), and Bonnie Fu Yuk-Jing and Ken Lo Wai-kwong.

Alternate titles: *Gei Ba Ba De Shen*; *Jet Li's The Enforcer*; *Kap Ang Ang Dik San*; *Letter to Daddy*.

High Risk (Upland Films, 1995) Color, 104 minutes.

Producer: Wong Jing. Directors: Wong Jing and Corey Yuen [Yuen Kwai]. Screenplay: Wong Jing. Art director/Costumes: Jason Mok Siu-kei. Music: Richard Yuen Cheuk-fan. Action directors: Corey Yuen and Bruce Law Lai-yin. Camera: Tom Lau Moon-tong. Editor: Angie Lam On-yee.

Cast: Jet Li (Kit Li), Jacky Cheung Hok-yau (Frankie Lone), Charlie Cho (Charlie), Chingmy Yau Suk-ching (reporter), Wu Ma (Frankie's father), Charlie Yeung Choi-nei (Joyce), Valerie Chow (Fai Fai), Billy Chow Bei-lei (henchman), Vincent Kok (cameraman), Kwan Suki (Li's wife), Ben Lam Kwok-bun (killer with sunglasses), Kelvin Wong (the doctor), Yang Chung-hsien (Joyce's boyfriend), Bobby Yip (ugly stuntman), and Corey Yuen and Yuen Tak.

Alternate titles: *Meltdown; Sue Daam Lung Wai; Shu Dan Long Wei*.

Dr. Wai in the Scripture With No Words (Newport Entertainment, 1996) Color, 90 minutes.

Producers: Charles Heung Wah-keung and Tiffany Chen Lan. Executive in charge of production: Chan Lam. Director: Ching Siu-tung. Screenplay: Sandy Shaw, Roy Szeto Cheuk-hon, and Lam Wai-lun. Production designer: Yee Chung-man. Art director: Jason Mok Siu-kei. Costumes: Willam Fung Kwun-man and Mok Gwan-git. Music: Frankie Chan Fan-kei. Action directors: Ching Siu-tung and Ma Yuk-sing. Camera: Tom Lau Moon-tong. Editors: Marco Mak Chi-sin and Angie Lam On-yee.

Cast: Jet Li (Dr. Wai/Chow Si Kit), Rosamund Kwan Chi-lam (Cammy/ Monica Kwan), Charlie Yeung (Yan Yan/Yvonne), Takeshi Kaneshiro (Wai's student/ Shing), Ngai Sing (the movie star/Hung Sing), Billy Chow Bei-lei (Chan/Japanese Embassy guard), Law Kar-ying (headmaster), and Johnnie Kong Yeuk-sing.

Alternate titles: *Dr. Wai and the Scripture Without Words*; *Mao Xian Wang*; *Mak Him Wong*; *The Scripture With No Words*.

Black Mask (Newport Entertainment, 1996) Color, 102 minutes.

Executive producer: Tsui Hark. Producer: Charles Heung Wah-keung. Associate producer: Teddy Chan Tak-sum. Executive in charge of production: Tiffany Chen Lan. Director: Daniel Lee Yan-gong. Screenplay: Tsui Hark, Hui Koan, Teddy Chan Tak-sum, Koan Hui, and Joe Ma Wai-ho. Art directors: Eddie Ma Poon-chiu and Bill Lui Cho-hung. Costumes: William Fung Kwun-man and Mabel Kwan Mei-bo. Music: Teddy Robin Kwan. Action directors: Yuen Woo-ping, Deon Lam Dik-on, and Guk Hin-chiu. Camera: Tony Cheung Tung-leung. Editor: Cheung Ka-fai.

Cast: Jet Li (Tsui Chik/Black Mask), Lau Ching-wan (Inspector Shek), Karen Mok Man-wai (Tracy), Françoise Yip Fong-wa (Yeuk Laan), Patrick Lung Kong (Commander Hung), Anthony Wong Chau-sang (King Kau), Moses Chan-ho and Michael Ian Lambert (701 squad members), Lawrence Ah Mon (operating room doctor), Chung King-fai (police commissioner), Henry Fong (Tai), Russ Price (Rocket), and Hung Yan-yan.

Alternate titles: *Hak Hap*; *Hei Xia*.

Once Upon a Time in China and America (China Star Entertainment, 1996) Color, 98 minutes.

Executive producer: Tsui Hark. Presenter: Charles Heung Wah-keung. Associate producer: Dick Tso. Executive in charge of production: Rita Fung. Director: Sammo Hung Kam-bo. Screenplay: Sharon Hui Sa-long, Shut Mei-yee, Roy Szeto Cheuk-hon, So Man-sing, Philip Kwak, and Tsui Hark. Production designer: Horace Ma Gwong-wing. Art director: Lam Hark-ming. Costumes: Mabel Gwaan Mei-bo and William Fung Kwun-man. Music: Lowell Lo Koon-ting. Second unit director: Lau Kar-wing. Action director: Sammo Hung Kam-bo. Camera: Lam Fai-taai and Walter Gregg. Editors: Marco Mak Chi-sin and Angie Lam On-yee.

Cast: Jet Li (Wong Fei Hung), Rosamund Kwan chi-lam (Aunt Yee), Xiong Xin-xin [Hung Yan-yan] (Club Foot Seven), Chan Kwok-bong ("Buck Teeth"

Sol), Jeff Wolfe (Billy), Joe Sayah (Black Bart), Chyrsta Belle Eucht (Sarah, the Indian maiden), Joe Sayah (bandit leader), Roger Yuan (Dick), Richard Ng Yiu-hon (Han), Daniel Lujan (Flying Eagle), W. Glenn Malmskog (gang member), Jean Wang (Aunt May), and Danton Mew (inn keeper).

Alternate titles: *Huang Fei Hong Zhi Xi Yu Xiong Shi*; *Once Upon a Time in China VI*; *Wong Fei Hung Ji Sai Wik Hung Shut*.

Hitman (China Star Entertainment, 1998) Color, 103 minutes.

Executive producer: Gordon Chan Ka-seung. Producer: Charles Heung Wah-keung. Director: Stephen Tung Wai. Screenplay: Chan Hing-kar, Vincent Kok Tak-chiu, and Cheng Kam-fu. Art Director: Bill Lui Cho-hung. Costumes: Shirley Chan Goo-fong. Music: T. Two and Teddy Robin Kwan. Action directors: Tung Wei, Ku Huan-chiu, Ling Chi-wah, and Chan Siu-wah. Camera: Arthur Wong Ngok-tai. Editor: Cheung Ka-fai.

Cast: Jet Li (Tai Feng), Eric Tsang Chi-wai (Sam Wong), Simon Yam Tat-wah (Kwan), Gigi Leung Wing-kei (Kiki), Sato Keiji (Eiji, the billionaire's grandson), Kim Yip Kwong-kim (Martin, the corrupt attorney), Paul Rapovski (Tall Guy), and Hideri Melken and Timmy Ho Bo-sang.

Alternate titles: *Saai Sau Ji Wong*; *Sha Shou Zhi Wang*.

Lethal Weapon 4 (Warner Bros., 1998). Color, 127 minutes.

Executive producers: Steve Perry and Jim Van Wyck. Coproducers: J. Mills Goodloe and Dan Cracchiolo. Associate producers: Ilyse Reutlinger, Spencer Franklin, and Jennifer Gwartz. Director: Richard Donner. Based on characters created by Shane Black. Story: Jonathan Lemkin, Alfred Gough, and Miles Millar. Screenplay: Channing Gibson. Production designer: J. Michael Riva. Art director: David Klassen. Set decorator: Lauri Gaffin. Costumes: Ha Nguyen. Music: Michael Kamen, Eric Clapton, and David Sanborn. Martial arts choreography: Cory Yuen [Yuen Kwai], Huen Chiu-ku, and Chi Wah-ling. Special effects coordinator: Jon Belyeu. Camera: Andrzej Bartkowiak. Editors: Frank J. Urioste and Dallas Puett.

Cast: Mel Gibson (Martin Riggs), Danny Glover (Roger Murtaugh), Joe Pesci (Leo Getz), Rene Russo (Lorna Cole), Chris Rock (Lee Butters), Jet Li (Wah Sing Ku), Steve Kahan (Capt. Ed Murphy), Kim Chan (Uncle Benny), Darlene Love (Trish Murtaugh), Traci Wolfe (Rianne Murtaugh Butters), Eddy Ko (Hong) Steven Lam (Ping), Michael Chow (Benny's assistant), Tony Keyes (Ng's partner), Phil Chong (Yee), Roger Yuan (Chu), Qian Zu-wu (Uncle Chung), Elizabeth Sung (Hong's wife), and Richard Libertini (rabbi).

Romeo Must Die (Warner Bros., 2000) Color, 115 minutes.

Executive producer: Dan Cracchiolo. Producers: Joel Silver and Jim Van Wyck. Coproducer: Warren Carr. Associate producers: Mitchell Kapner and Ilyse A. Reutlinger. Director: Andrzej Bartkowiak. Story: Mitchell Kapner. Screenplay: Eric Bernt and John Jarrell. Production designer: Michael Bolton. Art director: Jim Steuart. Costumes: Sandra J. Blackie. Music: Stanley Clarke and Timbaland. Martial arts supervisor: Corey Yuen [Yuen Kwai]. Camera: Glen MacPherson. Editor: Derek G. Brechin.

Cast: Jet Li (Han Sing), Aaliyah (Trish O'Day), Isaiah Washington (Mac), Russell Wong (Kai), DMX (Silk, the club owner), Delroy Lindo (Isaak O'Day), D. B. Woodside (Colin O'Day), Henry O (Ch'u Sing), Jon Kit Lee (Po Sing), Edoardo Ballerini (Vincent Roth), Anthony Anderson (Maurice), Matthew Harrison (Dave, Roth's assistant), Terry Chen (Kung), Derek Lowe (messenger), Ronin Wong (new prisoner), Byron Lawson (head guard, Hsing Kang Prison), Chang Tseng (Victor Ho), and Franêoise Yip Fong-wa (motorcycle fighter).

Kiss of the Dragon (Twentieth Century-Fox, 2001) Color, 98 minutes.

Producers: Luc Besson, Steve Chasman, Jet Li, and Happy Walters. Coproducer: Bernard Grenet. Screen story: Jet Li. Screenplay: Luc Besson and Robert Mark Kamen. Production designer: Jacques Rufnoir. Costumes: Pierre Bechir and Annie Thiellement. Music: Craig Armstrong. Martial arts choreography: Corey Yuen [Yuen Kwai]. Camera: Thierry Arboast. Editor: Marco Cavé.

Cast: Jet Li (Liu Jian), Bridget Fonda (Jessica), Tcheky Karyo (Inspector Jean-Pierre Richard), Ric Young (Mister Big), Burt Kwouk (Uncle Tai), Laurence Ashley (Aja), Cyril Raffaelli (twin #1), Didier Azoulay (twin #2), John Forgeham (Max), Max Ryan (Lupo), Colin Prince (Lupo's assistant), Vincent Glo (Pluto), Vincent Wong (Minister Tang), Kentaro (Chen), Stefan Nelet (Tang's Aide #1), and Stéphane Jacquot (Richard's assistant).

Alternate titles: *Le Baiser Mortel du Dragon.*

The One (Columbia, 2001) color, 87 minutes.

Executive producers: Todd Garner, Lata Ryan, Tom Sherak, and Happy Walters. Producers: Steve Chasman, Glen Morgan, Charles Newirth, and James Wong. Director: James Wong. Screenplay: Glen Morgan and James Wong. Production designer: David L. Snyder. Art director: Paul M. Sonski. Costumes: Chrisi Karvonides-Dushenko. Music: Trevor Rabin and Paul Linford. Second unit director: Corey Yuen [Yuen Kwai]. Camera: Robert McLachlan. Editor: James Coblentz.

Cast: Jet Li (Gabe/Yulaw/Lawless), Carla Gugino (T. K./Massie Walsh), Delroy Lindo (Harry Roedecker/gas station attendant), Jason Statham (Evan Funsch), James Morrison (Aldrich/ "A" world inmate #1), Dylan Brung (Yates), Richard Steinmetz (D'Antoni), Steve Rankin (MVA supervisor), Tucker Smallwood (prison warden), Harriet Sansom Harris (Nurse Besson), David Keats (MRI technician), Dean Norris (Sergeant Siegel), Ron Zimmerman (Rotten Ronnie), Darin Morgan (Hugo), Mark Borchardt (Cesar), Joel Stoffer (Doctor Franklin), and Scott L. Schwartz (prisoner).

Invincible (TBS-cable, November 18, 2001) Color, 100 minutes.

Executive producers: Bruce Davey, Mel Gibson, Jet Li, and John Morayniss. Producers: Steve Chasman, Janine Coughlin, and Jim Lemley. Director: Jefery Levy. Story: Carey W. Hayes and Chad Hayes. Teleplay: Michael Brandt, Derek Haas, and Jefery Levy. Production designer: Michelle McGahey. Costumes: Noreen Landry. Music: Rupert Parkes. Martial arts choreographer: Tony Ching. Camera: John Stokes. Editor Keith Salmon.

Cast: Billy Zane (Os), Byron Mann (Michael Fu), Stacy Oversier (Serena Blue), Tony Kittles (Ray Jackson), Dominic Purcell (Keith Grady), David Field (Slate), Michelle Comerford (White Warrior), Simone McAullay (Harrison), Linal Haft (Howard Lancaster), Myles Pollard (Paul Beck), Barry Otto (professor), George Cheung (Tojo Sakamura), and David No (shadowman #1).

IN PRODUCTION

Hero (Miramax Films, 2002) Color.

Producer: Bill Kong. Director/Screenplay: Zhang Yimou. Art director: Huo Tingxiao. Costumes: Emi Wada. Character designer: Yang Shudong. Music: Tan Dun. Action director: Ching Siu-tung. Camera: Christopher Doyle, and Yong Hou.

Cast: Jet Li (Wu Ming), Maggie Cheung Man-yuk (Flying Snow), Tony Leung Chiu-wai (Broken Sword), Cheng Daoming (Emperor Ying Zheng), Zhang Ziyi (Ru Yue), Bai Shiquian (Six Finger Iron Hand), Zheng Tianyong (butler of Flying Snow), and: Donnie Yen Ji-dan.

Cradle 2 to the Grave (Warner Bros., 2002) Color.

Executive producer: Herb Gains. Producer: Joel Silver. Director: Andrzej Bartkowiak. Story: Reggie Rock Blythewood. Screenplay: John O'Brien and

Channing Gibson. Production designer: David F. Klassen. Art Director: Richard F. Mays. Costumes: Ha Nguyen. Camera: Daryn Okada.

Cast: Jet Li, DMX, Mark Dacascos, Anthony Anderson, Gabrielle Union, Tom Arnold, Sean Cory, Drag-On, Kelly Hu, and Woon Young Park.

DOCUMENTARIES

Footage of Jet Li as a youth and young adult appears in, among others, such documentaries as *Dragons of the Orient* [Dong Fang Ju Long] (1988), *Abbot Hai Teng of Shaolin* [Shao Lin Hai Deng Da Shi] (1988), *This Is Kung Fu* [Chung Wa Miu Sui] (1988), *The Lucky Way* [Daai Baat Gwa] (1992), *Shaolin Kung Fu* [Li Lian-Jie's Shaolin Kung Fu; Shao Lin Zhen Gong Fu] (1994), and *Top Fighters* (1994).

Bibliography

Key Articles

Baskin, Ellen. "Master of His Universes." *Newsday*, October 30, 2001.

Blair, Iain. "Li fights Fears for 'Weapon 4.'" *Sacramento Bee*, July 5, 1998.

Bottenberg, Rupert. "Jet Li Interview." *Fant-Asia*, 1998.

Burr, Martha. "Jet Li Interview." *Kungfu Qigong*, November/December 2001.

Corliss, Richard. "Chinese Movie Magic in Hong Kong, Taiwan and on the Mainland, Film Is a Fine, Ferocious Art." Time International, January 29, 1996.

———. "Fighter Jet." *Time Asia*, October 5, 1998.

Fleming, Michael. "Action man Li a monk at Miramax." ("Dish" column). *Daily Variety*, June 11, 2001.

———. "Li sees green for 'Hornet'." ("Dish" column). *Daily Variety*, June 22, 2000.

Foster, Damon, Garo Nigoghossian, Jeff Goodhartz, Alberta Martinez, and Linda Arroya. "The Movies of Jet Li." *Oriental Cinema* no. 16, Summer 1999.

Gardner, Chris and Zorianna Kit. "King is Bad Girl in 'Monk' thriller for MGM, Hunter." *Hollywood Reporter*, December 18, 2001.

Havis, Richard James. "Fired Up Over a Bad Jet." www.netasia.net/users/sgc_wdi/ articles/g5.htm (undated).

Hobson, Louis. "Reluctant Hero." *Calgary Sun*, March 13, 2000.

———. "Westbound Jet." *Calgary Sun*, March 22, 2000.

Jensen, Jeff. "Shop Talk: How Does Jet Li Get His Kicks." *Entertainment Weekly*, July 13, 2001.

"Jet Li" *Current Biography*, June 2001.

"Jet Li." *DVD*, no. 2, Summer 2001.

"Jet Li." *Oriental Cinema*, no. 16, Summer 1999.

"Jet Li." *People*, August 3, 1998.

"Jet Li." *People*, November 16, 1998.

"Jet Li." *Premiere*, September 2001.

Jet Li: A Biography

"Jet Li." *Wushu Kungfu*, May 1998.

Kachado, Mario, Michael Kai, and Wendy Chan. "Jet Li Interview." www.asianconnections.com (2000).

Kehr, Dave. "West Coast Story." *New York Times*, March 24, 2000.

Kim, Ellen A. "Li Kicks Back." www.Hollywood.com (June 25, 2001).

Kiss of the Dragon Presskit (2001).

Lee, Edmund. "Cool Jet." *Village Voice*, July 22, 1997.

Lyman, Rick. "Too Real for Children." *New York Times*, July 6, 2001.

Macaulay, Sean. "Jet Li puts the art in martial arts." *The Times* (London), November 8, 2000.

Noxon, Christopher. "Taking a Fast-Track Career in Stride." *Los Angeles Times*, July 4, 2001.

The One Presskit (2001).

Polly, Matthew. "Jet Fighter." *Playboy*, August 2001.

Rafferty, Terrence. "Wind from the East." *GQ*, March 2001.

Reid, Dr. Craig T. "Meet Corey Yuen." *Kungfu Qigong*, November/December 2001.

Roche, Eddie. "Jet Li's Fast-Food Kick." www.tvguide.com (March 15, 2000).

Romeo Must Die Presskit (2000).

Rowe, Douglas J. "Jet Li." *Detroit News*, July 11, 2000.

Salleh, Sujiah. "Will the Real One Please Stand Up." *Malaysia Star*, November 2, 2001.

Sherman, Betty. "Putting the Li in 'Lethal'." *Boston Globe*, July 11, 1998.

"Shooting Star." *Bangkok Post*, July 24, 1998.

Silverman, Stephen, M., and Blayne Jeffries. "Bridget Is Fonda Her 'Kiss' Costar." www.People.com (July 2, 2001).

Smith, Kyle. "Prepared for Takeoff." *People*, April 17, 2000.

Strauss, Bob. "Superstar Jet Li pilots a propulsive thriller." *Press-Telegram*, July 18, 2001.

"Supersonic: Jet Li Sets Flight Path to Hollywood Stardom." *Yolk*, September 30, 1998.

Villanueva, Annabelle, and Beth Laski. "Jet Li." *Cinescape*, July/August 1998

Wang, Julia. "He's the One." *aMagazine*, August/September 2001.

"Wireless action and the pool ball kick." www.actionadventure.about.com (July 1, 2001).

Wise, David. "Jet Li." *Total Film*, December 2001.

Wong, Martin, and Eric Nakamura. "Jet Li: The International Weapon." *Giant Robot*, no. 12, Winter 1998.

"The World Is My Oyster." www.TimeAsia.com (April 12, 2000).

Books

Bernstein, Matthew, and Gaylyn Studlar, eds. *Visions of the East: Orientalism in Film*. New Brunswick, NJ: Rutgers University. Press, 1997.

Bordell, David. *Planet Hong Kong: Popular Cinema and the Art of Entertainment*. Cambridge, MA: Harvard University Press, 2000.

Fitzgerald, Martin, ed. *Hong Kong's Heroic Bloodshed*. Harpenden, Hertfordshire, England: Pocket Essentials, 2000.

Frederic, Louis, and Paul Crompton, ed. *A Dictionary of the Martial Arts*. Rutland, VT: Charles S. Tuttle, 1991.

Gross, Edward. *Bruce Lee: Fists of Fury*. Las Vegas, NV: Pioneer, 1990.

Hammond, Stefan. *Hollywood East: Hong Kong Movies and the People Who Make Them*. Chicago, IL: Contemporary, 2000.

Hammond, Stefan, and Mike Wilkins. *Sex and Zen & A Bullet in the Head: The Essential Guide to Hong Kong's Mind-Bending Films*. New York: Fireside, 1996.

Logan, Bey. *Action Cinema*. Woodstock, NY: Overlook, 1996.

Morton, Lisa: *The Cinema of Tsui Hark*. Jefferson, NC: McFarland, 2001.

Nan Huai-chin. *Basic Buddhism: Exploring Buddhism and Zen*. York Beach, ME: Samuel Weiser, 1998.

Stokes, Lisa Odham, and Michael Hoover. *City on Fire: Hong Kong Cinema*. London: Verso, 1999.

Sullivan, Lawrence R. with Nancy Hearst. *Historical Dictionary of the People's Republic of China: 1947–1997*. Lanham, MD: Scarecrow, 1997.

Teo, Stephen. *Hong Kong Cinema: The Extra Dimension*. London: British Film Institute, 1997.

Weisser, Thomas. *Asian Cult Cinema*. New York: Boulevard, 1997.

Yau, Esther C. M., ed. *At Full Speed: Hong Kong Cinema in a Borderless World*. Minneapolis, MN: University of Minnesota Press, 2001.

Key Internet Websites

Action Adventure.Movies: www.actionadventure.about.com

Another Hong Kong Movie Page: www.kowloonside.com/

Asian Connections: www.asianconnections.com

China Online: www.chineseculture.about.com/mbody.htm

Collect Rare Stuff: www.collectrarestuff.com/jet%20li.htm

Hong Kong Entertainment News in Review: www.hkentreview.com

The Hong Kong Movie Database: www.hkmdb.com

Jet Li Homepage: www.netasia.net/users/sgc_wdi/news/0701-0901.htm

Movie World Hong Kong: www.movieworld.com.hk/zine/Office/index-en.

Official Jet Li Website: www.jetli.com

Raffi's Wushu Biog Page: www.beijingwushuteam.com.raffiwushu.html

PHOTOGRAPHS

Pages: iv, 2, 3, 34, 37, 38, 42, 46, 48, 51, 52, 54, 56, 60, 63, 64, 72. 80, 93, 95, 96, 114, 116, 117, 119, courtesy of Colin Geddes

Pages: 87, 132, 135, courtesy of Tai Seng Video Marketing

Pages: 142, 152, 166, 182, 189, photos by Albert L. Ortega

Pages: 5, 8, Courtesy of Photofest

Pages: 168, 175, Reuters/Getty Images

About the Author

JAMES ROBERT PARISH, a former entertainment reporter, publicist, and book series editor, is the author of over 100 published major biographies and reference books of the entertainment industry including *Hollywood Bad Boys*, *The Hollywood Book of Death*, *The Multicultural Encyclopedia of Twentieth Century Hollywood*, *Gus Van Sant*, *Jason Biggs*, *Whoopi Goldberg*, *Rosie O'Donnell's Story*, *The Unofficial "Murder, She Wrote" Casebook*, *Let's Talk!—America's Favorite TV Talk Show Hosts*, *The Great Cop Pictures*, *Ghosts and Angels in Hollywood Films*, *Prison Pictures from Hollywood*, *Hollywood's Great Love Teams*, and *The RKO Gals*. Mr. Parish is a frequent on-camera interviewee on cable and network TV for documentaries on the performing arts. He resides in Studio City, California.

Index